How the Jews
Defeated Hitler

How the Jews Defeated Hitler

Exploding the Myth of Jewish Passivity in the Face of Nazism

BENJAMIN GINSBERG

ROWMAN & LITTLEFIELD PUBLISHERS, INC.
Lanham • Boulder • New York • Toronto • Plymouth, UK

Published by Rowman & Littlefield Publishers, Inc.
A wholly owned subsidiary of The Rowman & Littlefield Publishing Group, Inc.
4501 Forbes Boulevard, Suite 200, Lanham, Maryland 20706
www.rowman.com

10 Thornbury Road, Plymouth PL6 7PP, United Kingdom

British Library Cataloguing in Publication Information Available

Library of Congress Cataloging-in-Publication Data
Ginsberg, Benjamin.
  How the Jews defeated Hitler : exploding the myth of Jewish passivity in the face of Nazism / Benjamin Ginsberg.
    pages cm
  Includes bibliographical references and index.
  ISBN 978-1-4422-2238-0 (cloth : alk. paper) — ISBN 978-1-4422-2239-7 (electronic) 1. World War, 1939–1945—Jewish resistance. 2. World War, 1939–1945—Participation, Jewish. I. Title.
  D810.J4G554 2013
  940.53089'924—dc23

                                                                    2012050050

∞™ The paper used in this publication meets the minimum requirements of American National Standard for Information Sciences—Permanence of Paper for Printed Library Materials, ANSI/NISO Z39.48-1992.

Printed in the United States of America

For Sandy

Contents

Acknowledgments

In writing this book I benefited greatly from conversations with my friends Robert Kargon and David Satter. David read the entire manuscript and Robert shared with me his knowledge of Soviet history. My thinking about this topic was also clarified by many classroom discussions with my students at Johns Hopkins. Indeed, during a class discussion of Nazism, one Hopkins undergraduate, Shane Pinzka, asked the question that launched the book. I am, of course, also very grateful to my agent Claire Gerus, my editor Susan McEachern, and my production editor Jehanne Schweitzer for their wonderful efforts at various stages of the project.

I should observe, too, that in telling me their life stories—and surviving the events described below—my late parents, Anna and Herman Ginsberg, not only inspired but quite literally made this book possible.

Benjamin Ginsberg
Potomac Maryland
February, 2013

1

Introduction

The Problem of Jewish Resistance

During a class discussion of Nazism, one of my students said he simply could not understand why the Jews hadn't resisted the efforts of the Germans to exterminate them. This assertion is, of course, quite common and not limited to undergraduates. The noted historian Raul Hilberg, for example, wrote, "The reaction pattern of the Jews is characterized by almost complete lack of resistance. Measured in German casualties, Jewish armed opposition shrinks into insignificance."[1] My response to the student, which became the topic of this book, was that the Jews had not only resisted but actually played a major role in the defeat of Nazi Germany. The question, I said, was not whether the Jews fought but where and by what means.

Let me make two points at the outset. First, Jewish resistance to the Nazis should be characterized as a form of cumulative rather than collective action. That is, for the most part, Jewish resistance lacked even a modicum of central coordination or leadership. It consisted of a host of disparate groups, individuals, and organizations on several continents mounting various responses, ranging from partisan warfare through nuclear research, to the threat of Nazism. These uncoordinated efforts, however, were channeled by a common threat and cumulated into what we shall see was a potent, albeit sometimes futile, response to the Germans.

A second point concerns the meaning and scope of the term "resistance." Jewish resistance is often defined narrowly to refer to the activities of Jews in the occupied lands of Europe. Yet, just as the French Resistance operated outside as well as inside France, Jewish resistance and opposition to the Nazis manifested itself in a number of settings both inside and outside German-occupied territory. To ignore this point is to risk distorting the historical record. The discussion of Jewish resistance normally focuses on villages, ghettos, concentration camps, and other locations where whatever resistance arose was certain to appear feeble and was usually futile. Desperate and unarmed Jews in Eastern European *shtetlekh* (villages), city ghettos, and death camps hardly had the means to resist. Unarmed individuals cannot exactly mount armed resistance. Some fought nonetheless. There was resistance in nearly every major ghetto, and revolts broke out in virtually every concentration camp. Jewish undergrounds were organized in, for example, the Warsaw, Minsk, Vilna, and Bialystok ghettos, and some Jews who survived the liquidation of those ghettos, as we shall see in chapter 5, joined partisan groups in the forests. And revolts broke out even at the Treblinka, Sobibor, and Auschwitz *Vernichtungslager* (extermination camps), among others.[2] These were, however, easily and quickly suppressed by the Germans.

There seems little doubt, though, that in the ghettos and death camps, hoping to save their own lives and those of their family members, more Jews cooperated and even collaborated with the Germans than resisted. How could it be otherwise? Without weapons or military training or outside support, and guarded by ruthless and heavily armed German paramilitary police and their Ukrainian, Croatian, or other *Hilfswillige* (non-German volunteers known as Hiwis who worked in various capacities for the German army), few would resist, whether they were Jews or Americans, Englishmen or Frenchmen. Most would cooperate hoping to live another day. Some would collaborate hoping to survive even longer.

Hannah Arendt claimed that the Nazis depended on the cooperation of the *Judenräte* (the Jewish Councils established by the Germans to administer the day-to-day life of the ghettos), the Jewish police, and so forth to administer the "final solution."[3] "To a Jew," said Arendt, "this role of the Jewish leaders in the destruction of their own people is undoubtedly the darkest chapter of the whole dark story."[4] Arendt's claim is certainly true, particularly in the case of the Lodz ghetto, led by Chaim Rumkowski, who insisted on cooperation with the Germans until the very bitter end. Arendt was correct to view this as an exceedingly dark story. But the part of the story that so offended her doesn't distinguish the Jews from anyone else.

The head of German security in Amsterdam, for example, said, "The main support of the German forces in the police sector and beyond was the Dutch police. Without it, not 10 per cent of the German occupation tasks would have been fulfilled."[5] Members of the Dutch police, along with thousands of Dutch Nazis, volunteered to serve in the Wehrmacht and formed the Thirty-fourth SS (Schutzstaffel) Volunteer Division, Landstorm Nederland. The same was true of the French. As many, if not more, collaborated as resisted.[6] Until the Americans, British, and Canadians landed at Normandy, the Germans had little trouble occupying France with 3,000 to 4,000 of their own military police officers and the assistance of 100,000 cooperative French policemen and 40,000 members of the French paramilitary Milice. As in the Netherlands, French volunteers, many drawn from the Milice, joined the German army, forming the Thirty-third Waffen SS Division, Charlemagne.

If the ghettos and camps are not the correct places to look for effective Jewish resistance, where then? My own family's story, in particular the different paths to survival taken by my mother and father, may offer an answer as well as an illustration of the limits and possibilities of resistance. One night toward the end of 1941, my mother's *stot* (town) was entered by Germans and their Ukrainian auxiliaries, who began rounding up Jews, beating and shooting many of them on the spot and collecting the others for what was euphemistically known as "resettlement." Some Jews ran while others hid, but few resisted. My mother hid in an empty barrel, and through sheer blind luck, no one looked into that particular refuge. She survived, but she may have been the only survivor of that particular night's *Aktion* (campaign to assemble and deport Jews). She saw her own mother taken away and never saw her again. Should she and the others have resisted? How exactly could a scattering of unarmed civilians resist troops armed with automatic weapons and only too happy to kill them, then and there?

My father, on the other hand, resisted strenuously, but the context was quite different. After escaping from a German labor camp in 1940, he fled east and managed to reach the Soviet army. He was promptly conscripted and trained to serve in an artillery regiment. When large numbers of Katyushas, the famous Soviet rocket artillery, began to be deployed in 1942 and 1943, he was assigned to fire salvos of rockets at the Germans. These Soviet rockets, developed as it happens by Jewish engineers, were very effective against German infantry. In response to Hilberg's comment regarding the insignificance of armed Jewish resistance, one might say that salvos of hundreds of deadly rockets developed by Jews and fired by a Jew represented an exceedingly robust form of armed Jewish resistance. Even Arendt would have had no reason to feel ashamed. The Germans feared the Katyushas, so they would have been compelled to agree if they had known who was shooting at them.

The moral of the story is that rather than look for armed resistance among unarmed civilians and express scorn at Jews for failing to do what could not be done, we should look for resistance where it was possible to resist. If we pursue this path, we come to a very different conclusion about the Jews and their efforts during the war.

The fact of the matter is that the Jews resisted very vigorously and quite effectively through four vehicles. The first was the Soviet army. Jews constituted a significant percentage of the fighting strength of the Soviet army, including both its combat and political officers, and, on a per capita basis, won more medals and decorations than members of any other ethnic group in the USSR. More importantly, as we shall see, Jewish engineers supervised the evacuation and reconstruction of Soviet military industry in 1941 and designed and built many of the weapons upon which the Soviet army depended during the war. These included the T-34 medium tank, generally seen as the best tank of the war, the La-5 fighter plane, the Katyusha rocket launcher, and others. These weapons allowed the Soviets to survive the disasters of 1941 and, in four years, to drive the Wehrmacht back to Berlin.

Second, the Jews resisted through their influence in the United States. During the 1930s, most Americans were isolationist, anti-British, or pro-German. This included significant numbers of German, Italian, Irish, and Scandinavian Americans. America's white Anglo-Saxon Protestant (WASP) elite, though, was pro-British, while the Jews were anti-German. With the encouragement of the Franklin D. Roosevelt administration and British intelligence, the Jews and WASPs forged an alliance that worked to bring about shifts in American public opinion, to discredit isolationist groups, and to give Roosevelt the political backing he sought for rearmament, the introduction of universal military training, and critical lend-lease aid to Britain and the USSR.

During the war itself, Jewish soldiers fought in every branch of the U.S. military. On the home front, Jews played a major role in maintaining popular morale, selling bonds, and organizing the economics of the war effort. At the same time, Jewish scientists worked to build the atom bomb, a weapon that became America's ace in the hole and eventually ended the war. Hitler had declared that the war would be a war of extermination (*Vernichtung*). He presumably had the Jews and other *Untermenschen* (subhumans) in mind, but had the Germans fought on just a few months longer, or had the Jewish scientists of the Manhattan Project completed their work just a few months sooner, the war would certainly have brought *Vernichtung*—for the Germans.

Third, Jews in the Soviet Union, United States, and Great Britain were very important in the realm of intelligence and espionage. The Soviet Union's major—and very effective—spy rings, including the Red Orchestra, were led by Jews who, in some instances, had been schooled in the arts of espionage by Soviet intelligence services before the war. In the United States, Jews were among the leading figures in the realm of cryptanalysis. In fact, the term "cryptanalysis" was coined by America's foremost cryptanalyst, William Friedman. Friedman's heavily Jewish group at the U.S. Army's Signals Intelligence Service (predecessor of today's National Security Agency) pioneered modern code breaking and designed the U.S. military's SIGABA cipher machine, whose encryptions were never broken during the machine's period of service, which ended in the 1950s.

Jews were also involved in the British cryptanalysis effort. In Britain, however, Jews were more important in the area of covert operations. In particular, the British Special Operations Executive (SOE) recruited a sizeable group of foreign-born Jews whose linguistic and cultural skills would help them operate in the German-occupied countries of Europe. These individuals became important actors in British covert operations in Europe. There were, of course, Jews in regular British and Commonwealth forces, including the famous Jewish Brigade, and many fought bravely.[7] The number of Jews in Britain, Australia, and so forth was, however, minuscule, so their number in the military was necessarily very small as well.

Finally, Jews played important roles in several of the major European anti-Nazi resistance movements. When Americans think of resistance to the Nazis, they tend to think of the French and, perhaps, the Norwegians and Danes. The Norwegians helped the British SOE destroy the German heavy water plant at Vemork, and both the Norwegians and the Danes heroically smuggled large fractions of their small Jewish communities to safety in Sweden. Generally, though, these two movements posed little threat to the Germans.[8]

The French, for their part, with the exception of the Jews and the Communist Party, did not resist very vigorously until after D-day. Asked at Nuremberg about the impact of French resistance on German military production, Reich armaments minister Albert Speer quipped that he wasn't aware that there had been any French resistance.[9] In both Western and Eastern Europe, however, Jews helped to lead resistance groups whose acts of sabotage and attacks on the always-fragile German supply lines to the east did hinder the Germans and help the Allies. This includes the Polish, Greek, and Yugoslav resistance movements and the most important of the World War II resistance movements, the partisans of the Soviet Union.

In these four ways the Jews not only resisted but played a major role in the defeat of Nazi Germany. Could the Allies have won without the help of the Jews? Perhaps. Did they win without the help of the Jews? No.

In 1945, Hitler was dead, the Germans had been defeated, and the Allies were victorious, but it cannot exactly be said that the Jews had won. More than 6 million Jews were dead. The several hundred thousand Jewish survivors in displaced person's camps were unwelcome almost everywhere, while former Nazis were given asylum in the United States and Canada and provided with humanitarian assistance by the Vatican and the Red Cross. In the Soviet Union, Stalin's anti-Semitic campaign, halted temporarily by the war, resumed with a vengeance. In the United States, Jews, who had been among the first to warn of the Nazi threat in the 1930s, were accused of "premature anti-Fascism" by various anti-Communist crusaders in the postwar period.

When he launched his postwar campaign against the Jews, even Stalin usually had the good grace to eschew outright anti-Semitism in favor of campaigns against "cosmopolitans" and the like. As the memory of the war and the Holocaust faded, however, as if to confirm Marx's well-known comment that history repeats itself—*das eine Mal als Tragodie, das andere Mal als Farce* (the first time as tragedy, the second time as farce)—a more overt anti-Semitism, containing more than an element of farce, reemerged in Western Europe in the odd form of liberal anti-Zionism. This time the question of Jewish resistance in Europe was moot, since there were hardly any Jews left.

2

The Soviet Union

The War of the Engineers

During the 1930s and 1940s, Jews were confronted by an existential threat from Nazi Germany. Not only was Germany the most powerful state in Europe, but it had fallen under the leadership of an individual who frequently proclaimed his desire to find a "final solution" to the Jewish problem. Hitler and his followers gradually developed a plan for bringing about this "solution" and managed to murder more than 6 million of Europe's Jews.

As they faced this ever-growing threat, the Jews lacked the conventional means of defense that might be available to a besieged nation. The Jews were a small group of perhaps 18 million persons scattered across Europe and North America and had no state or army with which to fend off the German assault. The Jews lacked even an informal instrument of coordination. There was no council of the elders of Zion to direct the Jewish response to Hitler. By the end of 1945, though, Hitler was dead and Nazi Germany defeated. And though the Jews had suffered grievous losses, they had survived.

Despite their handicaps, the Jews managed to defend themselves by working for, with, and through states and political leaders who shared their hostility toward Nazi Germany. The Jews' most important allies were the United States and the Soviet Union led by Franklin Roosevelt and Joseph Stalin, respectively. And just as the Jews needed allies, these allies needed the Jews. For the United States and especially the Soviet Union, the Jews' technical, scientific, administrative, and financial talents, as well as their high level of motivation, proved crucial to the war effort. Indeed, just as the Jews could not have survived without their allies, these selfsame allies, particularly the USSR, would very likely have been defeated without the Jews. Let us consider the Soviet case.

Prior to 1940, fewer than 3 million Jews lived in the Soviet Union, representing about 2 percent of the USSR's 160 million people. Under the tsars, the Jews had been subject to persecution and numerous disabilities, which perhaps explains Jewish support for various revolutionary movements in tsarist Russia. The Russian government, in turn, often sought to discredit revolutionary forces by linking them to the Jews.[1] For example, after Alexander II's assassination in 1881 by revolutionaries who included a Jew, Hessia Hellman, the government charged that political dissidents were agents of a Jewish conspiracy and fomented pogroms throughout southern Russia and the Ukraine. The Ignatiev Report of 1882 recommended that harsh measures be taken against Jews to quell popular protest. The resulting May Laws of 1882 severely limited areas of Jewish settlement, slashed Jewish quotas in schools and universities, and sought to dislodge Jews from trade and the professions.

Tsarist attacks on the Jews continued even into the twentieth century. In 1902 and 1903, under the command of Interior Minister Vyacheslav von Plehve, major pogroms were launched in Bessarabia and White Russia. Peter Stolypin, appointed minister of the interior in 1906, vowed to "drown the revolution in Jewish blood." Under Stolypin's direction, the paramilitary forces of the Union of the Russian People, known as the "black hundreds," carried out a series of assassinations of liberal and radical opponents of the regime as well as a campaign of terror against the Jews. In an effort to maintain the loyalty of peasants and workers, Stolypin repeated the familiar mantra, depicting opposition to the monarchy as a Jewish conspiracy.[2]

Many Russian Jews emigrated to the United States during this period, while others responded to the pogroms by throwing in their lots with revolutionary movements. Thus, Jews were among the founders of the Social Democratic Party in the 1890s. In addition, the Jewish Socialist Bund organized tens of thousands of workers in the Pale and played a major role in the unsuccessful 1905 revolution. And during the period leading up to the 1917 revolution, Jews were among the leaders of both the Menshevik and the Bolshevik parties.[3]

After the revolution, among the first official acts of the victorious Bolsheviks was outlawing the pogroms and anti-Semitic movements that Russian Jews had feared for centuries. In a radical break with the Russian past, moreover, the new regime provided Jews with the opportunity to participate fully in government and society. They quickly came to play major roles in the ruling Communist Party and the Soviet state. Jews were among the few supporters of the revolution with even a modicum of education and literacy. Thus they soon assumed positions of leadership in areas requiring such skills—foreign affairs, propaganda, finance, administration, and industrial production.

Three of the six members of Lenin's first Politburo, Leon Trotsky, Lev Kamenev, and Grigory Zinoviev, were of Jewish origin. Trotsky, in addition, was commissar of defense and organized and commanded the Red Army during the civil war that followed the October Revolution. Kamenev and Zinoviev became members of the triumvirate (along with Stalin) that ruled the Soviet Union immediately after Lenin's death in 1924. Other prominent Jews in the early Soviet government included Yakov Sverdlov, president of the Communist Party Central Committee; Maxim Litvinov, commissar for foreign affairs; and Karl Radek, who served as press commissar. Lazar Kaganovich was one of Stalin's top aides and served as commissar of heavy industry during World War II and as a member of the Politburo.

During the early decades of Communist rule, Jews were especially prominent in the security services and in the Soviet army, both of which served as bulwarks of the new regime's power. Like the Sikhs and Gurkhas of British India, Jews had traditionally been at the margins of Russian society and hence were prepared to staff and direct the security instruments upon which the state relied to control its citizens. Genrikh Yagoda, for example, served as head of the secret police during the 1930s. Yagoda had been a pharmacist before the revolution and specialized in preparing poisons for his agents to use in liquidating Stalin's opponents.

Other high-ranking Jewish secret police officers included M. T. Gay, who headed the special department that conducted mass arrests during the "Great Terror" of the 1930s, and A. A. Slutsky and Boris Berman, who were in charge of Soviet terror and espionage abroad. As to the Red Army, in addition to Trotsky, prominent Jewish generals included Mikhail Frunze, who succeeded Trotsky as commissar of defense; Yona Yakir, a member of the Communist Party Central Committee; Dmitri Schmidt, a civil war hero and commander of the Kiev area; and Yakob Kreiser, who was later a hero of the defense of Moscow during World War II.

In all realms, the revolution opened educational and career opportunities to talented Jews who had been largely excluded from both under the tsarist regime. Jewish students flooded into the universities, including the excellent engineering schools to be found in Moscow, Leningrad, Kiev, and Kharkov, where they quickly comprised a large percentage of the student population. Though making up less than 2 percent of the overall populace, between 1929 and 1939, Jews constituted 11 percent of the students in Soviet universities. This included 17 percent of all university students in Moscow, 19 percent in Leningrad, 24 percent in Kharkov, and 35.6 percent in Kiev.[4] As we shall see, engineering graduates of these schools became major figures in the Soviet armaments industry, designing and producing the tanks, aircraft, and artillery with which the USSR defeated Nazi Germany.

Indeed, from the universities Jews streamed into the professions, especially those that were needed by the new regime. These included science and engineering, particularly in such fields as aircraft design, industrial production, and transport. For example, several of the Soviet Union's most prominent aircraft designers were Jews. These included Semyon Lavochkin, a 1927 Moscow State Technical University graduate, who developed the La series of fighter planes, which became the mainstay of the Soviet air force, as well as Mikhail I. Gourevich, designer of the famous MiG fighters. By the 1930s, Jews had also become the backbone of the Soviet bureaucracy and constituted a large percentage of the nation's physicians, dentists, pharmacists, and other professionals, as well as nearly 20 percent of the scientists and university professors in such major cities as Moscow and Leningrad.[5]

Also important to the government were film, journalism, and publishing, which were seen as key instruments of propaganda. Jews soon became important figures in the Soviet cultural apparatus. Mikhail Koltsov was the USSR's most important journalist. Yuri Levitan became Soviet radio's official announcer.[6] Semyon Lozovsky was deputy chief of the government's information bureau and chief Soviet press spokesman during World War II. The writer Ilya Ehrenburg became the leading publicist for Russian nationalism and wartime anti-German sentiment. Vasily Grossman was the Soviet army's leading war correspondent. Jews dominated the Soviet film industry. Prominent Jews in this area included directors Sergei Eisenstein, Mikhail Romm, Mark Donskoy, Leonid Lukov, and Yuli Reisman.[7]

Thus, while they had no state of their own, within a few years after the Bolshevik revolution, Jews had a good deal of influence within the new Soviet state. And though this state seemed weak and backward in many respects relative to the industrialized states of Western Europe and North America, it did appear to possess one very important asset—a large and powerful army. The Red Army had been built during the 1918–1921 civil war that followed the 1917 October Revolution. During this period, the new Soviet state faced a variety of enemies, including White Russian forces seeking to restore the old regime; German forces supporting efforts by the Baltic states to secure their independence; a Polish army dispatched to promote Ukrainian independence; British, French, and American troops sent to support the White Russians; an anti-Bolshevik army of former Czech and Slovak war prisoners; and a variety of dissidents and brigands who took advantage of the chaos to seize control of bits and pieces of territory.

In response to these developments, Lenin issued a decree in 1918 introducing compulsory military conscription and effectively establishing the Red Army. Lenin appointed Leon Trotsky to the newly created post of people's commissar for war and assigned him the task of creating an army. Over the objections of many Bolsheviks, Trotsky asserted the importance of constructing a professional army and appointed to senior command positions in the new military thousands of experienced tsarist officers, such as Generals Alexander Svechin and Joachim Vatsetis, who had offered their services to the new regime. A number of party leaders feared that the tsarist officers and peasant conscripts would be disloyal and favored the formation of a people's militia of Communist workers led by "Red Guard" officers. Trotsky, however, asserted that there were not enough Communist workers to build an army of requisite size and that a successful army must be led by what he called "military specialists" chosen for their training and experience rather than their ideological purity.[8]

To ensure the army's loyalty, however, Trotsky agreed to the formation of party cells and organizations inside the army to provide spies and informers as well as to stiffen morale. In addition, political commissars were assigned to every unit, essentially to watch military commanders for signs of disloyalty. The commissars shared authority with the military commanders and had the power to countermand military orders. This system impaired military discipline but was considered essential given the makeup of the officer corp. With this exception, Trotsky insisted on strict military discipline and, when push came to shove, backed the military specialists against the political commissars.

By 1921, the Red Army had managed to prevail over its various foes, after very nearly being defeated by the Poles in 1920, and had become a large and formidable fighting force with a cadre of experienced officers and a sophisticated operational doctrine emphasizing rapid maneuver, deep penetration, and encirclement of enemy forces.[9] Implementation of this doctrine required mobile forces. During the civil war these took the form of cavalry and infantry carried from front to front by train. Later, the necessary level of mobility was achieved by the use of armored cars and, eventually, tanks.

Over the next several years, Red Army doctrine and equipment evolved and matured. In 1924, as an outgrowth of his leadership struggle with Stalin, Trotsky was replaced as commissar for war by a general of Jewish origin and civil war hero, Mikhail Frunze. Frunze imposed discipline upon the army— drill, the wearing of uniforms, obedience to orders—and began the modernization of equipment and logistics. Though Frunze had supported Stalin against Trotsky, Stalin never trusted the general and had him murdered while he underwent a surgical procedure in 1925. Nevertheless, the army continued to improve its tactical doctrines and equipment. Soviet strategists developed the concept of "deep operation." This concept required combined-arms operations in which mechanized forces, aircraft, artillery, and engineers worked in conjunction with infantry to penetrate enemy defenses.[10]

To implement this concept, the Soviet government invested heavily in arms development and production, building large quantities of tanks, warplanes, artillery, and other arms. By 1932, three years before Germany fielded its first armored division, the Red Army had already formed two mechanized corps and led the world in the construction of mechanized forces.[11] In addition, the Soviet Union constantly expanded its military industries so as to possess a strong economic and industrial base from which to wage modern war.[12]

Thus, in the aftermath of the Bolshevik revolution, the Jews of the new Soviet Union, at least, might appear to have secured the protection of a powerful state that they helped to build and in which they exercised significant influence. However, before Soviet Jews could help to defeat Hitler, they would first have to survive Stalin. In the wake of Lenin's death in 1924, a succession struggle erupted between Leon Trotsky and Joseph Stalin. Stalin's main political base was the party *apparat* (bureaucracy), while Trotsky commanded the Red Army. Stalin, who personally had considerable antipathy for Jews, made use of anti-Semitic appeals to the party's rank and file to defeat Trotsky as well as Kamenev and Zinoviev, both Jews, who were his main rivals within the party leadership.

Much of the invective used by Stalin in the intraparty battles of this period was designed to appeal to anti-Semitic sentiment inside and outside the party, a sentiment that Stalin shared. For example, the label "left opportunist" used by Stalin to castigate his enemies was a euphemism for Jew. In a similar vein, Stalin's advocacy of the doctrine of "socialism in one country" was partly designed to limit the influence of foreign Jewish Communists, who often had ties to Jewish Communists within the Soviet Union itself.

During the 1930s, Stalin moved to consolidate his power by intimidating or eliminating all potential sources of opposition within the Communist Party, the army, the secret police, and the administrative apparatus. Jews exercised a great deal of influence within all these institutions and, as a result, constituted a large and important group of victims of the Stalinist purges.[13]

In the show trials during this period, the key Jewish officials of the Communist Party and Soviet state were accused of plotting against the revolution and were systematically killed. These included Kamenev, Zinoviev, Radek, and Alexei Rykov. Important Jewish military commanders such as Yona Yakir were liquidated. The diplomatic service was cleared of Jews. The secret police forces used to implement these purges often were led by Jews who were killed in their turn, until the influence of Jews within the secret police was substantially diminished. Those liquidated included Yagoda, Slutsky, and Karl Pauker, as well as Matvei and Boris Berman, brothers who had played lead roles in the development of the gulag prison system.

Given the paucity of other educated individuals, even Stalin was compelled to continue to rely to some extent upon the talents of Jews in the party, the state bureaucracy, and the security services. Their influence, however, was greatly reduced. Before the purges, Jews had comprised about 10 percent of the membership of the Communist Party Central Committee. After the purges, barely 2 percent of the committee's members were of Jewish origin.

This elimination of potential rivals gave Stalin complete control of the party apparatus and allowed him to broaden its base by increasing the representation of other nationality groups in the party leadership.[14]

Not only did the Stalinist purges reduce the influence of the Jews, but they also did great damage to the Soviet army—the key institution upon which the Jews, and the USSR as a whole, would rely in the coming years. After Hitler rose to power in Germany in 1933, most observers assumed that strengthening the Soviet army would be Stalin's highest priority. Indeed, in response to the new German threat, Stalin authorized an increase in the size of the Red Army and, in 1935, decreed a reorganization of the army that increased the authority of senior officers and reduced the power of the army's political commissars.[15]

Stalin, however, was ultimately more concerned with the loyalty of his officers than with external events and, among other things, suspected a number of senior officers of having opposed agricultural collectivization and possibly supporting his rival, Nikolai Bukharin, during the power struggles that erupted within the Communist Party leadership during the early 1930s. Accordingly, in June 1937, Stalin ordered the arrest of eight senior officers, including the army's commander in chief, Marshal Mikhail Tukhachevskii. All eight were quickly condemned for treason and executed. A ninth senior officer, Yan B. Gamarnik, was said to have committed suicide when faced with arrest.[16]

Over the course of the next several years, halted only by the German invasion, more than 30,000 Soviet officers, out of 75,000 to 80,000, were imprisoned or executed. This total included 3 out of 5 marshals, all 11 deputy defense commissars, all commanders of military districts, the commanders and chiefs of staff of the navy and air force, 14 of 16 army commanders, 60 of 67 corps commanders, 136 of 199 division commanders, 221 of 397 brigade commanders, and 50 percent of all regimental commanders.[17] By rank, 90 percent of all Soviet generals and 80 percent of all Soviet colonels were removed.[18]

The Soviet army's vitally important armored forces were especially hard hit by the purges. Marshal Tukhachevskii had been the army's chief proponent of armored warfare. After his arrest and execution, all the officers and even engineers and planners associated with him came under suspicion and were then arrested themselves. Many thousands of engineers, technicians, and even factory foremen associated with the construction of tanks were sent to remote prison camps. This virtually put a halt to the development and construction of new tanks in 1937.[19] In 1938 and 1939, virtually all the senior officers of the Red Army's armored forces were purged, often leaving brigades and even divisions under the command of officers who had been junior lieutenants a year earlier.[20] And after the commander of the air force was purged, many experienced officers, as well as aircraft designers and engineers, were arrested, stripping the military of experienced pilots and leaving the Soviet air force with obsolescent and ageing equipment.[21]

Thus, even as Hitler planned his attack, the Soviet army was thrown into disarray and its morale shattered. This became evident during the army's poor performance against Finland in 1939–1940. In 1938 the army had fought well under Georgy Zhukov's leadership against the Japanese. In the Finnish campaign, however, inexperienced officers were afraid to exercise independent judgment or take the initiative, allowing the vastly outnumbered Finns to impose heavy casualties on the disorganized Soviet forces. In some respects, Stalin had done more damage to the Soviet army's officer corps than would later be inflicted by Hitler's Wehrmacht. Indeed, the Germans watched gleefully as Stalin reduced the Soviet army from a powerful armed force to what the chief of the German General Staff, General Ludwig von Beck, dismissed as "an inert military machine" that would easily be crushed.[22]

WAR AND THE JEWS

The Germans struck in June 1941, hoping to quickly destroy Soviet military resistance. Hitler believed that the defeat of the Red Army and the occupation of the European portion of the Soviet Union would provide Germany with vast new agricultural lands, as well as supplies of fuel and raw materials. The tens of millions of inhabitants of the USSR would become slave laborers for the German settlers who would eventually take over the land. Those Soviet citizens who would or could not work, along with Jews, Communists, and other undesirables, would be put to death. The only force standing in the way of this grandiose plan was the demoralized and weakened Soviet army.

When the German attack commenced, the Soviet government and military seemed taken by surprise even though there had been ample warning of Germany's intentions. Initially, the Germans were enormously successful, occupying much of European Russia and the Ukraine, killing or capturing millions of Soviet troops and overrunning or destroying the most important portions of the USSR's industrial base. During the first weeks of the German attack, the Wehrmacht destroyed more than 17,000 Soviet aircraft, 20,000 tanks, and 100,000 heavy guns and mortars. As many as 5 million Soviet troops had been killed or captured or were missing in action. Briefly, German tanks were nine miles from Moscow and within sight of the Kremlin. Territory containing 40 percent of the Soviet population had come under German control. For millions of Jews unfortunate enough to find themselves under German occupation, the result of the Germans' battlefield achievements was a sentence of death in one of the many ways devised by Nazi ingenuity.

After the first year, however, the German advance was thwarted, and by 1943 the Soviet army had begun a series of offensives that, within two years, destroyed the Wehrmacht and brought Soviet forces into the heart of Berlin itself. Some historians have attributed this turn of events to such factors as the USSR's inexhaustible supply of manpower, the severe Russian climate, and even American and British aid sent to the Soviets via the lend-lease program. None of these explanations is fully satisfactory. The Soviet Union did have a larger population than Germany—more than 180 million Soviet citizens to roughly 80 million Germans. However, considering Russian losses, including the rapid loss of territory containing some 60 million people, as well as the populations of Germany's allies, Italy, Hungary, Finland, and Romania, and the support given to the Germans by Stalin's unhappy subjects in the Ukraine, the Baltic states, and elsewhere, the USSR's advantage in underlying manpower was hardly overwhelming. Indeed, during the course of the war, the Wehrmacht was supported by two Ukrainian divisions, an SS division recruited in Galicia, 150,000 Latvians, Lithuanians, and Estonians, and 250,000 Cossacks.[23] If the USSR was usually able to put more soldiers in the field than the Germans, this was the result more of the Soviet Union's superior capacity to mobilize the military potential of its population than the underlying inequality of numbers.[24]

As for the Russian winter, its severity hampered the Soviets as well as the Germans, and it is hard to see why it should explain the difficulties encountered by one army but not the other. The Soviets did not fight their war from Palm Beach; they were simply better able than the Germans to adapt their weapons and tactics to the harsh climate. For example, the Soviet counterattack that saved Moscow took place in severe weather that hampered the operations of both armies. The Soviets, however, had supplied their troops with winter equipment, including snow suits and goggles, which the German troops lacked, not because they failed to anticipate the need but because of the Wehrmacht's logistical shortcomings, which will be discussed more fully in chapter 5. The Soviet air force generally employed heated hangars while German planes stood in the open. Soviet tanks and other vehicles were designed for winter operation and used lubricants that would not freeze. The Germans had not yet adapted their own machines in this way.[25] Hence, it was not the winter per se but their superior preparation for winter fighting that helped the Soviets.

American and British assistance, on the other hand, was quite important. To be sure, the bulk of the tanks, aircraft, and artillery at the heart of the Soviet war machine were produced under the most adverse of conditions by the USSR itself, rather than provided by the West. Nevertheless, the United States provided the USSR with 400,000 trucks and jeeps, 1,900 locomotives, thousands of airplanes, thousands of tons of explosives, radios that allowed Soviet units to communicate with one another, and 14 million pairs of boots that allowed Soviet soldiers to remain on the march. This American lend-lease assistance was critical to the Soviet war effort. Stalin himself was said to have doubted whether the USSR could have survived without American material aid.

As we shall see in the next chapter, organizations in which American Jews played important roles, such as the Century Group, helped bring about the enactment of the lend-lease bill and later helped to thwart congressional efforts to prevent the use of lend-lease funds to aid the Soviet war effort.[26] In this way, American Jews played a significant role in helping to sustain the Soviet war effort. For the most part, though, the Soviet Union defeated Nazi Germany because of the resilience of its military forces, its capacity to produce huge quantities of armaments often superior to those fielded by the Germans, and the USSR's ability to mobilize its society for war to a degree far greater than that achieved by Nazi Germany. In each of these realms, Soviet Jews were critically important.

JEWISH SOLDIERS IN THE RED ARMY

Prior to the war, Jews were well represented in the Red Army. More than 4 percent of the army's officers were of Jewish origin, as were more than 10 percent of its political officers.[27] More than 300 Jews held the rank of general.[28] Some 169 of these Jewish generals fell victim to Stalin's purges. These included two commanders of the first rank (lieutenant general), Yona Yakir and Yan Gamarnik; five commanders of the second rank (major general); and twelve army corps commanders. Several of these men were quite famous and had gained a good deal of experience fighting against the Germans during the Spanish Civil War, when the USSR sent aid to the Republican forces while German soldiers fought alongside Franco's army.

Thus, among the Jewish officers liquidated by Stalin were General Grigory Shtern, who had been the chief military advisor for the Spanish Republicans; General Yakov Smushkevich, who had commanded the Soviet pilots who constituted the Republican air force; and General Semyon Krivoshin, who commanded Soviet armored units in Spain.[29] Shtern and Smushkevich had also fought against the Japanese in 1938, and both had been awarded the USSR's highest medal, Hero of the Soviet Union, for their efforts.

Given Stalin's antipathy for the Jews, it seems more than likely that most remaining Jewish officers would sooner or later have been purged—as was nearly the case after the war. However, the German invasion brought about an immediate change in policy. Not only were the military purges brought to a halt, but those purge victims—Jews and Gentiles alike—fortunate enough to still be alive in the NKVD's prisons were quickly rehabilitated and sent to fight the Germans. For example, in the wake of the German invasion, General Konstantin Rokossovsky, a non-Jewish officer who had been accused of treason and was awaiting an uncertain fate, was rushed from his NKVD cell to lead the Sixteenth Army in the defense of Moscow. Rokossovsky ended the war as a marshal of the Soviet Union commanding a *front*, the Soviet equivalent of an army group.

Soviet anti-Semites often averred during the war that no Jews were to be found on the front lines.[30] This charge was repeated after the war by no less a personage than Alexander Solzhenitsyn.[31] No doubt, many Jews, along with Russians, Ukrainians, and others, sought whatever refuge they could find and preferred rear-echelon assignments. However, the 200,000 Jews who were killed while serving in the Red Army, out of some 500,000 who served, were apparently unable to find such places of safety.[32] In point of fact, Jews included some of the most highly motivated and effective troops in Soviet uniform. Jewish soldiers, for example, received some 160,000 medals and

awards during the war, ranking fourth among all nationality groups in absolute numbers.[33]

Some 150 Jewish soldiers received the highest Soviet medal, Hero of the
Soviet Union, placing Jews first on a per capita basis among the various
Soviet nationality groups.[34] In absolute terms, Jews earned the third highest
number of these medals, behind only the rather more numerous Russians
and Ukrainians. It should be noted that the official medal tally undoubtedly
underestimates the extent of Jewish battlefield valor since the Soviet regime
in 1943 ordered that fewer medals should be awarded to Jews. The order read,
"Medals for distinguished conduct are to be awarded to men of all nations,
but within limits with regard to the Jews."[35]

But just as it is incorrect to view Jews as more cowardly than others, it is
also incorrect to interpret these numbers as demonstrating that the Jews were
somehow inherently braver than other Soviet soldiers. It would perhaps be
more accurate to say that Jewish soldiers were more highly motivated and,
importantly, more desperate than their fellow soldiers to avoid surrender
to or capture by the Germans. In the confused early months of the German
invasion, millions of Soviet troops, finding their positions overrun and units
encircled, simply surrendered or deserted. Many, particularly from non-
Russian nationality groups but including Russians as well, had little love for
the Stalinist regime and no desire to die defending it.

After a few months, however, the problem of surrender and desertion
diminished. Not only did the Red Army begin to reorganize and reassert
control over its soldiers, but soldiers became aware of the brutality of the
Germans toward Soviet prisoners and accordingly had less desire to surrender.[36] Moreover, the murderous practices of the Germans in the areas they
occupied, seen by the soldiers themselves and highlighted by the Soviet press,
generated a desire for revenge among Red Army troops.[37]

For Jewish soldiers, both factors were a powerful incentive to fight. Though
it was not discussed in the Soviet press, the German effort to annihilate the
Jews of Russia and the Ukraine soon became a matter of common knowledge
and gave Jews, especially those whose families had been murdered, a special
incentive to fight. As historian Catherine Merridale observes, "In 1941, Jews
signed up in the thousands for the Soviet cause. Students from Moscow set
their books aside, young Communists in government roles asked to be assigned to the front. Jews were among the keenest volunteers for every kind

of army service."[38] Some Jewish soldiers also felt compelled to disprove anti-Semitic assertions about Jewish cowardice. "I knew that I was a Jew," said one veteran interviewed by Merridale, "and so I had to prove that I was not afraid."[39]

Jewish soldiers, moreover, soon learned that if captured by the Germans and identified as Jews, they would almost certainly be shot. Even Jewish prisoners who sought to hide their identities from the Germans knew that they might at any time be denounced by an anti-Semitic fellow prisoner. As a result, even more than other Soviet soldiers, Jews had every incentive to fight to the end rather than surrender. Indeed, many of the Jewish medal winners whose biographies are reported by Gershon Shapiro received their awards posthumously for actions undertaken in hopeless situations where surrender to the Germans might have seemed the only reasonable course of action—and would have been for a non-Jewish soldier.

Because of their unusually high levels of education, a disproportionate number of Jews, perhaps as many as one-fifth of the Red Army's Jewish personnel, according to some estimates, held officers' commissions. During the course of the war, Jews commanded roughly 130 Soviet regiments.[40] Nine Jewish generals commanded armies, twelve commanded corps, twenty-three were chiefs of staff of army groups, and thirty-four commanded divisions.[41] Among these generals were such famous officers as Jakov Kreyzer, who commanded the First Moscow Motorized Infantry Division in the defense of Moscow. Kreyzer's division, for the first time, employed the new T-34 tanks, which proved very effective against the Germans, delaying their advance for several days while the Soviets established a defensive line along the Dnieper River. When the Germans learned that their opponent was a Jew, they dropped leaflets on Kreyzer's troops reading, "Russian soldiers! Into whose hands are you putting your lives? Your commander is the Jew, Yankel Kreyzer. Do you believe Yankel will save you from us?"[42] Kreyzer subsequently commanded a number of other Soviet forces, including the Fifty-first Army on the Baltic front.

Also as a function of the Jews' relatively high levels of education, Jewish generals were particularly prominent in the military's technical and political services. Until they fell from favor Yakov Smushkevich commanded the air force, and Yan Gamarnik headed the army's political administration. Jewish officers were also prominent in the Soviet army medical corps and in engineering, artillery, and armor, which, along with the air force, were services that required education and technical skills.

Although no precise numbers are available, Jews seem to have been especially important in the Soviet air force, which included many hundreds of Jewish pilots.[43] A number of Jews commanded air force squadrons, and several of the USSR's best-known fighter pilots were Jews. For example, Captain Vladimir Levitan is credited with shooting down twenty German planes in air-to-air combat. Captain Abrek Barsht shot down eighteen. Captain Yakov Vernikov destroyed sixteen German opponents. Captain Mikhail Plotkin was the first Soviet pilot to bomb Berlin. In August 1941, twelve aircraft mounted the Soviet equivalent of the Doolittle Raid on Tokyo—militarily insignificant but an important morale booster for a civilian populace desperate for good news. Plotkin was killed the next year when his plane was hit by antiaircraft fire while he was laying mines at the entrance to a German port on the Baltic. A number of Jewish women also distinguished themselves in the Soviet air force. These include two Heroines of the Soviet Union, Polina Gelman and Lily Litvak. Gelman flew hundreds of combat missions, piloting a light bomber, and survived the war. Litvak was shot down in 1943, but the wreckage of her plane was not actually recovered until 1990.[44]

THE JEWS AND SOVIET MILITARY PRODUCTION

No matter how determined and effective Jewish soldiers and officers might have been, one could not say with any confidence that their role was conclusive in bringing about the defeat of Nazi Germany. As soldiers, the Jews played an important role but hardly determined the outcome of the war. In the realm of military production, however, the role of Jewish engineers and managers was decisive.

Prior to the purges of the 1930s, the Soviet armaments industry had begun to produce excellent weapons, including modern tanks and aircraft equal to the best in the world. Industrially backward in the 1920s, Soviet industry had taken a "great leap forward" by signing technical assistance contracts with American and European firms that called for these companies to build factories in the USSR and train Soviet citizens in their operation.[45] By the late 1930s, the Soviet Union possessed modern plants and industrial equipment. Foreign training, coupled with the expansion of Soviet universities and the opening of university places on the basis of merit, produced growing numbers of individuals educated in engineering and technical subjects, including a large number of Jews. These developments provided the Soviet Union with the basis for a first-class armaments industry.

The purges of the 1930s, as discussed earlier, resulted in the liquidation of many military officers and the arrest and imprisonment of large numbers of engineers and technical experts. This left major Soviet military industries, along with the army itself, in disarray. Tactical doctrines were revised and discarded before anyone even understood them. Plans for new weapons languished, while even maintenance of existing armaments fell by the wayside owing to poor planning and a lack of skilled personnel. When the Germans attacked, for example, new tanks were still in development, and large numbers of existing tanks were not only obsolete but in need of serious repair. In June 1941, 29 percent of the army's tanks needed overhaul, and 44 percent needed major repairs. Only 27 percent of the Red Army's tanks were actually in working order.[46] Of course, to make matters even worse, the German invasion engulfed or threatened the major centers of Soviet industrial and arms production—Moscow, Leningrad, Kiev, Stalingrad, and so forth. If these factories were captured or destroyed, there would be no possibility that the Soviet Union could recover from its initial reverses, and the war would almost certainly be lost.

To be sure, some Soviet planners had considered this very problem and developed contingency plans for the evacuation of industries and people from the predictable path of a German attack. One such planner was a Jew, Boris Vannikov, a graduate of the High Technical Institute in Moscow and the people's commissar for armament. Vannikov had given some thought to this problem and developed preliminary ideas regarding the evacuation and reorganization of factories in secure areas east of the Urals. The Soviet leadership, Stalin in particular, had insisted that, in any war, the Red Army would adopt an aggressive "forward" strategy and carry the war to the enemy. Hence, the notion that evacuations might be needed was considered heretical. Vannikov, in fact, fell under suspicion of disloyalty and, as it happened, just a few weeks before the German invasion, was arrested, accused of being a German spy, and beaten and tortured by the NKVD in Moscow's infamous Lubyanka prison.

Several weeks after his arrest, according to Soviet historian F. D. Sverdlov, Vannikov was visited by an NKVD officer, who asked him, apparently hypothetically, if in the event of a successful German attack, there would be any possibility of evacuating important Soviet factories to some safer region.[47] Vannikov replied that, given a few days, he could sketch out the general outline of such a plan. The NKVD officer expressed great interest in the idea; he gave Vannikov a notebook and pencils and said he would be interested in seeing Vannikov's ideas when he returned the day after next. Two days later, Vannikov showed the officer a hypothetical plan for the evacuation of Soviet factories to the east. The officer took the notebook and departed. Soon thereafter, Vannikov was removed from his cell, and the wounds incurred during his torture were treated. As soon as Vannikov had been outfitted in a new uniform, he was taken to the Kremlin and presented to Joseph Stalin himself, who was accompanied by Lavrenty Beria and Vyacheslav Molotov.

Vannikov quickly learned that the German invasion was real, not hypothetical. Stalin held Vannikov's notebook, declared that the evacuation plan was excellent, and appointed Vannikov deputy people's commissar for armament with full authority to implement the plan. As to the charges that had led to Vannikov's arrest and torture, Stalin dismissed them with a wave of his hand, saying that they had been found to have been based on lies made up by "scoundrels." Stalin told Vannikov that he should not be upset or offended by the whole matter and had him driven immediately to the Commissariat for Armament, where he began organizing the evacuation of Soviet factories.

Over the course of the next half year, many industrial plants were destroyed or lost to the Germans, but some 2,500 Soviet factories—mainly those involved in military production—and their several million workers were evacuated from the western industrial regions of the USSR to locations east of the Ural Mountains, thousands of miles from the front lines. In October and November 1941, 498 plants were removed from Moscow alone, along with their 210,000 workers.[48] This prodigious effort, accomplished under German bombing, required the coordinated use of tens of thousands of railroad cars that were also needed to bring troops and supplies to the front and to evacuate wounded soldiers. Whenever possible, to achieve maximum efficiency, an entire factory and its workers would be loaded onto a single train.[49] Responsibility for the transport plan fell to another Jewish commissar, Lazar Kaganovich, commissar for transport. During the critical first months of the war, Kaganovich presided over the Council for Evacuation, which was responsible for planning and coordinating the operations of the Soviet rail system.

Responsibility for the rebuilding of the evacuated factories was assigned to the Commissariat for Construction, directed by Semyon Ginsburg, another Jewish graduate of Moscow's High Technical Institute, who served as people's commissar for construction. Ginsburg was in charge of the construction of defense plants and making certain that the evacuated plants began producing military equipment as quickly as possible.[50] A number of other Jewish engineers also played vital roles in coordinating Soviet military production. Semyon Reznikov was deputy commissar for steel production, Solomon Sendler was deputy commissar for the aviation industry, Grigory Kaplun was deputy commissar for naval construction, and Leon Lokshin served as deputy commissar for the chemical industry. During the war years, Jewish deputy commissars were also in charge of electricity, heavy industry, and the fuel industry.[51]

The evacuation and reconstruction of industrial plants was an enormous success. In 1941, while factories were being evacuated and rebuilt, Soviet industrial production came to a virtual halt. Tanks, aircraft, and artillery lost in battle could not be replaced, and ammunition was in short supply. By 1942, however, Soviet military production accelerated dramatically as factories began to manufacture military supplies using multiple shifts of workers on a twenty-four-hour basis even before their walls and roofs were finished. Workers lived in caves and tents until housing could be built. By the end of 1942, 96 percent of the factories evacuated to the east were in full operation.[52] And, astonishingly, in 1942 the Soviet Union built more tanks, aircraft, and artillery pieces than Germany. Further, although Germany stepped up its level of industrial production in the following years, it was outproduced by the USSR in these three vital categories every year until the end of the war, ensuring that Soviet battlefield losses of equipment could be replaced while German losses could not.[53] As a result, in the four-year campaign of attrition that characterized the Russo-German war, the USSR was eventually able to overwhelm the Germans, not with manpower but with weapons.[54]

Tanks

Soviet superiority in weapons was not only quantitative but, in many areas, qualitative as well. The most important of these realms was tank design. Before the war, both Germany and the USSR had experimented with a variety of different tanks as well as doctrines for their use. Indeed, prior to 1933 Germany and the USSR cooperated in the design and production of tanks and in training tank officers. The basis for cooperation was obvious. Germany was prohibited by the Versailles Treaty from producing tanks, while the Soviets benefited from German technology. Hence, the Germans helped the Soviets develop tanks in the USSR, while the Soviets provided the Germans with training in their use. This cooperation ended when Hitler came to power, but, ironically, Germany's first three Panzer divisions were led by tankers who had learned their trade in the USSR.[55]

Over the next several years, the Soviets built thousands of tanks of various types. Indeed, just before the German attack, the Soviet Union nominally fielded more than 15,000 tanks in its western military districts, while the German army on the Soviet border boasted only some 5,200. As noted earlier, however, only about one-fourth of the Soviet tanks were actually operational, and many of the others were obsolete. Thanks also to the Stalinist purges, the majority of experienced tank officers had been arrested by the secret police, and the Soviet tank corps was in complete disarray. Thousands of Soviet tanks were destroyed or captured by the Germans in the early weeks of the war, reducing the strength of Soviet armored forces by as much as 90 percent.[56]

Just before the war, however, the USSR had deployed small numbers of two new tanks. These were the KV heavy tank and T-34 medium tank. These tanks, particularly the T-34s, caused some consternation among the Germans when, on first encountering them on the battlefield, they discovered that their antitank guns were ineffective against the Soviet machines.[57] In the early weeks of the war, shortages of ammunition and fuel, coupled with the general disorganization and lack of leadership of Soviet forces, limited the effectiveness of the new Soviet tanks. As the front stabilized, though, and the Soviets realized the superiority of their new machines, they turned all their attention to the construction of T-34s and KVs.

The T-34, which became the mainstay of the Soviet armored forces, weighed 30.9 tons, initially carried a 76-mm gun, had a top speed of 55 kph, could traverse almost any terrain, and was protected by thick armor ingeniously designed to deflect rounds that might strike it. The early T-34s manifested several problems, but these were rectified, the tank's armor strengthened, and a larger, more powerful 85-mm gun introduced. This T-34/85 outgunned and outperformed every German tank it faced and is generally considered to have been the best tank of World War II. Not only was the T-34 effective, but it was relatively inexpensive to produce and easy to maintain and operate. And, to make things worse from the German perspective, the Soviets built tens of thousands of T-34s once the evacuated factories went into full operation. More than 60,000 T-34s were built during the war.

The designers of the T-34 included a number of Jewish engineers, such as Yaakov Vikhman and Yaakov Nevyazhesky, who were among the USSR's leading designers of diesel engines. The chief builder of T-34s, however, was Isaak Zaltzman, people's commissar for tanks. Zaltzman, the son of a Jewish tailor from an isolated *shtetl* (village) in the Ukraine, was a graduate of Odessa's Polytechnic Institute. In 1938, Zaltzman was appointed director of the Kirov Works in Leningrad, the Soviet Union's major center for the production of tanks, locomotives, and artillery.[58] Kirov designers had proposed the construction of a new heavy tank whose armor would be more difficult to penetrate than that of existing Soviet tanks. These tanks were produced and called KVs after the initials of Soviet defense minister Kliment Voroshilov. The KV tanks were very effective in the Finnish war and went into mass production in 1940.

As the Wehrmacht approached Leningrad, an evacuation of the Kirov Works was ordered. The factory and its workers were relocated to the Cheliabinsk tractor factory in the Urals, which eventually employed 75,000 persons, producing an average of ten tanks per day every day until the end of the war. Though initially the goal was continued production of KV tanks, the German capture of Stalingrad where the T-34s were built required a shift in production to meet military demand for the T-34s. Under Zaltzman's supervision, T-34s were also produced by the Urals Railcar Factory in Nizhny Tagil, to which Kharkov's tank factory had been evacuated.[59] These two factories were supported by a large group of evacuated plants. Tank engines, for example, were produced by the Urals Turbo Motor Factory, which had also been evacuated from Leningrad.

Managers like Zaltzman often had to improvise to overcome difficulties in obtaining parts and raw materials in wartime. In 1941, a large group of KV tanks was scheduled to be delivered to the army defending Moscow. The factory, however, could not obtain starter motors for the tanks. The starter motors were manufactured by a plant within range of German aircraft, and the Soviet planes sent to pick them up had twice been shot down. Zaltzman resolved this problem by sending the tanks, along with a group of assembly workers, by rail to Moscow. At a station near the capital, they met a train carrying the starter motors and assembled them on the spot. Zaltzman then delivered the tanks to Marshal Zhukov.[60]

In the Soviet Union, the T-34 was, quite properly, often called "the tank that won the war." Isaak Zaltzman, for his part, was known as "the king of the tanks."

Aircraft

Some Jewish engineering and technical school graduates designed tanks. Others designed aircraft, playing major roles in the design and production of such important Soviet combat aircraft as the La-5, the Il-2, the Yak-3, and the MiG-3. At the beginning of the war, the Soviet military fielded some 15,000 aircraft of various types, with about two-thirds assigned to the USSR's western military districts.[61] As in the case of Soviet tanks, however, a large percentage of the combat planes were obsolete, not fully operational, or flown by inexperienced pilots. The Germans, moreover, destroyed a large fraction of the Soviet air force in the first days of the war, quickly achieving air superiority.

In the late 1930s, Soviet aircraft designers had developed plans for new combat aircraft. Their efforts were hindered by Stalin's purges, which led to the arrest and deportation of hundreds of aircraft designers and engineers.[62] However, small numbers of new planes had been delivered to the air force just before the German invasion. These deliveries, unfortunately, only added to the air force's confusion since pilots and ground crews had not yet had time to familiarize themselves with the new equipment when the Germans attacked.[63] Since the main centers of Soviet aircraft production were in the west and in the direct path of the Germans, production of new planes came to a virtual halt until factories could be evacuated to the Urals. There, Soviet aircraft plants started work, utilizing new designs, and quickly began to produce planes that were equal to or better than those flown by the Germans. And, as in the case of tanks, the USSR produced many more aircraft than Nazi Germany. In 1942, relying on the evacuated factories, the Soviet Union produced 10,000 more airplanes than Germany—and continued to outproduce the Germans for the remainder of the war.[64]

One of the new Soviet aircraft that began to appear in large numbers in 1942 was the La-5, designed by Semyon Lavochkin, a Jewish engineering graduate of Moscow State Technical University. Lavochkin was assisted by a

team that included two other Jewish designers, Leonid Zak and Mikhail Ar-
lozorov.[65] The La-5 replaced an earlier plane, the La-3, also designed by Lavochkin. The La-5 (along with its successor, the La-7) was an air-superiority
fighter designed to engage the various German fighters, such as the Fw-190
and Me-9, as well as to destroy German bombers and ground-attack planes.
Soviet pilots regarded the La-5 and La-7 as the equal of the top German
fighter planes and their superior at low altitudes, where most aerial combat
actually took place.

Some 15,000 of the La series fighters were produced during the war, and
about 2,500 were lost in combat. In 1942, the La-5s more than held their own
against the Luftwaffe in the skies over Stalingrad and prevented the German
Sixth Army from being supplied by air. In the decisive 1943 Battle of Kursk,
both the German and Russian air forces sustained extremely heavy losses. In
the initial days of the battle, the Luftwaffe managed to achieve local air superiority, but this proved short-lived, and the La-5s, which appeared in large
numbers over the battlefield during fifty days of fighting, eventually won
control of the skies.[66]

After 1943, the Soviet army was generally able to maintain air superiority
over the battlefield thanks in no small measure to the La fighters and their pilots.[67] These included the USSR's top air ace, Ivan N. Kozhedub (called "Ivan
the Terrible"), credited with sixty-two victories in his La-5 and La-7 fighters.
In addition to designing the La fighters, Jewish engineers were important in
the planes' production. At the assembly plant, the head engineer was David
Reznikov, the chief technician was Semyon Zaichyk, and the factory's deputy
directors were Arkady Shulman and Alexander Joffe.[68]

A second very important Soviet aircraft to appear in 1941 was the Il-2, a
two-seat ground-attack plane produced in enormous numbers—more than
42,000 were built—during the course of the war. Among the chief designers of the Il-2 were several Jews, including Victor Shaivin, D. V. Leshchiner,
and A. M. Vulman. Yaakob Khaevsky was chief engineer of the evacuated
factory that produced the planes, and I. Shenkman was the factory director.
No less a personage than Joseph Stalin viewed the Il-2 as one of the most
important weapons in the Soviet arsenal, "as essential to the Red Army as air
and bread."[69] Stalin railed at the factory directors when Il-2 production fell
behind schedule and threatened dire consequences if more planes were not

produced.[70] The importance of the Il-2 was its capacity to provide close air support for Soviet troops and, in particular, to destroy German tanks.

A fighter like the La-5 is designed to engage other aircraft. A ground-attack plane like the Il-2, on the other hand, is designed to engage enemy tanks and infantry in order to provide air support for its side's armor and infantry. Close air support is the most difficult and dangerous of all air operations since it requires the pilot to operate at low speed and altitude, where the craft is vulnerable to ground fire as well as to fire from opposing fighter planes.

The main German ground-attack plane, the Ju 87, or Stuka, was hampered by thin armor and weak defensive armament, which made it quite vulnerable both to antiaircraft fire and to Soviet fighters. Stukas were most effective when attacking unprotected cities or already-demoralized troops fleeing from the battlefield and unable to mount an air defense. The Il-2, known as the Shturmovik, on the other hand, was strongly armored and mounted heavy machine guns, front and rear, with which to defend itself against German fighters. Armor plates protected the Shturmovik's pilot, engine, fuel tanks, and other critical components so that the aircraft was quite resistant to ground fire. This mode of construction anticipated the American A-10 Warthog ground-attack plane of the 1990s, whose pilot was protected by titanium plates. Some Il-2 pilots reported that their aircraft had not been brought down even after being hit by hundreds of German bullets. They called the Il-2 a "flying tank." German troops reportedly referred to the Il-2 as "Der Schlachter" (The Slaughterer), and Luftwaffe pilots called the Il-2 "Eiserner Gustav" (Iron Gustav) because of the difficulty of destroying it. Despite all its armor, the Il-2 was, of course, not invulnerable, and many were lost, especially to German fighters.

In battle, the Shturmovik was an extraordinarily effective weapon against German tanks. After the Soviet air force mastered the plane's various characteristics, made modifications, and developed appropriate tactics, the Il-2's rockets, canon, and cluster bombs were used to penetrate the upper armor of German tanks with devastating effect. The Shturmovik's main weapon was the deadly NS-37 antitank cannon, whose chief designer was another Jewish engineer, A. E. Nudelman.[71] Typically flights of thirty to forty Shturmoviks launched coordinated attacks on tank columns, infantry formations, and other targets, while other groups of Il-2s worked to suppress antiaircraft fire. The Shturmovik was also able to fly in all weather conditions—clouds, fog, and even snowstorms.[72]

The Il-2 played a major role in defeating the Wehrmacht in the decisive 1943 Battle of Kursk in which the Germans absorbed huge losses of tanks from which they were never able to recover. According to Soviet studies, a great many of these German tanks and other armored vehicles were destroyed by the Shturmoviks.[73] For example, the Ninth Panzer Division lost seventy tanks in twenty minutes to air attacks. Similarly, the Third Panzer Division lost 270 tanks in two hours, and the Seventeenth Panzer Division lost 240 of its 300 tanks during four hours of continuous air attack by multiple flights of Shturmoviks.[74] The Shturmoviks were also used to attack the German rear and prevent reserves from being brought forward to block Soviet breakthroughs.[75]

Two other aircraft in whose design and production Jews played important parts were the Yak-3 and the MiG-3. The Yak-3 was an air-superiority fighter introduced in 1944. Among its leading developers were two Jewish engineers, Yosef Zaslavsky and Leonid Schechter. The evacuated factory that produced Yak (Yakovlev) fighters was directed by Israel Levin. The Yak was considered an outstanding fighter and was extremely effective against German aircraft when deployed. Even the Germans regarded it as an "exceptional" aircraft.[76]

Unfortunately, development work on the Yak-3 had been abandoned when the Germans captured Stalingrad, site of the Yakovlev factory. Though work resumed in the evacuated factory in far-off Saratov, the production of other aircraft was given priority, and the Yak-3 did not enter service until the last year of the war. The MiG-3, on the other hand, had begun to be deployed just before the German invasion. The plane was developed by the Mikoyan-Gourevich design bureau. Mikhail Gourevich was an aeronautical engineer trained at the Kharkov Technological Institute. His partner, Artem Mikoyan, had no engineering training but had important political connections. He was the brother of Anastas Mikoyan, Stalin's minister of trade. Some years later, Anastas became first deputy premier under Nikita Khrushchev, a promotion that did no harm to the interests of the Mikoyan-Gourevich aircraft enterprise.

The MiG-3 was especially effective at high altitudes, where it was superior to most German fighters.[77] Several hundred had been deployed in the first half of 1941, but most were destroyed on the ground when the Germans attacked. Subsequently, production of MiGs was delayed in favor of La fighters and especially Il-2s, whose engines were produced in the same transplanted factories as those of the MiGs. After the war, of course, the MiG design team produced the USSR's first jet fighter. Successive generations of MiG fighters became international symbols of Soviet air power.

Artillery

A third area of weapons design and production in which Jewish engineers and managers played important roles is the realm of artillery. During the course of the war, the Soviet Union produced nearly 500,000 artillery pieces of all types—nearly five times as many as were built by the Germans.[78] One important site of artillery production was the Lenin Machine Factory, evacuated to Perm in the Ural Mountains, which was directed by a Jew, Abraham Bikhovsky. This one factory produced 48,000 heavy guns during the war, including 152-mm self-propelled guns and 122-mm howitzers.[79] Similarly, the Barrikady Factory, which had been evacuated from Stalingrad, was directed by a Jew, Lev Gonor, with production under the direction of L. N. Eisenberg. This factory was one of the Soviet army's major suppliers of 210-mm and 305-mm guns. Antiaircraft guns were built in Kalinin Factory No. 8 under the direction of a Jewish engineer, Boris Fratkin. The chief designer of the guns was another Jewish engineer, Grigory Avtsin. The factory was evacuated from Moscow to the Urals in October 1941 and began production one month later.[80]

In 1942, three Jewish engineers, Leonid Shvarts, Mosei Kommisarchik, and Yakov Shor, were awarded the Stalin prize for "the development of a new type of weapon."[81] This new weapon, which came to be called the "Katyusha" and had been introduced at the end of 1941, was a mobile multiple rocket launcher that could fire between fourteen and forty-eight rockets from the back of a vehicle. The preferred vehicle was the lend-lease Studebaker truck contributed by the Americans. The Katyusha was not especially accurate, but grouped together, a number of Katyusha batteries firing simultaneously could saturate a target with hundreds or even thousands of rockets and cause considerable destruction. While the rockets were relatively ineffective against tanks or fortified targets, they were deadly to German infantry caught in the open; accordingly, they were greatly feared by the Germans. Katyushas were also inexpensive to manufacture and easy to use. More than 10,000 were built during the war. The rocket fuel for the Katyushas was developed by two Jewish scientists, Yakov Zeldovich and Yulii Khariton, who later became important Soviet nuclear weapons designers.[82]

POPULAR MOBILIZATION

A third reason the Soviet Union was able to defeat Nazi Germany is that the USSR was better able than Germany to mobilize the energies of its citizens for total war. Until the final months of the war, Nazi Germany sought to preserve a veneer of normalcy for its citizens. Even as cities were bombed and news from the front became increasingly grim, factories worked only one shift and continued to produce consumer goods, children attended school, and women remained at home. One author characterized the Germans as maintaining a "peace-like wartime economy."[83] In the USSR, by contrast, factories worked around the clock producing tanks and fighter planes. Women worked in the defense plants or in the fields if they were not among the 2 million women in the Soviet military; 250,000 women actually served as frontline troops or combat pilots. Children, too, worked in the factories and fields. And, for all, the workweek was seven days, sixty-six hours per week, with one day of rest per month.[84]

A particular problem faced by the USSR at the beginning of the war was that many of its citizens hated the regime and were not prepared to sacrifice for it. As noted above, millions of Soviet soldiers surrendered or deserted in the early months of the war, and in many regions, including the Ukraine, German troops were greeted as liberators. Even in Russia proper, millions of peasants had been uprooted and dispossessed by the regime's policies of agricultural collectivization and had little interest in fighting for communism and Stalin. How could a regime that was despised by many of its citizens secure their cooperation in what became a long and bloody war of attrition?

The answer is that every regime seeks to elicit popular cooperation through a mix of coercion and persuasion—the stick and the carrot. The Stalinist regime was no exception. Its stick was heavy. Immediately after the German attack, Stalin declared martial law in the western USSR. He also announced a labor-conscription law and a "ruthless campaign" against "disorganization of the rear by enemy spies, diversionists and parachutists." Officers and soldiers who surrendered or allowed themselves to be captured were declared "traitors to the motherland." Their families were subject to arrest and imprisonment. Later, Stalin issued his famous Order No. 227, declaring "Not a step back!" and decreeing summary execution, imprisonment, or service in penal battalions for soldiers deemed guilty of cowardice. This order sparked a large number of executions.[85] In battle, NKVD "blocking units" were deployed behind the frontline troops to prevent desertion. During the course of the war, 158,000 soldiers were shot for cowardice and related offenses, 436,000 were imprisoned, and 442,000 were assigned to penal battalions, where they performed the most dangerous duties, such as clearing mine fields. A soldier wounded while doing penal duty could be reinstated into the regular army. He was deemed to have "atoned with his own blood."[86]

As for persuasion, beginning in 1942 Soviet propaganda shifted from socialist to nationalist themes in an effort to mobilize Russian patriotism. Russia and the Motherland replaced the USSR and communism as the entities to be defended.[87] A new national anthem was written and played in place of the Communist "Internationale." Russian Orthodox churches were reopened. The war was presented in the press, motion pictures, and lectures to the troops by their commissars and *politruks* (political workers) as a fight to prevent the Russian motherland from being defiled by German beasts.[88] According to most observers, these propaganda themes were extremely effective in building morale among the troops and maintaining the spirit of the hard-pressed civilian population.[89]

Jews played important roles in both these realms, especially the second. In terms of the stick, Jews continued to serve in the NKVD and other security services, but their influence had diminished since the purges of the 1930s and the rise of Lavrenty Beria as head of the NKVD. Nevertheless, in the initial months of the war, the army's political commissars were assigned new powers and given authority to implement Stalin's edicts concerning surrender and retreat. The head of the army's political officers was Lev Mekhlis, a prominent Jewish Communist who had played a major role in the military purges of the 1930s. Mekhlis was now assigned the task of making certain the soldiers fought and did not surrender. Mekhlis was himself fired (but not liquidated) in 1942 for his part in a disastrous military operation in the Crimea.

It was in the realm of persuasion that Jews were most prominent. Within the army, the *politruks* not only enforced discipline but also lectured the troops on their duties to the motherland and the bestiality of the Germans. During the first eight months of the war, more than 130,000 political workers were mobilized and assigned to combat units.[90] More than 10 to 15 percent of these *politruks* were Jews. Their efforts were generally thought to have played an important role in stiffening the will of Soviet soldiers to fight against terrible odds in the early months of the war.[91] In terms of more general forms of persuasion, Jews had been major figures in the prewar Soviet film and media industries and now turned their talents to exhorting the frightened and exhausted citizenry to fight the Germans. Sergei Eisenstein's film *Alexander Nevsky*, the story of a Muscovite prince who defeated the Teutonic Knights in the thirteenth century, had been produced in 1938 but withdrawn in 1939 after the Nazi-Soviet pact. In 1942, it became required viewing.[92] Mikhail Romm's *Girl No. 217* showed Russian audiences the brutal treatment of a Russian girl held as a slave by a German family.[93] Mark Donskoy's *How the Steel Was Tempered* tells a story of Ukrainian resistance to the Germans in 1918.[94] Donskoy's *The Rainbow* is about a woman partisan, Olena, who is brutally tortured by the Germans but refuses to betray her comrades.[95] These films and hundreds of others like them were shown throughout the war to fan feelings of Russian nationalism and hatred for the Germans.

Equally important were the press accounts in *Pravda* and the official army newspaper, *Red Star*, edited by David Ortenberg. These accounts emphasized the heroism of Soviet troops and the bestiality of the Germans and were often accompanied by commentary from Ilya Ehrenberg, a Jewish writer who became one of the most famous newspaper writers in all the Soviet Union during the war years. Ehrenberg's accounts from the front lines and published in *Red Star* called upon every Soviet citizen to kill the Germans. "If you have killed one German," he wrote, "kill another. There is nothing jollier than German corpses."[96] Ehrenberg's articles were read by every literate soldier in the Red Army, as well as by millions of civilians, and helped to crystallize popular feelings and hatreds, particularly in 1941 and 1942 when all seemed to be lost. Ehrenberg's articles helped inspire the hundreds of thousands of popular militiamen and -women, or *opolchenie*, who turned out to dig trenches, build fortifications, and fight to defend Soviet cities.

Jewish propagandists also worked abroad to build support for the Soviet cause. The major vehicle for this effort was the Jewish Anti-Fascist Committee (JAFC) composed of prominent Soviet Jewish political figures and intellectuals. The JAFC raised money in the United States and Great Britain for the Soviet war effort and worked to create a favorable picture of the USSR abroad. Though nominally an independent entity headed by the famous Soviet Jewish actor Solomon Mikhoels, the JAFC was actually part of the Soviet Information Bureau and closely monitored by a Jewish NKVD official, Sergei Shpigelglaz.[97]

THE JEWS AND SOVIET VICTORY

Jews were a small and often persecuted group in the Soviet Union but made a major contribution to the USSR's victory in World War II. Jews fought, commanded troops, and bolstered popular morale. Even more importantly, Jews played a major role in designing and building the enormous quantities of superb weapons—tanks, aircraft, and artillery—that made Soviet victory possible.

Could the USSR have defeated Nazi Germany without the Jews? This question, of course, cannot be answered. However, in the Soviet Union of that era, the Jews were by far the best educated and most literate and numerate segment of the populace. There were none to take their places. The Soviet Union was vast and rich in resources but poor in talent. In the absence of educated native talent, the tsars had, for centuries, recruited talented outsiders, usually Germans, to serve as administrators, managers, and military officers. In 1941, the Germans were not available for these purposes. The Jews were.

The United States

The Anti-Nazi Coalition

In the 1930s, Europe's Jews were surrounded by foes. They faced the grim beginnings of Adolf Hitler's "final solution" and bore the brunt of Joseph Stalin's purges. Fascism and anti-Semitism seemed to be sweeping the European continent.

America's Jews, on the other hand, found a very important ally in the person of Franklin Delano Roosevelt. In the decades before FDR's New Deal, Jews had been pushed to the margins of American society. Their access to higher education had been restricted, with top universities and professional schools seeking to prevent "excessive" Jewish enrollment and limiting Jews to no more than 3 or 4 percent of entering classes.[1] Employment discrimination was the norm, with major corporations, law firms, and universities declining to offer positions to Jews. Housing discrimination was commonplace. Jews were denied membership in and admission to business and social clubs, as well as resorts and other institutions that, by referring themselves as "exclusive," indicated that they were *Judenrein* (free of Jews). Academic and literary proponents of eugenics, like prominent zoologist Charles Davenport and popular author Houston Stewart Chamberlain, justified Jewish exclusion by asserting that Jews lacked the character, loyalty, and leadership ability of Anglo-Saxons.[2]

Beginning in the 1930s, though, Jews began a long climb to power and prominence in the United States as members of a coalition of forces assembled by Franklin Roosevelt under the banner of the Democratic Party.

When elected in 1933, Roosevelt and the Democrats were opposed by much of the nation's established elite. As a result, Jewish attorneys, economists, statisticians, and other talented professionals became an important source of leadership and expertise for the Roosevelt administration, much as they had for Lenin and his Bolsheviks.

In the Soviet case, the problem was a nationwide shortage of talent. America, for its part, was hardly bereft of talent. Outside the Jews, however, administrative, academic, and intellectual talent was concentrated in the Republican camp. Accordingly, more than 15 percent of Roosevelt's top-level appointees were Jews—at a time when Jews constituted barely 3 percent of the nation's citizenry and were objects of considerable popular antipathy.[3] Jews were also important among Roosevelt's political advisors and functionaries. Jewish labor leaders like Sidney Hillman, for example, became major figures in Roosevelt's political campaigns.[4]

The majority of FDR's Jewish appointees were given positions in the new agencies created by the White House to administer New Deal programs. In these agencies Jews came to constitute a large and highly visible group and prompted FDR's enemies to refer to the New Deal as the "Jew Deal." Anti-Semites would not have been surprised to learn that the term "New Deal" was actually coined by one of Roosevelt's Jewish aides, Samuel Rosenman.[5] For their part, Jews found the Roosevelt administration and New Deal programs to be a major route to power, status, and employment in a society that otherwise subjected them to severe discrimination in virtually every occupational realm.

Roosevelt, as well as his Jewish advisors, have been criticized for their failure to take any action on behalf of Europe's Jews.[6] And, indeed, Roosevelt's Jewish staffers and appointees were concerned more with the fate of America's Jews than with that of their European brethren. FDR, well aware of the depth of anti-Semitism in the United States, was cautious about taking actions that might provide ammunition to those who accused him of placing Jewish interests ahead of America's.

At any rate, quite a number of Jews achieved positions of considerable influence in the Roosevelt administration. Henry Morgenthau was named secretary of the treasury. Felix Frankfurter, Harvard's only Jewish law professor and a Roosevelt advisor, was appointed to the Supreme Court in 1939. Even after he joined the High Court, Frankfurter remained a key presidential adviser and consultant. From the bench, Frankfurter played a central role in formulating New Deal programs and channeling large numbers of bright young Jewish lawyers to Washington to work in New Deal agencies and programs. These individuals came to be called "Frankfurter's happy hot dogs."[7]

Among the most important of these "hot dogs" was Benjamin Cohen. Frequently advised by Frankfurter, Cohen was instrumental in writing major pieces of New Deal legislation, including the Securities Act of 1933, the Securities and Exchange Act of 1934, the Public Utility Holding Act of 1935, the Federal Communications Act, the 1933 Tennessee Valley Authority Act, the 1935 Wagner Act, and the 1938 Minimum Wage Act. Other Jews who played significant roles in the Roosevelt administration included Supreme Court Justice Louis Brandeis; attorney Abe Fortas at the Securities and Exchange Commission; Isador Lubin, who served as head of the Bureau of Labor Statistics and also as Roosevelt's chief economic advisor; Charles Wyzanski in the Department of Labor; and White House special assistant David Niles.

Jews, including lawyers and other professionals, were also prominent in the Department of Labor, the Justice Department, the Securities and Exchange Commission chaired by Jerome Frank, the Tennessee Valley Authority chaired by David Lilienthal, the U.S. Housing Authority administered by Nathan Straus, the National Labor Relations Board, the Social Security Administration, and the Agricultural Adjustment Administration. For Jewish professionals, New Deal agencies were a critical source of employment and a vital route to professional status and successful careers.[8] Jews faced significant discrimination in the private sector and previously had few career options in the public sector. Talented Jews were more than able to hold their own in college, graduate school, and professional school—if they could gain admission. Jews found, however, that academic success did not give them access to jobs and careers. Nowhere in the country would major corporations or law firms hire Jews, except under the most extraordinary circumstances. Service with the Roosevelt administration, though, gave status, and ultimately power, to bright Jewish professionals who had few other options. FDR, for his part, was happy to take full advantage of this pool of underemployed talent to develop ideas and staff his agencies.

As a result of all these factors, the New Deal provided Jews with numerous opportunities and advantages, and by the end of Roosevelt's first term in office, most Jews had given the president and his party their allegiance. To this

day, America's Jews largely remain in the Democratic camp as voters, activists, and financial contributors.

FORMING AN ANTI-NAZI COALITION

During the late 1930s, Jews and the Roosevelt administration became linked
in still another way. The administration and the Jewish community became
close allies in the struggle against isolationism and pro-Axis sentiment in the
years preceding World War II. Roosevelt and the Jews had a common set of
enemies—right-wing, pro-German, and isolationist organizations. Some, like
the America First Committee, sought to avoid any identification with Nazism
or anti-Semitism, though they inevitably attracted Nazis and anti-Semites.[9]
Others, like the German American Bund, were less scrupulous.

The Roosevelt administration was anxious to enhance America's military
strength, to intervene in support of Great Britain, and to prevent Germany
from dominating Europe and the North Atlantic. FDR, however, viewed
isolationism as a powerful political force both in Congress and among the
public at large. Roosevelt was generally reluctant to engage in an all-out battle
with the isolationists and noninterventionists, lest he give credence to their
charge that his administration placed British and other interests ahead of
America's. Accordingly, the president relied on proxies to do battle for him in
a campaign to discredit the opponents of his foreign policy goals. America's
Jews became among the most important of these proxies. In the years before
World War II, the efforts of the Jewish community helped in a number of
important ways to bring isolationism into disrepute and to turn American
opinion against Germany. This, in turn, helped to make it possible for the
Roosevelt administration to provide aid to Britain and the Soviet Union and
to prepare the United States for war.

The struggle against Nazi Germany and its friends also united Jews and
the so-called Eastern Protestant establishment, whose members later would
be colloquially known as WASPs, an acronym for white Anglo-Saxon Protestants. Upper-class Protestants generally disdained association with Jews and
had built the "exclusive" schools, clubs, and enterprises mentioned above.
However, on the basis of education, economic interest, and often family
connections, the Eastern Protestant establishment was strongly Anglophilic
and found among members of the Jewish community virtually the only
reliable American allies for the British cause. Indeed, Jews and upper-class

Northeastern Protestants were the two groups in American society that most vehemently opposed Germany and supported England at a time when large segments of the American public, including Americans of German, Italian, Irish, and Scandinavian descent, either supported Germany, opposed England, or were against any form of American intervention in European affairs.

Jews and members of the Eastern establishment united during the 1930s to create the Century Group, which worked vigorously for American intervention against the growing power of Nazi Germany. Jewish members of this group included financier James Warburg, film producer Walter Wanger, and Harold Guinzburg, president of the Viking Press. Establishment members of the organization included the prominent manufacturer Ward Chaney, journalist Joseph Alsop, diplomat Frank Polk, and well-known attorneys and public servants Dean Acheson and Allen W. Dulles.[10] The Century Group advocated increased American preparedness via stepped-up production of military equipment and universal military training.

The Century Group sponsored public speeches and radio addresses by such luminaries as Colonel William J. Donovan, a winner of the Medal of Honor and one of America's most famous heroes of World War I. Donovan's typical theme was that universal military training was designed to save American lives by ensuring that American boys would be well trained if the nation was attacked. He pointed out that a lack of training had led to many casualties when American troops had gone to Europe in World War I. Donovan described conscription and training as giving the American soldier "a fair chance for his life" rather than as an imposition by the government.[11] This campaign played an important role in paving the way for the enactment of a selective service law and beginning American preparation for the war to come.

After the defeat of France in 1940, the Century Group called for the United States to declare war against Germany without waiting to be attacked. The group issued a proclamation, titled "A Summons to Speak Out," which was widely circulated in the press. The summons declared, "Nazi Germany is the mortal enemy of our ideals, our institutions and our way of life." The defeat of America's allies, the summons went on to say, would mean that at some point in the future, America would have to fight alone. Accordingly, America must declare war now before it was too late. The summons was condemned by the isolationist and pro-German press, but it did provoke a good deal of public discussion and marked the beginning of a major effort to use the press to condition public opinion to the necessity of providing aid to Britain, including U.S. naval support for the defense of the British Isles.

Working closely with a second and overlapping advocacy group, the Committee to Defend America, the Century Group was also among the main forces promoting the famous destroyers-for-bases deal, in which the United States transferred fifty of its older destroyers to the British navy in exchange for several naval bases in the Atlantic and Caribbean, including in Bermuda, the Bahamas, Newfoundland, and Labrador. Britain asked for the American destroyers because Royal Navy losses to German U-boats and mines had been severe and Britain badly needed more destroyers for convoy duty. The American destroyers eventually sent to the British required extensive refitting before they could be used by the Royal Navy, but the transfer of the naval bases actually helped Britain immediately by shifting responsibility for their protection to the United States, thus freeing British naval assets for other duties.

Isolationist and pro-German groups in the United States were bitterly opposed to this exchange, viewing it as a step toward U.S. involvement in the war. Isolationist speakers such as Charles Lindbergh attacked the proposal and sought to build public opposition to it. The Century Group responded with its own celebrity speakers in what it called a "radio program of education." One of the group's first such educators was General John J. Pershing, commander of the American Expeditionary Force in World War I. The elderly general made a speech to the nation on the Mutual Broadcasting System in which he declared that "all the things we hold most dear are gravely threatened" because "more than half the world is now ruled by men who despise the American idea and have sworn to destroy it."[12] Pershing urged rearmament, universal selective service, and the immediate transfer of destroyers to Great Britain. "If the destroyers help save the British fleet," he said, "they may save us from the danger and hardship of another war." Pershing's speech was widely heard and discussed. The newspapers associated with the Century Group, such as the *New York Times*, gave it front-page billing while relegating opposing points of view, such as those expressed by Charles Lindbergh, to the back pages.

In the Congress, where isolationists held important positions, there was considerable opposition to the idea of providing England with any aid whatsoever. And though Franklin Roosevelt strongly favored aid to the beleaguered British, he had no confidence that Congress would approve the destroyer deal. However, at the suggestion of Felix Frankfurter, Benjamin Cohen sent the president a memorandum arguing that under his constitutional power as commander in chief, he had the legal authority to release the destroyers without consulting Congress. Roosevelt was at first dubious, but observing in the wake of the Century Group's "radio program of education" that public opinion seemed to be shifting toward support of sending Britain the destroyers, FDR decided to move forward. It is worth noting that FDR was the first president to regularly consult the polls and particularly worked with pollster Hadley Cantril to monitor shifts in public opinion.[13] Citing legal opinion as to its validity, Roosevelt on September 2, 1940, signed an executive agreement with the British government and released the destroyers to the British navy. Subsequently, the Century Group worked to sway public opinion in favor of the lend-lease bill developed by the Roosevelt administration to assist Britain in financing its war effort.

Another organization that brought together Jews and members of the Eastern establishment was the Fight for Freedom Committee (FFF). Though some individuals were active in both groups, the FFF viewed itself as a more "all-out" movement for American military intervention than the Century Group, which had become focused on aid to Britain. "There are greater evils than war," read an FFF statement, "and among them are submission to or acquiescence in tyranny."[14] Jewish members of the FFF included Warburg and Guinzburg of the Century Group as well as Hollywood producers Jack and Harry Warner, labor leader Abe Rosenfield, and New York restaurateur Mac Kreindler (owner of "21"). A number of labor unions led by Jews, such as the International Ladies Garment Workers Union, became active participants in the FFF. The FFF was chaired by Episcopal bishop Henry Hobson and included such establishment luminaries as Allen Dulles, Grenville Clark, Sinclair Weeks, and Walter White. The FFF organized a nationwide effort—with the tacit support of the White House and the behind-the-scenes support of the British embassy—to discredit isolationists and to mobilize public opinion against Germany and in support of American participation in the war.

One FFF tactic that turned out to be quite effective was a campaign aimed at casting a negative light on the leading spokespersons for the isolationist movement. Each of the major isolationist figures was repeatedly branded a

Nazi, a Fascist sympathizer, or a "dupe" of the Axis. These labels were most frequently attached to Charles Lindbergh, America's most prominent isolationist, who often expressed respect for Germany and had even received a medal from Hermann Goering. The FFF distributed tens of thousands of cardboard replicas of the medal and added the inscription "For Services Rendered to the Third Reich." FFF claimed that Lindbergh wanted to become the puppet president of the United States under German rule and accused Lindbergh, not entirely without cause, of being a vicious anti-Semite.

In a similar vein, the FFF accused Robert R. McCormick, publisher of the *Chicago Tribune*, of being pro-Nazi. "Hitler likes him" was their slogan. To deal with McCormick, the FFF helped Chicago businessman Marshall Field launch a rival newspaper, the *Chicago Sun*. This effort had the personal blessing of President Roosevelt, who hated McCormick. The FFF declared the Senate's two most outspoken isolationists, Burton K. Wheeler and Gerald P. Nye, to be Nazi sympathizers or dupes. Wheeler, in particular, was said to be a "twentieth-century Benedict Arnold" for revealing that American troops were to be sent to protect Iceland.

The FFF also collected information showing that several isolationist members of Congress, including Nye and Wheeler, as well as Congressmen Hamilton Fish, Stephen Day, Jacob Thorkelson, and George Tinkham, regularly allowed their franking privileges to be used by pro-Nazi groups. Wheeler's frank had been used by two avowed Fascists to distribute their literature. Nye's frank had been used by a pro-Nazi unit of the Steuben Society of America. Fish's frank was being used by the "Silver Shirts" to distribute the *Protocols of the Elders of Zion*. After a federal investigation, it became apparent that Fish's office had become a haven for Nazi sympathizers, working with two German agents, to distribute pro-Nazi literature. Fish's secretary, George Hill, was ultimately sent to prison for his role in the matter, as was George Viereck, a naturalized American citizen born in Germany who sent weekly reports to German intelligence and served as Hill's paymaster.[15] Though Fish himself escaped prosecution, his patriotism, as well as that of the other isolationist legislators, was thrown into question.[16]

In a number of instances, the FFF worked closely with British intelligence services. The various British intelligence agencies operating in the United States, generally with the knowledge and cooperation of the FBI, were organized under an umbrella organization called British Security Coordination

(BSC). Agents of the BSC believed that the America First group was a serious menace to British interests and found in the FFF a useful ally to help them discredit America First.[17] Frequently, the BSC provided newspaper editors associated with the FFF with information that appeared to show that prominent America Firsters actually had pro-Nazi views and appeared to be involved in treasonous activities. BSC also coordinated efforts with the FFF to disrupt America First rallies.

For example, when Representative Hamilton Fish spoke at an America First rally in Milwaukee, the FFF, alerted by the BSC, turned the speech against the congressman. At the conclusion of his talk, just before he left the podium, someone handed Fish a large card, which he held up to examine. On the card was written, "Der Fuehrer thanks you for your loyalty." As Fish stared at the card, photographers came forward, photographed Fish with his apparent greeting from Hitler, and sent copies to waiting newspapers. This type of action by the FFF, in covert alliance with the BSC, was frequent and helped to undermine the isolationist movement.[18]

The interventionist alliance between Jews and the Eastern establishment was also a factor underlying Roosevelt's appointment of Henry Stimson as secretary of war in 1940. Stimson, a Republican and pillar of the establishment, was a partner in an elite Wall Street law firm once headed by Elihu Root. He had served as secretary of war under President William Howard Taft and secretary of state under Herbert Hoover. Though Stimson opposed Roosevelt's domestic program and had voted against FDR in both 1932 and 1936, he strongly supported an interventionist foreign policy and believed that American security required support for England and defeat of the Axis. Stimson had not been among those initially considered for a cabinet post after Roosevelt's 1940 electoral victory. Roosevelt and Stimson, however, were brought together by Justice Felix Frankfurter for a luncheon discussion of foreign policy. After this meeting Frankfurter lobbied strongly for Stimson's selection to the War Department post and ultimately prevailed upon the president to make the appointment.[19]

In addition to their involvement with groups like the FFF, Jews worked in their own organizations to discredit pro-German and isolationist forces. Indeed, several Jewish organizations worked closely with national security agencies in the years before the war. The Roosevelt administration had tasked the FBI and other security services with monitoring politicians and public figures it suspected of having pro-Nazi sympathies, and Jewish organizations were happy to help with this effort. The Anti-Defamation League (ADL), for example, engaged in an active and extensive program of surveillance directed against pro-German and isolationist groups and individuals.

The ADL monitored the activities of such organizations as the German American Bund, the America First Committee, and the anti-Semitic National Economic Council, as well as such prominent isolationists as Charles Lindbergh, General Robert Wood of Sears, Montana senator Burton Wheeler, North Dakota senator Gerald Nye, Mississippi senator Theodore Bilbo, North Carolina senator Robert Reynolds, New York representative Hamilton Fish, and many others. The ADL also monitored the activities of such overtly pro-Nazi or anti-Semitic politicians as Gerald L. K. Smith, Gerald Winrod, Laurence Dennis, and Father Charles Coughlin.

The ADL often employed investigative agents who secretly infiltrated isolationist and anti-Semitic organizations and collected potentially damaging or incriminating information. One ADL agent, Marjorie Lane, became an active and trusted member of a number of isolationist and anti-Semitic groups, including Women for the USA, Women United, and Mothers Mobilize for America. The ADL's opponents responded with their own espionage activities. On one occasion an ADL investigator married a young woman after a whirlwind courtship. At the end of his first day of work after their honeymoon, the agent found that his new wife had disappeared along with all his files. Within a few days, the files surfaced in the offices of Senator Burton Wheeler.[20]

Information secured by the ADL was often turned over to federal agencies such as the FBI and the Immigration Bureau for possible criminal action. The ADL also worked closely with such sympathetic newspaper columnists and broadcasters as Walter Winchell and Drew Pearson. Winchell and Pearson publicized and criticized the activities of isolationist and pro-Nazi groups and politicians, relying heavily on the information supplied to them by ADL investigators. For example, an ADL agent who had worked his way into Mississippi senator Theodore Bilbo's inner circle provided a flow of embarrassing information on the senator's personal and political conduct, as well as contacts for Winchell's Sunday radio exposés and Pearson's national column.[21]

The American Jewish Committee (AJC) also conducted surveillance of the activities of groups that appeared to exhibit pro-German sympathies. This effort was directed by George Mintzer, a former assistant U.S. attorney. Detectives working for the AJC infiltrated anti-Semitic and pro-German groups and, over a period of five years, compiled a card index listing 50,000 individuals associated with these organizations. This index was frequently used by the FBI and army and navy intelligence offices.[22]

On one occasion, an AJC investigator pirated the files of a German agent calling himself Baron von Stein, who had been sent to the United States by the Gestapo to bring about a greater degree of cooperation among the various pro-German groups in the United States. After his arrival in the United States, the "baron" made contact with Royal Gulden, leader of the Order of 76; William Dudley Pelley, leader of the Silver Shirts; George Deatheridge, head of the Knights of the White Camelia; and a number of others, including well-known anti-Semites James True, Robert Edmundson, and Representative Louis T. McFadden of Pennsylvania, who made a viciously anti-Semitic speech after, as it happened, he had conferred with von Stein. The AJC turned over von Stein's files to the FBI, but the baron had already fled the country.[23]

The activities of pro-German organizations, particularly the German American Bund, were also attacked by a Jewish congressman from New York, Samuel Dickstein. The so-called Dickstein Resolution, adopted in 1934, called for a congressional investigation of all groups in the United States with ties to Nazi Germany. The House established a committee cochaired by Dickstein and John McCormack of Massachusetts to investigate "un-American activities." The committee, known by the acronym HUAC, worked to harass and intimidate Bundists and other pro-German groups. Ironically, after the war, under the leadership of Martin Dies, HUAC turned its attention to investigating allegedly pro-Communist groups and often harassed Jewish labor leaders and Hollywood personalities.

THE MOVIES

In addition to the aforementioned activities, Jews played a very important role in producing films and other forms of entertainment that echoed the Roosevelt administration's anti-German and pro-British stance. Most of America's major film studios—Paramount, Twentieth Century Fox, MGM, Warner Brothers, and so forth—had been founded and were owned by Jews.[24] Jewish filmmakers, as well as newspaper columnists and radio personalities, especially those associated with the FFF, were quite happy to attack Nazism and present Great Britain in a positive light. During the early and mid-1930s, to be sure, Jewish filmmakers and broadcasters had been reluctant to take a strong position on Germany for fear of sparking an anti-Semitic backlash in the United States.

Joseph Breen, head of Hollywood's Production Code Administration (PCA), often warned Hollywood's Jews against using their influence in the industry to make anti-Nazi and "Communistic" propaganda films.[25] Breen's predecessor, Will Hays, held a similar view and had blocked production of several films deemed offensive to Nazi Germany, such as an adaptation of Sinclair Lewis's *It Can't Happen Here*, as well as the antiwar film *Idiot's Delight*, which criticized Mussolini's invasion of Ethiopia. The film was eventually shown but only after scenes to which the Italian government objected were cut.[26]

In 1938, though, independent filmmaker and FFF member Walter Wanger produced *Blockade*, a film that criticized Francisco Franco, and *Personal History* (later re-released as *Foreign Correspondent*), which questioned German treatment of the Jews. Both films touched off a good deal of controversy and were condemned by isolationists and pro-German groups as "Jewish propaganda," but the dam had been breached. Wanger's films effectively led the way for the major Hollywood Jewish executives, particularly Jack Warner, to take on the same topics. At the end of 1938, Warner Brothers released *Confessions of a Nazi Spy*. The film was inspired by the actual case of a group of German spies who had come to the United States and were subsequently caught and convicted of espionage. When the film project was first being discussed, the German consul in Los Angeles wrote to the PCA urging that the project not be undertaken lest it lead to unspecified "difficulties."[27] Warner went ahead with the film and, indeed, put it in the hands of a staunchly anti-Nazi production crew. *Confessions* was directed by Anatol Litvak, a German Jewish émigré, and starred Edward G. Robinson, a Jewish actor active in the Hollywood anti-Nazi movement, and Paul Lucas, another German Jewish émigré. In the film, Nazi Germany is depicted as intent on world domination and presenting a clear and present danger to the United States. Robinson, in the role of an FBI agent, asserts that through espionage and subversion, Germany has already embarked on a war against the United States. Toward the conclusion of the film, the audience is warned that continued isolationism will leave the United States and its way of life vulnerable to German attack from within and without.

By 1940, Hollywood studios were producing many feature films and film shorts promoting American rearmament and attacking Germany. Warner Brothers offered to make any film short on the need for military preparedness free of charge. At the Roosevelt administration's request, MGM produced a film on foreign and defense policy titled *Eyes of the Navy*, which dramatically presented the importance of a strong national defense and an activist foreign policy. Other studios followed with films bearing such titles as *I Wanted Wings*, *Dive Bomber*, *Flight Command*, *Navy Blues*, *Buck Private*, and *Tanks a Million*. Even the comedy team of Abbott and Costello promoted preparedness with their humorous depiction of national military service, *Caught in the Draft*. Other important films presenting anti-German themes or warning of the need for preparedness included *A Yank in the R.A.F.*, in which a young American flier shows his countrymen how to fight the Nazis, and Warner Brothers' *Sergeant York*, the story of America's greatest World War I hero, Alvin York, who put aside his pacifism to serve his country. York himself attended the film's New York premiere along with Eleanor Roosevelt and General John Pershing. York declared that if Americans stopped fighting for freedom, "then we owe the memory of George Washington an apology."[28]

President Roosevelt personally thanked the movie industry for its "splendid cooperation with all who are directing the expansion of our defense forces." The White House showed its gratitude to Hollywood by ordering the Justice Department to settle, on terms favorable to the studios, an antitrust suit it had brought against the major film producers a few years earlier. Roosevelt also intervened to secure a reduced sentence for Joseph Schenk, head of Twentieth Century Fox, who had been convicted of income tax evasion.[29]

The increasingly anti-German and interventionist perspective presented by the film studios in 1940 was echoed by important segments of the news media, particularly the radio networks. Two of the most important networks, CBS and NBC, embodied the pro-British, anti-German alliance between America's Jews and establishment Protestants. These networks were owned by Jews, while their most important news broadcasters and journalists were such establishment figures as Edward R. Murrow and William Shirer. Murrow's broadcasts from London during the Blitz brought the war and the plight of the British people into every American home.

In 1938, 1939, and even early 1940, isolationism had been a powerful force in the United States. When the European war began, even many Americans who had little love for Nazi Germany were dubious of American involvement in Europe and reluctant to spill American blood for the defense of Great Britain or, particularly, Soviet Russia. By late 1940 and early 1941, however, the relentless media and public information campaign conducted by the FFF, ADL, AJC, and other groups had weakened and discredited isolationist and anti-interventionist forces, as well as those who advocated appeasement of Nazi Germany. By late 1940 and early 1941, the polls showed increasing public support for the administration's desire to intervene in the war on behalf of Great Britain.[30]

LEND-LEASE

This shift in public sentiment in turn emboldened the president to act with increasing forcefulness to bolster American military strength, to aid Great Britain, and, later, to take the politically risky step of providing help to the Soviet Union in the wake of the German invasion. Thus, in the summer of 1940 the administration secured the enactment of legislation authorizing an expansion of the navy and stepping up military production. During the same period, the president pushed a universal military training bill through Congress over isolationist objections. The subsequent draft touched off little resistance among potential conscripts—in and of itself suggesting that popular sentiment supported military preparedness—despite isolationist claims that conscription was another step toward war.[31]

In December 1940, responding to an urgent letter from Winston Churchill, Roosevelt declared in one of his "fireside chats" that the United States should become the "arsenal of democracy" and introduced the concept of lend-lease. The president proposed supplying Britain with war materials but, since the British could not currently afford to pay, postponing payment until after the war. Once again, isolationists objected vehemently, but Roosevelt had seen the shift in poll data and counted votes in Congress and was now reasonably confident of winning congressional support for his proposal. The president, nevertheless, asked the Century Group to mount an immediate effort to build popular support for lend-lease and to put pressure on Congress to enact the proposal.[32] The Century Group responded with enthusiasm and launched a campaign of radio addresses, newspaper columns, and advertisements making the case that opponents of lend-lease were, in effect, covert Nazi agents. As the debate reached a crescendo, opinion polls indicated that more than two-thirds of all Americans now believed that helping Britain was more important than keeping out of the war.[33] The lend-lease bill passed with sizeable majorities in the House and Senate.

The flow of American food and military supplies to Britain that began in 1941 under the lend-lease program eventually supplied more than one-fourth of Britain's wartime needs and almost certainly played a major role in preventing Britain's defeat by the Germans.[34] During the first few months alone, the United States sent Britain 1,000 tanks and more than 13,000 trucks. Most of these vehicles went directly to British forces in Egypt, where they helped to repulse the Afrika Korps. Also during the first few months, Britain received more than $1 billion worth of guns, bombs, and ammunition and more than 1 million tons of American food. Before American aid began to arrive, British ammunition stocks had been running low, and Britain had fewer than three weeks of rations on hand. American supplies ended England's food crisis and the looming threat of starvation.[35]

As it had a quarter of a century earlier, America's shipment of goods to Britain led inevitably to closer military ties between America and England and to confrontations between German U-boats and American vessels. In March 1941, the U.S. Navy began intensive training in antisubmarine warfare and by September had begun escorting ships en route to England. That same month, a German U-boat fired a torpedo at the American destroyer USS *Greer*, which retaliated with depth charges.[36] This incident increased coordination between the U.S. Atlantic fleet and the Royal Navy. The president authorized arming of American merchant ships, and American warships were ordered by the president to "shoot on sight" at German submarines menacing merchant ships. Playwright Robert Sherwood called the Anglo-American naval alliance of this era a "common-law alliance" rather than a formal marriage.[37]

Far more controversial than lend-lease aid to Britain was the issue of extending lend-lease assistance to the Soviet Union. After Germany invaded the USSR, both Churchill and Roosevelt favored providing aid to the Soviets. In July 1941, Roosevelt sent Harry Hopkins to Moscow to assess the military situation and determine whether the Soviet Union could survive long enough to benefit from the delivery of American military supplies. After meeting with Stalin and other Soviet leaders, Hopkins reported that the USSR had suffered devastating defeats but would continue to fight so long as it possessed the means.

Roosevelt was concerned that Congress and the public at large would not accept the idea of assisting the Soviets. A Gallup poll in June 1941 showed that only 35 percent of those responding favored aid to the USSR, while 54 percent were opposed.[38] American Catholics were particularly hostile to the Soviets, whom they saw as enemies of religion and the church. Isolationists asserted that there was little difference between Hitler and Stalin and that the two ought to be encouraged to destroy one another. Charles Lindbergh went a bit further, acknowledging that though Germany might have some faults, he would rather see his country ally itself with the Third Reich "than with the cruelty, the Godlessness, and the barbarism that exist in the Soviet Union."

Consistent with his usual tactics, Roosevelt turned to Fight for Freedom and other proxies to prepare public opinion for aid to the Soviets. The FFF proceeded cautiously, not wanting to be accused of sympathy with communism. Indeed, some isolationists already averred that Jewish Communists in the FFF were the driving force behind the idea of helping the Soviets, and it seemed that Communist front organizations actually were active in several FFF chapters.[39] Nevertheless, the FFF launched a media blitz on behalf of aid to the Soviet Union. FFF speakers declared that U.S. security was enhanced by assisting any country that fought Germany, while newspapers associated with the FFF printed numerous articles on the heroism of the Russian people and the barbarism of the Germans. An FFF advertisement appearing in newspapers throughout the United States asserted that Hitler's campaign against the Soviets was an effort to secure his rear for a final assault against Britain and the United States.[40] Hence, by supporting Russia, America was enhancing its own security.

This campaign was successful. Within a few months, public opinion had shifted significantly, with a majority of Americans coming to favor help for the Soviets.[41] Roosevelt then defeated congressional efforts to prohibit lend-lease assistance to the USSR and in November 1941 declared that such assistance would begin forthwith. By this point, 51 percent of Americans surveyed approved of aiding the Soviet Union, while only 13 percent were opposed. One Virginia congressman expressed the opinion of most Americans when he cited a Romanian proverb: "It is permissible to walk with the devil until the bridge is crossed."[42]

In the last month of 1941 and first months of 1942, the United States shipped 2,000 light and medium tanks and 1,800 military aircraft of various types to the Soviets. This was in addition to thousands of jeeps and trucks, thousands of tons of ammunition, more than 100,000 field telephones, 45,000 tons of barbed wire, and 75,000 Thompson submachine guns.[43] A flood of war material followed in the ensuing years. Lend-lease supplies played a critical role in keeping the USSR in the war until its own factories, evacuated to the Urals, were able to resume production of military equipment.

Of course, isolationist and pro-German forces bitterly attacked the Jews for their interventionist efforts. Charles Lindbergh warned in a 1940 speech, "Instead of agitating for war the Jewish groups in this country should be opposing it in every possible way, for they will be among the first to feel its consequences. A few farsighted Jewish people realize this and stand opposed to intervention. But the majority still do not. The greatest danger to this country lies in their large ownership and influence in our motion pictures, our press, our radio and our government."[44] Similarly, Joseph P. Kennedy, U.S. ambassador to Great Britain and outspoken advocate of American appeasement of Nazi Germany, warned American Jews to halt their support of U.S. intervention on Britain's behalf. In 1940, Kennedy met with a number of Jewish film producers and urged them to stop making anti-Nazi films. Kennedy suggested to the Jewish producers that they learn from the experience of their brethren in Europe to avoid behavior that might offend their non-Jewish neighbors.[45]

For his part, isolationist senator Burton Wheeler, who chaired the Interstate Commerce Committee, appointed a subcommittee to investigate efforts by the movie industry to lead America into the war by inflaming opinion against Germany. The first witness called by the subcommittee was Wheeler's close ally, Senator Gerald Nye of North Dakota. Nye castigated the producers of anti-German propaganda films, whom he described as a small group of foreign-born Jews who "came to our land and took citizenship here" while "entertaining violent animosities toward certain causes abroad."[46] The force of Nye's testimony was undercut by his admission that he had not actually seen many of these films and could not remember anything specific about those he had seen.

The hearings and the entire issue of Jewish propaganda became moot on December 7, 1941, when the Japanese bombed Pearl Harbor. In the wake of the attack, the Roosevelt administration was freed to destroy anti-British, anti-Semitic, and pro-German groups through indictments, arrests, and deportations. All public talk of clandestine Jewish efforts to delude Americans halted, albeit only temporarily.

THE WAR

As in the case of the Jews of the Soviet Union, hundreds of thousands of American Jews donned the uniforms of America's various military services. Many fought bravely, won medals, and were wounded and died in their nation's service. Like other Americans, Jews fought in a number of combat theaters opposing the Japanese and Italians as well as the Germans. Not all fought directly against Hitler. World War II, however, was a global war in which events in one theater profoundly affected events everywhere. Had the United States been defeated by the Japanese in the Pacific, it would hardly have been in a position to wage war against the Germans in Europe.

GI Jew

More than 600,000 Jews served in America's armed forces during World War II. Jews accounted for about 4 percent of Americans in uniform, a bit more than their percentage of the general population. About 10,500 Jews died in the service, most as a result of wounds received in combat, and another 25,000 were wounded.

Many Jewish soldiers and sailors reported having encountered anti-Semitic prejudice on the part of their comrades in arms, though some attributed negative attitudes toward Jews more to ignorance than to malice.[47] Nevertheless, anti-Semitism remained widespread in the United States during the 1940s, and it was not unusual for Jews in the military to be the objects of taunts and insults from their fellow GIs, who might assert that Jews were cowards, that Jews were seldom to be found in the front lines, or, occasionally, that Jews had started the war. A number of senior military officers were not at all reticent about expressing their own anti-Semitic views. One 1940 U.S. Army War College study, authored by a Colonel Dean Hudnutt, claimed that the rapid collapse of the Polish army was due in part to the fact that it included large numbers of Jewish soldiers. Hudnutt said the lesson to be learned from this was that the U.S. Army should not be allowed to become a home to the "scum of Europe."[48] Many Jewish soldiers and sailors felt compelled to always show bravery under fire in order to refute anti-Semitic stereotypes. One Jewish sergeant discussed by Deborah Moore was wounded several times but always came back to his unit, determined to disprove the idea that Jews were unwilling to fight.[49]

Perhaps because of this motivation, during the course of the war, some 36,000 Jews received a total of 61,448 military decorations, including 5 Medals of Honor, 74 Distinguished Service Crosses, 37 Navy Crosses, 1,627 Silver Stars, and 6,090 Bronze Stars.[50] One Jewish officer, Colonel (then Captain) Matt Urban, received over a dozen major combat decorations, including the Medal of Honor, and was one of the most decorated soldiers in the U.S. Army. Urban received the Medal of Honor for his actions in June 1944, when he single-handedly destroyed two German tanks and, though severely wounded, refused to be evacuated until he had led his infantry battalion in a successful attack on a German position.[51] Another Jewish Medal of Honor winner, Lieutenant Raymond Zussman, captured ninety-two German soldiers and killed eighteen others in a battle near the town of Noroy-le-Bourg, France, in September 1944.[52]

A number of Jews served as officers in the various military services. One of the highest-ranking Jews in the U.S. armed forces during World War II was Major General Maurice Rose, commander of the Third Armored Division. Rose was raised in an Orthodox Jewish home and spoke Yiddish. During World War I, however, Rose decided to pursue a military career, and knowing that Jews were not welcome as regular army officers, Rose began to claim that he was a Protestant. During World War II, Rose's tanks were the first American forces to penetrate Germany's Siegfried Line, and Rose, known for his aggressive leadership, later became one of the highest-ranking American officers killed by enemy fire during the war. In the last week of March 1945, Rose was shot and killed by a German tank commander when his jeep encountered a column of German Tiger tanks.[53] The army subsequently conducted an investigation into the matter, believing that the German officer had killed Rose after the general had already been disarmed, perhaps having discovered that he was a Jew. Nothing ever came of the inquiry.

Another notable Jewish officer was Colonel Robert Rosenthal, commanding officer of the 350th Bomber Squadron. Rosenthal flew a B-17 Flying Fortress on a total of fifty-three missions over Germany, volunteering to extend his tour after completing the twenty-five missions that normally concluded a pilot's obligation. Rosenthal was shot down twice, suffered numerous injuries, and was heavily decorated. After Germany's surrender, Rosenthal, a graduate of the Brooklyn Law School, served as an assistant to the U.S. prosecutor at Nuremberg and helped to interrogate Hermann Goering.[54]

Lieutenant General Mark Clark, commander of the U.S. Fifth Army during the Italian campaign, had been baptized as an Episcopalian while attending West Point, but his mother was Jewish. Clark's choice of religions also seemed to be a function of his desire to pursue a military career.[55] Had he not converted, Clark would have been the highest-ranking Jew in the U.S. military during the war.

Again, it cannot be said that Jewish soldiers were more or less heroic than their Gentile counterparts or that, on a per capita basis, their contribution to the war effort was more or less significant than that made by others. Of 600,000 Jewish soldiers who fought, many died or were wounded, and many comported themselves honorably. The contribution of Jewish soldiers and sailors was important but, given their numbers, hardly decisive. In three other realms, though, American Jews did play a special role in the war effort. These included the financing of the war, the production of the wartime propaganda that helped to maintain the morale of the public and America's troops, and, as in the Soviet case, weapons production.

FINANCING AMERICA'S MILITARY EFFORT

America spent nearly $300 billion to defeat Germany and Japan in World War II. Most of this enormous sum, more than eight times the cost of World War I and the equivalent of more than $4 trillion today, was raised by the U.S. Treasury through individual and corporate income taxes and through the sale of war bonds. The personal income tax, which had only brought in $1 billion in 1939, was generating nearly $40 billion per year by 1945.[56] The sale of war bonds yielded more than $185 billion in revenues between 1941 and 1945. In the realms of both taxation and bond sales, Jews played major roles.

Federal taxation and revenue were, of course, the province of the Treasury Department, headed by America's only Jewish cabinet secretary, Henry Morgenthau. Among those working for Morgenthau at Treasury were large numbers of Jewish economists and statisticians, including such contemporary and future luminaries as Jacob Viner, Walter Salant, Herbert Stein, and Milton Friedman, who helped to fundamentally change America's tax system to meet wartime needs. It should be noted that Treasury was also the only agency of the federal government to challenge the State Department's adamant opposition to any efforts on behalf of the European Jews being slaughtered by Hitler.

Among Treasury's most outspoken critics of the State Department's anti-Semitism was Morgenthau's chief tax advisor, Randolph Paul, one of the authors of a report denouncing the U.S. government's failure to take action on behalf of the Jews of Europe.[57] Paul was a Christian, but his enemies claimed that he actually must be a Jew. What else could explain his extraordinary sympathy for the plight of Europe's Jews (as well as the fact that many of his speeches on tax policy were written by Milton Friedman)?

At any rate, a number of Jewish economists, as well as Paul and Morgenthau himself, championed the introduction of payroll withholding, or "collection at the source," which to this day ensures a smooth, regular flow of billions of dollars into the federal government's coffers. Ironically, one of the most important members of this group was Milton Friedman, an individual who would later become the nation's most famous conservative economist. In his memoirs, Friedman is apologetic for having helped to develop a system of tax collection that continues to serve as a major revenue engine for the expansion of the national government's power.[58]

The Constitution's Sixteenth Amendment, allowing the levying of an income tax, was ratified in 1913. Prior to the New Deal, however, a high tax threshold and numerous exemptions meant that only about 3 percent of American adults were subject to the tax. These individuals were expected to file a tax return on which they reported their previous year's income and to make whatever payment might be required. The system depended on more or less voluntary compliance by a small number of well-to-do individuals. This, coupled with low rates, meant that income taxation was not at first a major source of federal revenue.

During the 1930s, the Roosevelt administration raised rates and closed a number of loopholes but did not fundamentally change the reach of the federal income tax.[59] By 1940, however, the government faced sharply increased costs for military preparedness and possible mobilization for war. President Roosevelt and the Congress reached a consensus on the need for higher tax rates and the development of a tax system that would expand the number of individuals subject to income taxation.[60] Hence, the 1940 Revenue Act lowered the income threshold for taxation, adding nearly 2 million new taxpayers, and the 1941 Revenue Act lowered the threshold again, adding another 2 million taxpayers, so that about 5 million Americans would now be subject to income taxation.[61]

The 1942 Revenue Act, adopted in the wake of the Pearl Harbor attack, was a turning point in the history of American income taxation. The act raised rates, cut exemptions, and lowered the threshold for income subject to taxation so that some 40 million Americans would now be required to pay income taxes.[62] This expansion of America's tax base meant that tens of millions of lower- and middle-income Americans with no prior experience in this realm would now need to file income tax returns, an idea that most found confusing and daunting. And given the numbers involved, the Internal Revenue Service (IRS) would be hard-pressed to enforce the law. The IRS lacked the administrative capacity or data base to allow it to assess the accuracy and veracity of the tax filings of tens of millions of Americans.

Anticipating that collection could be a major problem, Treasury officials launched a two-pronged campaign to encourage taxpayer compliance. First, the Treasury Department presented tax payment as a patriotic duty and launched an extensive propaganda campaign to convince Americans that paying taxes was a form of sacrifice required to win the war. In this campaign, Jewish film studios and radio networks, as well as Jewish composers and media personalities, played an active role. For example, at Secretary Morgenthau's behest Irving Berlin wrote a song performed by Danny Kaye and played incessantly on the radio, titled "I Paid My Income Tax Today," aimed at lower-income Americans who previously had not been asked to pay federal income taxes:

> I said to my Uncle Sam,
> "Old Man Taxes here I am."
> And he was glad to see me.
> Lower brackets that's my speed.
> Mr. Small Fry, yes indeed.
> But gee—I'm proud as can be.
> I paid my income tax today.
> I'm only one of millions more.
> Whose income never was taxed before.
> A tax I'm very glad to pay,
> I'm squared up with the USA.
> You see those bombers in the sky?
> Rockefeller helped to build them, so did I.
> I paid my income tax today.[63]

Secretary Morgenthau and Treasury's economists, however, were not confident that appeals to patriotism alone would be enough to ensure tax compliance. Accordingly, Morgenthau and his economic advisors, including Milton Friedman and Elisha Friedman, strongly supported the adoption of a permanent system of payroll withholding—already used for Social Security taxes and, briefly, for the 1942 Victory Tax—which would increase the efficiency of collection and sharply reduce noncompliance. Payroll withholding would produce a steady rather than episodic flow of income into the government's coffers and provide data from employers via the soon-to-be ubiquitous third-party information return to compare with taxpayers' own accounts of their incomes. These data would allow the IRS to easily determine whether taxpayers' filings were truthful and accurate. The idea of payroll withholding was presented by Treasury as a device designed to help taxpayers by allowing them to meet their obligations, as Randolph Paul told Congress, "with a maximum of convenience and a minimum of hardship."[64] Treasury's main goal, of course, was to increase taxpayer compliance and generate more revenue. Payroll withholding was the central feature of the 1943 Revenue Act, which raised rates yet again and mandated "collection at the source."

The result of the gradual increase in tax rates mandated every year between 1940 and the end of the war, accompanied by payroll withholding, was conversion of the income tax from a minor tax levied on wealthy Americans into a major tax levied on all Americans—from a class tax to a mass tax. Before 1940, the federal income tax had barely produced $1 billion per year, but by 1945, the income tax was generating $40 billion per year in revenue. During the course of the war, federal income tax receipts were $164 billion, more than half the cost of the conflict.[65] Treasury congratulated itself on having accomplished this enormous increase in taxation with a minimum of the taxpayer resistance that had been widely feared. According to Elisha Friedman, one key, in addition to collection at the source, was gradualism. Raising taxes gradually, Friedman told the Congress, "got the people's minds accustomed to things" and lessened the chance of tax resistance and political opposition.[66]

War Bonds

During the war years, the Treasury Department raised more money through bond sales than through income taxation. Seven bond drives, as noted above, generated $185 billion in revenues. More than 85 million

Americans purchased war bonds of varying maturities, which were typically sold at a 25 percent discount. Bond sales were directed by the Treasury's War Finance Committee, which worked through the War Advertising Council to promote bond sales. Bond sales were especially important in 1942, before tax increases actually produced significant new revenues.[67]

Many of America's major artists, such as Norman Rockwell, along with singers and actors, contributed their time and energy to the effort. However, the two names most closely associated with World War II bond sales are Irving Berlin and Bugs Bunny. At the behest of Secretary Morgenthau, Berlin wrote the song "Any Bonds Today?" based on his popular tune "Any Yams Today?," which had been sung by Ginger Rogers in the 1938 musical *Carefree*. The Berlin song, for four years, served as the anthem of America's war bond drives and was performed by the era's most famous bands and singers, including the Andrews Sisters, the Tommy Dorsey Orchestra, Dick Robertson, and Kay Kyser.[68]

> The tall man with the high hat and the whiskers on his chin
> Will soon be knocking at your door and you ought to be in.
> The tall man with the high hat will be coming down your way.
> Get your savings out when you hear him shout, "Any bonds today?"
>
> Any bonds today?
> Bonds of freedom,
> That's what I'm selling.
> Any bonds today?
> Scrape up the most you can.
> Here comes the freedom man,
> Asking you to buy a share of freedom today.
>
> Any stamps today?
> We'll be blest
> If we all invest
> In the U.S.A.
> Here comes the freedom man.
> Can't make tomorrow's plan,
> Not unless you buy a share of freedom today.

First came the Czechs and then came the Poles,
And then the Norwegians with three million souls.
Then came the Dutch, the Belgians, and France,
Then all of the Balkans with hardly a chance.
It's all in the Book if only you look.
It's there if you read the text.
They fell ev'ry one at the point of a gun.
America mustn't be next.

Any bonds today?
All you give
Will be spent to live
In the Yankee way.
Scrape up the most you can.
Here comes the freedom man,
Asking you to buy a share of freedom today.

For his part, Bugs Bunny became involved in bond sales not long after Pearl Harbor. Bugs, along with his animated friends Elmer Fudd and Porky Pig, was created by a Jewish producer, Leon Schlesinger, for the Jewish-owned Warner Brothers Studio. Bugs had been designed in the late 1930s to compete with the *Judenfrei* Disney Studio's popular animated character Mickey Mouse. As opposed to the all-American Mickey, Bugs sported a thick Brooklyn accent, was sarcastic and disrespectful, and was said to have been born in a rabbit warren under the Brooklyn Dodgers' old stadium, Ebbets Field. The Treasury Department asked Warner's to produce a ninety-second cartoon in which Bugs might encourage movie theater audiences to purchase defense bonds, and the studio responded by developing such a cartoon at its own expense.

The first version of the cartoon aired soon after the Japanese attack and featured the Brooklyn rabbit singing a verse of Berlin's "Any Bonds Today?." Before Bugs finishes the song, he is joined by Porky Pig in navy uniform and Elmer Fudd in army uniform to endorse the rabbit's patriotic message.[69] This cartoon became among the most famous and most frequently screened of the Word War II era.

Jews not only marketed bonds but also bought them in large quantities.[70] Jewish religious and fraternal organizations bought bonds. Individual Jews bought bonds. For example, Billy Rose, the theatrical producer, bought $100,000 worth of bonds; Julius Klorfein, a cigar manufacturer, bought $1 million in bonds, while his wife purchased bonds worth another $175,000. The Gimbel brothers, owners of the eponymous department store, were major bond purchasers and called bond sales "democracy's answer to Hitler." Buying bonds was also the Jews' answer to Hitler and to continuing anti-Semitism in the United States.[71]

WARTIME PROPAGANDA

During the war, the Roosevelt administration established a number of agencies designed to mobilize popular sentiment, bolster civilian morale, and encourage military service. The largest of these was the Office of War Information (OWI), whose mission was the enhancement of public understanding of the war, coordination of government information activities, and oversight and liaison with the press, radio, and motion pictures.[72] In other words, the OWI was in charge of coordinating wartime propaganda. The OWI's Bureau of Publications, which employed a number of Jewish writers, such as Samuel Lubell, produced pamphlets and essays on topics relevant to the war effort.

Lubell, who later became a well-known pollster, wrote a 123-page pamphlet titled *Battle Stations for All*, designed to explain to ordinary Americans how taxation, rationing, and bonds contributed to winning the war.[73] Similarly, the OWI's Domestic Radio Bureau worked with the radio networks to encourage popular entertainers to incorporate war-related themes into their acts. At the OWI's behest, Jack Benny told his audience, "When we buy those bonds, remember we're not doing the government a favor. We're the government! This is my war, and your war! So let's get rolling."[74]

Among the most important offices within the OWI was the Bureau of Motion Pictures (BMP), which was charged with seeking to ensure that the movie industry would help to promote the nation's war effort. According to published BMP guidelines, the first question filmmakers were to ask themselves before beginning a project was, "Will this picture help win the war?"[75]

Not unlike their Russian counterparts, Hollywood's large cadre of Jewish studio heads, producers, and directors needed little urging to join the war effort. Between 1941 and 1945, the studios focused on such themes as the danger posed by Nazi Germany and its Japanese ally, the threat of foreign spies and saboteurs, the need for national unity, the importance of American leadership in the world, patriotism and sacrifice, and, above all, the indomitable American spirit. Once aroused, said Hollywood, Americans would show their mettle and bring Hitler and his friends to their knees. To be sure, not all wartime movie propaganda was produced by Jews. The Italian-born Frank Capra's Why We Fight series of short documentaries is an obvious example. But most of the great propaganda films of this era were written, produced, or directed (or all three) by Hollywood's Jewish filmmakers. Indeed, even several of Capra's films were written by Julius and Philip Epstein.

A film that presents many of the main themes of World War II propaganda is, of course, Warner Brothers' 1942 feature *Casablanca*, starring Humphrey Bogart and Ingrid Bergman. *Casablanca* was produced by Hal Wallis, directed by Michael Curtiz, and written by Julius and Philip Epstein and Howard Koch, all members of Hollywood's Jewish film community. In this film, Bogart portrays Rick Blaine, an embittered American who owns Rick's Café in Casablanca, then under the rule of the Vichy regime. Gathered at the café are refugees from Nazism from many lands. Though Rick claims to be an apolitical cynic, it turns out that he, like America itself, fought against the Germans before and only needs to be reminded of his duty. The reminder comes in the form of Ilsa Lund (Ingrid Bergman), Blaine's long-lost love, who arrives at Rick's with her husband, Czech freedom fighter Victor Laszlo (Paul Henreid). Laszlo reawakens Rick's latent heroism and resolve. Rick decides to reenter the fight against Nazism, even though it means giving up Ilsa. He tells her that the stakes outweigh their own love and lives. Rick tells Ilsa he has a "job to do," a phrase often heard by Americans in the military.[76]

Rick even inspires the sleazy, collaborationist French commandant, Captain Renault (Claude Raines), to join him in the battle against the Germans. Thus, the film intimates, Americans need to be reminded of their duty and must put personal concerns aside for the duration of the war. Inspired by American leadership, moreover, the other nations of the world—even the sometimes craven French—will do their duty as well. With America reawakened, the outcome is no longer in doubt. "I know our side will win," Laszlo tells Rick as they part.

Another well-known film that presents a number of propaganda themes is Paramount's 1943 *So Proudly We Hail!*. Directed by Mark Sandrich (born

Mark Goldstein), the film tells the story of a group of military nurses sent to the Philippines at the beginning of World War II. The nurses' convoy is attacked by the Japanese; when they reach their destination, their camp is shelled; they suffer many hardships as they endeavor to provide care for wounded soldiers. In a dramatic scene, one nurse gives her life to allow her friends to escape the advancing Japanese. The surviving nurses are finally evacuated and dream of someday resuming their normal lives. The film depicts Americans as heroic and ready to sacrifice for their friends and country. The enemy is shown as brutal and merciless. An idyllic future is possible if Americans continue to work together to win the war. *So Proudly We Hail!* was the only World War II film to give women a lead role in combat settings. The presence of the women underscores the film's theme of national unity. One nurse receives a letter from her husband explaining, "You were kids from all walks of life—all classes—all kinds of people. This is . . . the people's war because they have taken it over and are going to win it."[77]

For the most part, the Hollywood studios operated more or less independently of the government, though they submitted scripts for review and consulted with various civilian and military agencies on their propriety. One 1942 feature film, however, was actually commissioned by the OWI. This was the documentary film *The World at War*, produced and edited by Samuel Spewack and distributed to theaters through MGM, Twentieth Century Fox, Paramount, Warner Brothers, and RKO. The film makes use mainly of newsreel material to trace the origins and history of the war and to explain to Americans the need to fight the Axis. The film revisits the years before the war when the German American Bund and isolationists, such as senators Nye and Wheeler, sought, according to the film, to confuse Americans and leave them unprepared to defend their nation. *The World at War* goes on to show German and Japanese atrocities, some of the footage taken directly from Nazi films. After viewing the film, *New York Times* film critic Bosley Crowther wrote in 1942, "Spread across the face of America, *The World at War* should stimulate a grim resolve."[78]

Retrospectively, World War II is sometimes seen as "the good war," a conflict that united Americans in the face of an existential threat. In point of fact, Americans were deeply divided before the Japanese attack and not definitively united after Pearl Harbor. Partisan and ethnic differences could well have become the basis for wartime division, especially as the human and pecuniary costs of the war escalated.[79] One key to American unity during the war was the fact that Americans were the recipients of a steady diet of material emphasizing the need to support the war effort. From the radio, the cartoons, and the movies, the nation learned that Americans must buy bonds, pay taxes, serve in the military, and fight until "the job" was done. As for the Jews, part of their job was to make sure the nation focused on its job.

WEAPONS

The Soviet Union, as we saw, relied heavily on its Jewish scientists and engineers for the development and production of the aircraft, tanks, and other weapons with which it defeated the Germans. In America too, despite anti-Semitic quotas, Jews played an important role in science and technology and turned their talents to military research. For example, Isidor I. Rabi, head of the MIT Radiation Laboratory, was responsible for major advances in radar technology during the war, including the development of the H2X radar, which greatly improved the accuracy of American bombers. One rather improbable Jewish weapons designer was Hollywood actress Hedy Lamarr, born Hedwig Kiesler in Vienna. Lamarr, who had become intrigued by weapons when she was briefly married to an Austrian arms manufacturer in the 1930s, designed and patented a remote-controlled torpedo whose transmitter and receiver were capable of randomly changing frequencies together, so that an enemy would find it difficult to jam the signal. Lamarr called this technique "frequency hopping." Lamarr's torpedo was never used during World War II but was later employed by the U.S. Navy and remained in use until the 1960s.[80]

Of course, the most important American weapons project of World War II was the Manhattan Project, which led to the building of the atomic bomb. The overwhelming majority of the Manhattan Project's key scientists were Jews. Some, like J. Robert Oppenheimer, had been born in the United States, but most were refugees from Europe, where they had experienced Nazism firsthand. In 1933, Germany had promulgated the Law for the Restoration of the Professional Civil Service, which effectively barred Jews from holding teaching positions at German universities. The immediate effect of this legislation was to drive one-fourth of Germany's physicists from their university posts with a promise of further indignities to follow.[81] The two leading universities, Berlin and Frankfurt, lost one-third of their physicists. Among these newly unemployed Jewish physicists were eleven contemporary or future Nobel Prize winners.

Many of these physicists sought opportunities abroad, especially in the United States; they were soon joined by Jewish refugee scientists from Hungary, where Jews were also increasingly subject to disabilities. In the United States, a number of prominent intellectuals, including John Dewey, created the Emergency Committee in Aid of Displaced German Scholars to find positions for refugee scientists and to secure their admission to the United States. During this period, many of the world's most famous scientists found refuge in America. They included Albert Einstein, Leo Szilard, Hans Bethe, Edward Teller, John von Neumann, and many other Jewish scientific luminaries, as well as Enrico Fermi, who left Italy because his wife was Jewish.

In 1939, Szilard and Einstein, in consultation with fellow Jewish refugees Edward Teller and Eugene Wigner, sent a letter to President Roosevelt in which they described the possibility that a new type of weapon of unprecedented power could be built based on the principle of nuclear fission. Such a weapon, they said, might potentially destroy an entire city with one blast. Moreover, the letter went on to say, there was reason to believe that Germany had already begun work on a nuclear bomb.

Roosevelt received the Einstein-Szilard letter a few days after the German invasion of Poland and was sufficiently concerned to authorize the creation of an advisory committee, which in turn funded the first stages of work on what would become an atomic bomb. Over the ensuing years, for the Jewish scientists, both native born and refugee, who joined the project, the defeat of Nazi Germany was an overriding objective. "After the fall of France," Hans Bethe wrote, "I was desperate to do something—to make some contribution to the war effort."[82] And Oppenheimer wrote, "I had a continuing, smouldering fury about the treatment of Jews in Germany."[83]

The first atomic bomb was tested on July 16, 1945, two months after the German surrender, and, of course, two bombs were used against Japan, destroying the cities of Hiroshima and Nagasaki in August 1945 to end the war. It is always dangerous to speculate about what might have been, but two bits of speculation seem warranted. First, it seems clear that if the Germans had not been so blinded by Nazism that they felt compelled to drive their best scientists into exile, Germany might have come into possession of the atom bomb and changed the war's outcome. Of course—and this is why historical speculation can be futile—if the Germans had not been blinded by Nazism, they might not have launched the war in the first place.

A second bit of speculation, though, seems to leave us on firmer footing. Hitler declared many times that the war he launched would be a war of annihilation, or *Vernichtung*. He presumably meant to imply that Germany would exterminate the Jews and Hitler's other enemies. Yet, as I observed earlier, if Germany had managed to fight a few months longer, or the Jewish scientists of the Manhattan Project had completed their work a few months sooner, World War II could well have led to *Vernichtung*—for the Germans.

4

Jewish Intelligence

During World War II, Jews played important roles in intelligence and espionage, serving the Soviet Union, the United States, and Great Britain. Intelligence, of course, has many facets. These include human intelligence and counterintelligence; signals intelligence, which includes cryptography and cryptanalysis; covert operations, such as sabotage and assassinations; and intelligence analysis and evaluation. Jews possessed a number of skills and resources that helped to make them important figures in all these areas.

First, German Jewish refugees in England and, to a lesser extent, the United States possessed linguistic and cultural backgrounds and anti-Nazi motivation, which made them ideal instruments of espionage and covert operations against the Germans, as well as knowledgeable analysts of German capabilities and intentions. Second, during the 1920s and 1930s, the Soviet Union had trained Communist activists throughout Europe, including quite a number of Jews, in techniques of espionage and subversion. These trained cadres later built the main Soviet espionage networks in Nazi-occupied Europe. Third, a number of Jews with backgrounds and aptitudes in such fields as mathematics and engineering became important figures in wartime code making and code breaking, particularly in the United States. Finally, as we saw in chapter 2, Jews had figured prominently in the prewar Soviet security services, and though many had fallen victim to the purges of the 1930s, the survivors included a number of the leading officers in wartime Soviet counterintelligence agencies. In these ways, Jews contributed to the intelligence efforts of the major Allied powers.

SIGNALS INTELLIGENCE

Cryptography and cryptology (code making and code breaking) have played a role in military and diplomatic affairs through much of recorded history. The ancient Egyptians, Hebrews, and Greeks used codes in their communications, and Julius Caesar employed a cipher involving the transposition of letters.[1] Codes, however, became especially important with the advent of electronic communications. Messages broadcast via the radio can be heard by foes as easily as by their intended recipients. In the Russo-Japanese War of 1904, the Japanese navy made what are believed to be the first combat intercepts of an adversary's communications.[2] And during World War I, all the major combatants began to make use of radio communications to coordinate and direct the activities of their far-flung armies. Of course, their opponents would listen with interest, hoping to learn of plans and troop movements and glean other useful bits of military intelligence.

Radio communications were generally coded but many of the early codes were easily broken. The French, British, and Germans devoted a good deal of effort to intercepting and decoding one another's radio communications, an effort that bore fruit on a number of occasions. Communications intercepts helped the Germans rout the Russians at Tannenberg in 1914. The Germans, in turn, were defeated by intercepted communications in 1918. Prior to the decisive Second Battle of the Marne, French cryptologists broke the German code and gave the French army advance warning of the precise deployment of German forces in Germany's final effort to capture Paris and win the war.[3]

The French made good use of this information and positioned their own forces in such a way as to defeat the German assault and launch their own devastating counterattack. For its part, the U.S. Army Signal Corps became adept at intercepting German radio communications, while the army cryptographic section of military intelligence was tasked with reading the intercepts and coding America's own radio traffic. The United States, however, lagged far behind the other combatants in its ability to decipher coded messages or to develop codes that would protect American communications from unfriendly ears.

After World War I, the major and some minor powers worked to improve their capacity to intercept and decipher one another's coded transmissions.

Even before the Nazi era, German military intelligence (the Abwehr) built many monitoring stations and trained intercept staff to listen in on other nations' radio communications. After he came to power, Hitler expanded this capability, adding monitoring stations outside Germany, and used intercepted communications to gauge likely British and French responses to his remilitarization of the Rhineland, Anschluss (unification) with Austria, and annexation of the Sudetenland. Reading secret French radio traffic, Hitler knew that his adversaries were not prepared to act and so was confident that he could proceed with his plans without fear of their intervention.

The British, for their part, established the Government Code and Cipher School (GC&CS) in 1919 to monitor and decode radio traffic. For several years GC&CS was mainly concerned with communications between the Soviet Union and Communist Party activists and sympathizers in England. It was not until 1936 that the British turned their attention away from the USSR to the growing danger posed by Nazi Germany and Japan. The actual interception of German and Japanese radio messages was the province of the army and navy, which operated intercept stations throughout the world. Within England itself, radio intercepts were handled by the Post Office and the Air Ministry. All these agencies sent encrypted messages to GC&CS for decoding.

The United States had closed its code-breaking operations at the end of World War I, but in 1919 the army and the State Department cooperated in the formation of the Cipher Bureau, sometimes known as the "Black Chamber." The Cipher Bureau was disguised as a private civilian corporation and had some success in decoding the diplomatic communications of other nations. In 1921, for example, the Cipher Bureau decoded a number of intercepted Japanese communications, which helped the United States obtain a very favorable outcome at the Washington Naval Conference of that year. In 1929, Secretary of State Henry Stimson famously declared, "Gentlemen do not read each other's mail," and withdrew State Department support from the Cipher Bureau, forcing it to close.

The army, however, was apparently not troubled by Stimson's principles and established the Signals Intelligence Service (SIS), led by William (Wolf) Friedman, a Russian Jewish immigrant who became America's premier cryptanalyst (a term coined by Friedman), to carry on the work of the Cipher Bureau. The SIS was the forerunner to today's National Security Agency. The U.S. Navy maintained its own cryptology section, and both services gradually built an extensive system of radio intercept stations throughout the world using increasingly sophisticated receivers, some mounted on warships. In the 1930s the army and navy were mainly concerned with Japanese radio traffic.[4] It was not until 1939 that the army began to regularly monitor communications between the United States and Germany. The army, however, kept its domestic monitoring stations a secret for fear that they were in violation of the 1934 Communications Act, which made such spying on American citizens a crime.

It might almost go without saying that the army and navy kept their intelligence operations secret from one another and refused to share whatever radio intercepts or decrypts they might acquire. Normal interservice rivalries were exacerbated by the fact that the navy's intelligence officers did not wish to cooperate with an army unit that was headed by a Jew and that, as we shall see below, employed a number of Jews in its upper echelons. The U.S. Navy was thought by many to be even more anti-Semitic than the U.S. Army, and according to a British naval officer who visited the U.S. Navy's cryptology unit, "The dislike of Jews prevalent in the U.S. Navy is a factor to be considered" in the prevailing animosity between army and navy code-breaking operations "as nearly all the leading Army cryptographers are Jews."[5]

During the 1930s, new technologies made interception of radio transmissions an increasingly simple matter. At the same time, though, technological advances made reading those transmissions, if they were encoded, increasingly difficult. The Germans, in particular, had begun to make use of an electromechanical code machine invented by a German engineer, Arthur Scherbius, who named his device the "Enigma."

The Enigma resembled a typewriter. It was a box with a keyboard and contained a set of rotors, each containing the twenty-six letters of the alphabet. The original version of the Enigma had three rotors, while a later version used by the German navy had as many as eight rotors. When the operator typed a communication, the machine, through its rotors and various elements of electrical circuitry, electronically scrambled the message prior to transmission. The message could only be read by a receiver whose own Enigma machine's rotors had been set identically to those of the sender, based on a key that could be changed as frequently as wanted. During the war, settings were changed on a daily basis and sometimes every eight hours. With hundreds of trillions of possible rotor and electrical settings, the Germans were completely confident that without the key, a message coded by the Enigma could not be deciphered.[6]

British Cryptanalysis

At the beginning of the war, British cryptologists were inclined to agree with the German assessment of the impossibility of breaking the German code. Though the British had little difficulty breaking French, Italian, Soviet, and, for that matter, American codes, they were unable to decrypt messages that had been enciphered by the Enigma.[7] And to make matters worse, the Germans seemed to be having little difficulty breaking most British codes and reading thousands of intercepted British messages.

The first of these problems, breaking the German code, was eventually solved by the cryptologists of Bletchley Park, who included quite a number of Jews. In 1939, British code-breaking efforts moved to the Bletchley Park estate, which had belonged to Sir Herbert Leon, a Liberal member of Parliament, and was conveniently located on the rail line between Oxford and Cambridge.[8] Admiral Sir Hugh Sinclair, head of British military intelligence, bought the estate himself when he was unable to secure government funding for the purchase. Sinclair, known as "C," was very likely the model for the spymaster "M" in Ian Fleming's James Bond novels.

The head of GC&CS, Commander Alistair Denniston, set about recruiting and training individuals who might have a talent for cryptology. For the most part, Denniston relied on the academic and military "old boy's" network to identify individuals who might show some aptitude in the realm of math and puzzles.[9] Some of these individuals, like the great mathematician Alan Turing, proved to be talented cryptologists, while in other cases math ability did not translate into a talent for codes. Only after the first year did military intelligence broaden its recruitment efforts to include chess and bridge champions and others whose interests and skills suggested that they might have a knack for cryptology.

Despite the best efforts of the British code breakers, if the Enigma machine had always been used properly, it might have been impossible to decrypt its communications. However, German operators often made mistakes that provided useful clues to the machine's operations. Most importantly, Marian Rejewski of Poland's Cipher Bureau had, with the help of stolen German manuals, been able to deduce many of the operations of the Enigma device.

Rejewski and two of his colleagues escaped from Poland and in late 1939 presented the British with the results of their work, greatly advancing the British effort.

At any rate, by the spring of 1940, the British were able to decrypt some of the Enigma codes used by the Germans, primarily by the German air force. In 1941, British code breakers were able to decrypt communications between Berlin and Erwin Rommel's army in North Africa. Though the Germans frequently changed their keys, by mid-1942 British code breakers had learned how to adjust to these shifts and were producing a steady stream of valuable information on U-boat movements and, later, on German troop movements in Italy and in France prior to the Normandy invasion.

There is some controversy about the precise contribution of this information, which the British called "Ultra," to the Allied victory. Winston Churchill claimed that Ultra intelligence hastened the end of the war by two years, while more recent analysts are inclined to make more conservative claims. But even the most conservative analysts agree that Ultra was extremely important. It is generally agreed, for example, that by exposing German submarine deployments, Bletchley Park's decrypts played a major role in the Battle of the Atlantic and in the defeat of the German U-boats in 1941 and again in 1942 and 1943. Similarly, decrypted German communications allowed the British to continually intercept Rommel's supplies and defeat the Africa Korps in 1942. In 1944, decrypts prevented an Allied disaster in Italy by revealing the precise German plans for a counterattack that might have overwhelmed the tenuous Allied beachhead in the first days after the Anzio landing. During the Normandy invasion, Ultra intelligence frequently revealed German troop deployments and capabilities.[10]

Approximately 150 Jews took part in the GC&CS effort at Bletchley Park.[11] This number may seem small, but it represents about 2 percent of the Bletchley Park staff at a time when Jews constituted less than 0.5 percent of the British population. Hardly any Jews, moreover, were to be found among the military and academic old boys who were recruited to form Bletchley Park's first group of code breakers. Among the Jews, two were especially important. These were Max Newman (born Neumann) and Rolf Noskwith (born Noskovitch).

Newman's father was originally from Germany and emigrated to England with his family in the late nineteenth century. A talented mathematician,

Newman had won a scholarship to Cambridge, where he was later a lecturer in mathematics, and came to Bletchley Park in 1942. He was assigned the task of breaking the German army's radio-teletype cipher, which depended upon adding rotors like those of the Enigma to ordinary radio-teletype machines to automatically encipher teletype communications. The two principle German enciphering machines were given the British code names "Tunny" and "Sturgeon."

By the spring of 1943, some slight progress had been made by British analysts in reading Tunny and Sturgeon encrypts, largely because of errors made by German operators that provided clues about the structure of the code.[12] However, the complexity of the code meant that it might be months or even years before cryptologists would be able to provide reliable decrypts. Newman suggested an alternative procedure. He argued in favor of constructing a machine that would have the capacity to sort more quickly than any group of humans through the various permutations and combinations that could be generated by Tunny's rotors. This heretical idea met with some initial opposition, but Newman convinced the military head of Bletchley Park that such a machine could be built.

The first automated decryption machine at Bletchley Park was an ungainly device that seemed to be composed of wheels, pulleys, and vacuum tubes. The staff named the machine "Heath Robinson," the British equivalent of "Rube Goldberg." Despite its appearance, Newman's machine worked, though it had a tendency to tear its teleprinter tapes and to produce clouds of noxious smoke. An improved version, code-named "Colossus," was built several months later. By allowing the British to read the German army's teletype traffic through part of 1943 and all of 1944 and 1945, Colossus told the Allies a good deal about German preparations for the threat of an invasion and helped the British and Americans anticipate and counter German troop movements.[13] Ten Colossuses were built during the war, but their existence was kept secret until the 1970s, as the British government was selling encryption devices to other countries and did not wish to make it known that it could easily read the communications encrypted by these devices.

A second important Jewish member of the Bletchley Park team was Rolf Noskwith, a German-born Cambridge student of mathematics. Noskwith was recruited by the chess champion Hugh Alexander and began work as a cryptologist in 1941.[14] Noskwith had worked on the German navy's version of

Enigma, which was considerably more complex than the other Enigma codes then in use. A particularly intractable problem was presented by the German navy's officers-only, or *Offizier*, code, which was re-enciphered by the operator after being initially enciphered using the day's Enigma code. When an *Offizier* message was received by a German warship, the initial coding would be deciphered by the radio operator, who would hand the ship's captain the still-coded message for the second, officers-only decipherment.[15]

Making use of captured codebooks from a German U-boat and several "cribs," examples of the plain and encrypted versions of a message, Noskwith in 1942 broke the *Offizier* code. Now able to read the instructions being sent to U-boats, the British navy began to route convoys away from the locations where the U-boats were waiting for them. Beginning in January 1943, the Germans noted a sharp drop in successful U-boat attacks against British and American ships. The Germans were so confident, however, that their *Offizier* code was unbreakable that they believed treason on the part of some high-ranking naval officer was more likely than a breach of the code to explain the U-boats' failures.

Nevertheless, the Germans made a number of changes in their code, which only briefly stymied British cryptologists, who now understood the main elements of the *Offizier* code.[16] The U.S. Navy made use of the British intercepts and decryptions to identify and attack the so-called milk cows, the fuel- and supply-carrying tanker submarines upon which the U-boat fleet depended. As these milk cows were being sunk, the Germans continued to refuse to believe that the *Offizier* code could have been broken.[17]

A third important British cryptanalyst of Jewish descent was Leo Marks, the son of a London bookseller. Marks did not work at Bletchley Park but instead was associated with the British Special Operations Executive (SOE), which conducted espionage and sabotage operations in German-occupied Europe. SOE agents generally communicated with their superiors in England via radio, which of course entailed the use of codes. The nature of the work and the clandestine character of the radio communications ruled out the use of complex coding machines. Agents relied on short broadcasts and codes that could easily be committed to memory, such as ciphers based on familiar poems. In his memoir, Marks explains that he gradually phased out the poetic ciphers, which the Germans easily broke, and introduced single-use ciphers printed on silk cloth that could be hidden in an agent's clothing.[18] Marks also developed procedures to reduce agents' risk in transmitting messages and to identify agent communications made under duress. In these ways, Marks contributed significantly to the work of the SOE, which will be discussed more fully later in this chapter.

American Cryptography and Cryptology

American cryptanalysts contributed significantly to the defeat of both Japan and Nazi Germany. Of course, the best-known triumph of American code breaking was navy commander Joseph Rochefort's decryption of the Japanese JN-25 naval code, which contributed directly to America's victory in the Battle of Midway.[19] Rochefort subsequently fell victim to a bureaucratic battle within the navy and was rewarded for his contribution to the victory at Midway with an assignment to command a floating navy dry dock in San Francisco.[20]

The heart of American cryptanalysis was the army's SIS, and America's chief cryptanalyst was the head of the SIS, William Friedman. Friedman was born in Russia and emigrated to the United States with his family in 1892. After studying genetics at Michigan State and Cornell—then one of the few major universities that did not restrict Jewish admission—Friedman was hired by an eccentric millionaire, George Fabyan, to head the Genetics Department at Fabyan's Riverbank Laboratories near Chicago. Though Fabyan pursued a number of conventional business and research interests, his true passion was cryptology. In particular, Fabyan was convinced that secret codes, which he believed were embedded in a number of texts, would prove that Francis Bacon was actually the author of Shakespeare's plays, and he was willing to spend tens of thousands of dollars in a fruitless effort to prove this point.[21] Fabyan assigned Friedman to this quixotic project, and while Friedman had little interest in the Francis Bacon issue (though many years later he demonstrated that Fabyan's conjectures were without merit), he became quite interested in codes and taught himself a good deal about the topic.

Pleased with Friedman's interest, Fabyan created a Department of Codes and Ciphers and made Friedman its director. In the years prior to World War I, Friedman wrote a number of papers on cryptology, collectively called the Riverbank Publications. These present a number of statistical methods for solving codes and are today seen as among the first systematic studies of cryptology. During World War I, the U.S. Army sent officers to Riverbank to be trained in the techniques of making and breaking codes.

The Riverbank Publications became Friedman's textbooks and were classified and not available to the general public for many years. In 1918, Friedman went to France with the army and served as General John J. Pershing's personal cryptanalyst. Upon his return to the United States in 1920, Friedman published another classified monograph, "The Index of Coincidence and Its Application in Cryptography." This index is a technique invented by Friedman that involves comparing a plain text with an encrypted text to determine the number of times that identical letters appear in the same positions in the two texts. Such coincidences provide a key to decrypting the enciphered text.

With Pershing's patronage, Friedman became the War Department's chief cryptanalyst, though he worked with other government agencies as well. For example, Friedman broke the code used by the conspirators in the Teapot Dome scandal.[22] When the army established the SIS in 1929, Friedman was named its director and was authorized to hire "three junior cryptanalysts" at $2,000 per year. There were no cryptanalysts—the profession did not exist—but Friedman hired three high school mathematics teachers and began to teach them the skills they would need. These budding cryptanalysts were Frank Rowlett from Virginia and Abraham Sinkov and Solomon Kullback from New York City.

Thus, three of the first four SIS cryptanalysts were Jews. In addition to code breaking, the mission of the SIS included creating new ciphers for the War Department, developing and printing codebooks, and training military officers in the use of codes.[23] Both Sinkov and Kullback earned doctorates in mathematics while working for SIS, and Sinkov was sent in 1942 to Australia to provide cryptanalytic support for General Douglas MacArthur, who used decrypted Japanese signals very effectively in his campaigns in New Guinea and the Philippines.

SIS grew slowly during the 1930s, as Friedman made use of then popular puzzle and code-breaking contests sponsored by newspapers and the American Cryptogam Association to identify potential recruits. Friedman was also one of the first to recognize the role that IBM's early sorting and punch card machines could play in cryptanalysis. Analyzing coded material often required analysts to spend months sorting through logical possibilities—a task an IBM sorter could accomplish in hours. During the 1930s, IBM leased rather than sold its machines, and Friedman calculated that with $2,250 he could lease enough equipment for six months to equal more than two years of full-time work by all his employees.[24] The War Department refused Friedman's request for funding. Friedman learned, however, that a newly appointed official of the Civilian Conservation Corps had inherited a great deal of IBM equipment from his predecessor but wished to discard what he saw as useless machinery, even before his lease expired. Friedman cheerfully helped this official by taking the equipment off his hands—and so was born the computer age in the realm of cryptanalysis. Once the value of automation was proven, the army and navy both leased hundreds of IBM sorters for cryptanalytic work.

SIS soon achieved a number of successes against Japanese codes. During the mid-1930s, Rowlett and Kullback broke the ciphers generated by the Japanese "Red" machine, a device similar to the German Enigma, used mainly by the Japanese foreign ministry. Red intelligence proved useful, but in 1938, the Japanese discarded the Red code in favor of a more complex cipher machine, which SIS dubbed "Purple." SIS determined that unlike Red or the German Enigma, Purple did not use rotors, but it was not clear what the Japanese were using in place of them. For several months, SIS cryptanalysts were stymied. In a flash of insight, however, one of SIS's Jewish engineers, Leo Rosen, built a device using telephone exchange stepping switches attached to an IBM sorter that provided the first clues to the Japanese encryption process.

After the war, SIS learned that Rosen had fortuitously chosen precisely the same switches that the Japanese used in place of rotors in their actual machine. Several months after Rosen's initial breakthrough, another SIS cryptanalyst, Genevieve Grotjan Feinstein, finally broke the code. This allowed Rosen to construct a machine that automatically deciphered Purple transmissions as they arrived, printing them out as though by magic. Indeed, the process by which this was accomplished seemed so arcane that the military dubbed the Purple decrypts "Magic."

It never occurred to the Japanese that their Purple code might have been compromised, and they were shocked when this was revealed after the war. Magic allowed the Americans to read virtually every bit of Japanese diplomatic traffic during the war. This capability gave the United States invaluable information regarding Japanese plans, and since the Japanese were often privy to the plans of their Axis allies, the United States learned much about German plans as well. For example, Magic intercepts of Japanese radio traffic foretold the 1944 German attack in the Ardennes, of which the Japanese had prior knowledge. In this case, however, American commanders refused to believe that the Germans had the capacity to mount a major offensive. The army's failure to pay heed to the decrypted information presented to it by SIS led to a near disaster in the so-called Battle of the Bulge. Magic intercepts, however, told the United States, which informed the USSR, that the Japanese had no intention of attacking the Soviet Union in 1942. This information emboldened Stalin to shift hundreds of thousands of troops from the east to the west, where they played a crucial role against the Germans.[25]

Of course, the most important event that Magic failed to prevent was the successful Japanese attack against Pearl Harbor on December 7, 1941. Magic intercepts on December 3, 1941, revealed that the Japanese ambassador to Washington had been ordered to destroy his codebooks and Purple machines. When this information was handed to President Roosevelt, he knew that it meant war. Magic intercepts, however, did not offer any precise information regarding the time or place of the likely attack. The Japanese naval code had not yet been broken, and the Imperial Navy had not provided this information to its own nation's diplomats. The Imperial Navy believed, correctly, that the best way to keep a secret was to tell no one.

Friedman and SIS not only spearheaded America's efforts at code breaking but were also at the forefront of American code making. In particular, in 1935 Friedman and Rowlett developed and built the SIGABA cipher machine, a rotor machine designed to be immune to any code-breaking techniques that Friedman could envision. During World War II, SIGABA became America's highest-security code machine. Even the navy swallowed its pride, after ignoring the SIGABA for two years, and built its own version of the machine. The navy, however, demanded that "civilians" (a euphemism for the army's Jews) be prohibited from using the machine. The army—which, as the navy well knew, employed many such civilians in SIS, including SIGABA's developer—saw this demand as an effort to cripple its cryptanalytic capabilities and rebuffed its sister service.

During the course of the war, American and British cryptanalysts cooperated closely, after overcoming some initial mutual suspicion. The Americans provided the British with Purple, while the British demonstrated to the Americans the workings of Enigma. By 1945, German and Japanese plans and the movements of Axis troops, warships, and aircraft were often known in Washington and London as soon as they were ordered in Berlin and Tokyo. The Germans and Japanese, however, were never able to decrypt material coded by SIGABA. This provided the Allies with an important advantage during several years of bitter fighting.

HUMAN INTELLIGENCE

Despite the value of signals intelligence, all the major powers also made extensive use of human intelligence—espionage—throughout the war. Human intelligence can provide indications of another nation's plans long before these are set into motion and communicated through channels vulnerable to electronic eavesdropping. Human intelligence may also offer a check on false or misleading signals and decrypts. Jewish espionage agents played important roles in the Soviet and British intelligence efforts and, albeit to a lesser extent, in the American intelligence effort as well. In some instances, they provided information that contributed to German defeats and setbacks. In other instances, they provided valuable information that was ignored or rejected because it was not consistent with their superiors' preconceived notions. This was a special problem for Soviet spies because intelligence that did not comport with Stalin's views was likely to be dismissed, or worse, declared to be the work of wreckers or saboteurs. Thus, when Soviet agents reported in 1941 that a German attack was imminent, their warnings were ignored because Stalin had declared that such an attack was not an immediate threat.

With regard to Soviet espionage, as noted above, prewar Soviet intelligence services had recruited and trained promising Communist activists, many of them Jews, from nearly every European country. The best prospects had been brought to Moscow and given advanced training in organization and espionage at one of several Soviet schools established for that purpose. After training they were returned to their home countries to serve as Soviet agents. After the German attack on the USSR, these same individuals became the backbone of Soviet espionage activities in Nazi-occupied Europe and in Nazi Germany itself.

One of the most important of these Soviet spies was Leopold Trepper, leader of an espionage ring the Germans named "Die Rote Kapelle," or "Red Orchestra." Trepper served as the orchestra's "conductor," while his various clandestine radio operators were dubbed "pianists." Trepper himself was a Polish Jew who had engaged in Communist Party activities in Poland, Palestine, and France before evading arrest in Paris and traveling to Moscow. In 1932, Trepper was enrolled in the Institute for Party Activists at Marchlevski

University, one of four schools where foreign Communist militants received special training.[26] Trepper studied Marxist theory, languages, and the history of workers' movements. He also received intensive weapons training. His wife, Luba, was also enrolled at Marchlevski and, after three years, assigned to serve as a *politruk* in the agricultural realm.

In 1938, the GRU (Soviet military intelligence) sent Trepper to Belgium to establish an espionage network. He spoke French and German and had good contacts from his days as a party activist. He was assigned the name "Adam Mikler" and a false identity as a Canadian industrialist seeking to establish a business in Belgium.[27] Once in Belgium, Trepper contacted another Jewish Communist, Leo Grossvogel, whom he had known in Palestine. Grossvogel had been working in his family's business, the manufacture of rainwear, but was apparently happy to give up his bourgeois pursuits to join Trepper in the business of espionage. The two men established a new firm, an import-export company that would nominally market Grossvogel's family's raincoats through branches in a number of European countries. Trepper and Grossvogel hired several front men, who were unaware that they were actually working for the GRU, to manage the business.

Quickly, Trepper's ersatz firm was able to establish branches and outlets throughout Western Europe, and the GRU sent additional personnel to join the effort. Among these were a number of Jewish activists such as Anatoli Gurewitsch, Hermann Isbutsky, and Isidor Springer, along with David Kamy, a radio operator, and Sophie Poznanska, a cipher expert. All were assigned code names and false identities. Trepper found a lawyer to obtain the release of another Jewish Communist, Abraham Raichmann, who was then in prison in Belgium. These were later joined by Hillel Katz, another Jewish Communist from Poland. Many years later, during Stalin's purges, when Trepper was accused by Soviet authorities of having surrounded himself with "a bunch of Jews," he replied that Jewish Communists were generally his most reliable agents.[28] Trepper's espionage ring was still in the process of becoming organized when the Wehrmacht swept through Western Europe. Rather than attempt to flee to safety in the Soviet Union, Trepper and his agents began following the Germans in a car to observe and document the German army's tactics.[29] Trepper's report, describing the Germans' use of tanks and dive bombers, was sent to Moscow via shortwave radio.

After the fall of France in 1940, Trepper moved his organization to Paris, where he established two new companies, Simex and Simexco, to serve as fronts for his activities. These two companies mainly resold surplus goods, sometimes purchased on the black market. One of their main customers was a German firm, which gave Trepper and his agents German passes and entrée into German commercial circles, where they were able to acquire a good deal of useful information pointing to German preparations for an attack on the USSR. Trepper also made contact with the French Resistance and with a variety of individuals throughout occupied Europe who could collect information about German plans and activities. Among the most important of Trepper's contacts was an anti-Nazi group in Berlin headed by Harro Schultze-Boysen, a German aristocrat who worked in the aviation ministry and as a Luftwaffe intelligence officer.

In early 1941, Trepper's various agents and contacts began observing that German forces that had been massing for an effort to cross the English Channel to invade Great Britain were being withdrawn from France and sent east. This shift of forces seemed a sure signal that Germany was preparing to attack the USSR. Schultze-Boysen confirmed that a German attack on the Soviet Union would come soon, and he was ultimately able to give Trepper the precise date of the planned attack.[30] Trepper sent numerous dispatches to Moscow detailing German troop movements and likely invasion dates.[31] Moscow, however, ignored the information provided by Trepper (which it was also receiving from other sources). As noted above, Stalin was convinced that the Germans would not attack, and he would not listen to intelligence reports inconsistent with his assumptions. And since none of his subordinates dared to challenge Stalin's views, inconvenient facts were ignored.

The Red Orchestra's most important intelligence had been ignored. However, for more than a year after the German attack, Trepper and his Orchestra transmitted hundreds of useful reports to Moscow. Because of its contact with Schultze-Boysen, the Orchestra was able to collect and forward a great deal of information about the plans of the German air force and the capabilities of German aircraft.[32] The Red Orchestra also sent Moscow information on German troop movements, arms production, and military plans. After the initial fiascos, the Soviet army generally made careful use of such intelligence.[33] The Germans claimed that Red Orchestra espionage cost the German armed forces as many as 200,000 lives, though this figure may be an exaggeration.[34]

The Achilles' heel of Trepper's network was the radio. The Red Orchestra's pianists transmitted their coded information to Moscow via their shortwave radio sets. This gave German intelligence and security services an opportunity to use direction-finding equipment to locate the transmitters. The procedure was tedious and time-consuming, but during the course of 1942, all the Red Orchestra's pianists were located and arrested. Trepper himself was captured in November 1942. Under interrogation, Trepper revealed the names and locations of several agents who had not yet been captured. However, when the Gestapo sought to use him to mount a *Funkspiel*, or radio broadcast conveying disinformation, Trepper managed to convey the fact that he had been captured and was broadcasting under duress. In September 1943, Trepper escaped and remained in hiding until the end of the war, when he returned to Moscow. He was there accused of having helped the Germans and imprisoned until 1955. At that point, Trepper was cleared of all charges and released. It has never been clear how Trepper survived when the Soviets executed so many others charged with lesser offenses. Proof was seldom a decisive criterion.

Another important Soviet espionage operation headed by a Jew was the so-called Dora group, which the Germans called the "Rote Drei," or "Red Three," directed by Alexander Rado, a Hungarian Jew. Before its destruction, Rado had worked with the Red Orchestra. Unlike his unfortunate fellow pianists though, Rado was located in Switzerland and thus beyond the reach of the Gestapo. As a result, even though the Germans had traced clandestine radio transmissions to near Rado's location, they were unable to arrest him as they had done with the others.

Until the end of 1943, Rado sent Moscow detailed information on German arms manufacture, including plans for the new Panther tank before it even went into production. Rado also transmitted the information gathered by another Soviet spy apparatus, code-named "Lucy," regarding the plans for the 1943 German offensive code-named "Zitadelle" (citadel), which ended with the decisive Battle of Kursk in which the Soviet army destroyed 3,000 German tanks and turned the tide of the war. A major factor in the Soviet victory was foreknowledge of a good deal of the German plan and order of battle, thanks in part to Rado.

The source of much of this information was an anti-Nazi German, Rudolph Roessler, code-named "Lucy," who in turn had been recruited by another Soviet spy ring headed by a Polish Jew, Rachel Dubendorfer, code-named "Sissy." Dubendorfer had been receiving a good deal of information on the German and Italian economies from several individuals working in the League of Nations International Labor Office. She forwarded this information, most of it mundane, to Moscow. One of her informants was an individual named Christian Schneider, who, beginning in 1941, began to pass Sissy extremely sensitive reports on German military planning.[35]

It turned out that Schneider's source was Roessler, a German who had become a fervent anti-Nazi when his family's business was confiscated by a covetous Nazi official. Subsequently, Roessler made contact with two anti-Nazi German intelligence officers, General Fritz Thiele and Colonel Rudolph von Gersdorff, both later involved in the 1944 plot to assassinate Hitler. Thiele was second in command of the communications department of the German High Command, where his superior, General Erich Fellgiebel, was also an anti-Nazi and later a member of the conspiracy to kill Hitler.

Thiele and von Gersdorff provided Roessler with an Enigma machine and decryption information through which they sent him, in code, top-secret German military data. Through still another covert operative, Roessler sent copies of the reports to Sissy, who in turn passed them to Dora, who transmitted them to Moscow. Dora's reports, like those sent by many other sources, warned of the planned German invasion and were ignored by the Soviets. Once Stalin overcame his own delusions regarding German intentions, however, reports from Lucy via Sissy and Dora were read with extreme interest in Moscow since they gave the Soviets up-to-date information on the German order of battle, including the disposition of the Luftwaffe, which proved to be highly accurate—and why not? The source of the intelligence was within the German High Command itself.

Among the most important of the Lucy-Sissy-Dora reports was the 1942 German plan for "Fall Blau," the attack on Stalingrad and the oil fields of the Caucasus. Hitler's entire directive, spelling out the plan, was transmitted to Moscow and proved invaluable to the Soviets, who were able to counter the Germans and to hand them an important defeat at Stalingrad.[36] During this same German offensive, Dora also passed information from other agents in Germany indicating Hitler's adamant refusal to consider withdrawing his encircled forces from Stalingrad. Toward the end of 1943, Swiss authorities, under pressure from the Germans, shut down Rado's transmitters and forced Rado into hiding until the end of the war.

Still another noteworthy Jewish spy working for the Soviets was Colonel Lev Manevich, a Soviet intelligence officer born in Byelorussia in 1898. Manevich lived for several years in Switzerland, where he became fluent in French, German, and Italian, and returned to Russia in 1917. During the civil war he served as a Red Army intelligence officer. Afterward, he trained as a pilot and planned to serve in the Soviet air force.[37] Because of his language skills, however, Manevich was recruited by Soviet military intelligence. In 1932, using the code name "Konrad Kartner," Manevich opened a patent registration office first in Vienna and then in Milan. As a pilot, Manevich was able to make good contacts in the aviation industry in several countries, including Germany.

From his contacts he learned a good deal about German and Italian aircraft design and production, which he transmitted to Moscow. These included detailed plans for several of the newest fighters and bombers. In 1937, Manevich was arrested by Italian authorities and later transferred to German custody. In 1945, when Manevich was incarcerated at the Ebensee concentration camp, the guards were planning to kill all the prisoners before the camp could be liberated by the American army. This was a common practice, and in many instances the SS moved prisoners from camps about to be liberated to locations further behind German lines in order to continue killing them for as long as possible. Manevich organized a prisoner revolt and managed to halt the Germans' death machinery until the SS guards were forced to flee ahead of the advancing Americans. Not many weeks later, Manevich died from the effects of his incarceration. He was posthumously named a Hero of the Soviet Union for his espionage work.

Soviet Counterintelligence

While Soviet intelligence services had a great deal of success against Nazi Germany, German intelligence was seldom able to learn much about Soviet capabilities, intentions, or plans. The Soviet Union was, of course, a society in which numerous secret police and intelligence agencies employed networks of agents and informants to spy on the populace and on one another. The slightest deviation from orthodoxy in word or deed, the slightest hint of suspicious conduct, was likely to be noticed and brought to the attention of the authorities. German agents sent into the USSR were generally arrested within a few days of their arrival, and Soviet citizens recruited by the Germans fared little better.[38] Between 1941 and 1945, Soviet security agencies questioned nearly 7 million individuals on suspicion of spying and arrested 2 million.[39] Presumably, hardly any of these individuals were actual spies. Indeed, the Germans only reported deploying about 44,000 agents during the war. Soviet intelligence services, however, had little to fear from punishing the innocent along with the guilty, and from their perspective, it was better to imprison a hundred innocent individuals than to allow one guilty person to go free.

The Soviet Union's lead counterintelligence agency was SMERSH, an acronym for Smert Shpionam, or "Death to Spies." SMERSH was formed in 1941 within Soviet military intelligence to ensure the loyalty of Soviet troops and to deal with the threat of German efforts to infiltrate the military and to deploy intelligence agents to rear areas to sow panic and confusion among the troops. Unlike civilian intelligence agencies, military intelligence had not been purged before the war and so still included large numbers of Jewish officers. Accordingly, Jews played an important role within SMERSH throughout the war.

Among SMERSH's most important Jewish officers were Nahum Eitingon, who had planned Trotsky's assassination, Iakov Serebrianski, Isidor Makliarskii, and Vilyam Fisher (also known as "Rudolph Abel"), who became famous many years later in the United States. Under the name Abel, Fisher was being held by the United States for his involvement in the Rosenberg atomic spy ring. In 1962, though, he was exchanged with the Soviets for U-2 spy-plane pilot Francis Gary Powers, who had been captured when his plane was shot down over the Soviet Union in 1960. During the course of the war, SMERSH alone killed or captured nearly 40,000 of the 44,000 agents the Germans acknowledge having sent into the USSR.[40]

JEWS IN THE BRITISH AND AMERICAN INTELLIGENCE SERVICES

Just as the Soviet Union made good use of Jewish Communists as espionage agents during the war, Great Britain and, to a lesser extent, the United States also employed Jewish intelligence operatives. For the most part, these British and American spies were not dedicated Communists but were instead fervent anti-Nazis. These were, after all, men and women who had been forced to flee Germany and German-occupied Europe and whose family members had been brutalized or murdered by the Nazis. In addition to their hatred of the Nazis, what made such Jewish refugees especially useful operatives was the fact that they could be given training and covert identities and assigned to countries where they would have little difficulty blending into the local populace linguistically and culturally.

Some of the German Jews had actually served in the German military during World War I. This experience helped them to understand the Wehrmacht's operations and procedures and to penetrate its ranks. Several of the German Jewish refugees resident in England actually owed their lives to a British intelligence officer. During the 1930s, Frank Foley, the Berlin station chief of Britain's MI6, apparently acting on his own authority, provided British visas and passports to thousands of German Jews, allowing them to leave Germany and emigrate to England.

Britain's main employer of Jewish agents was the Special Operations Executive. One of the wartime directors of the SOE was Sir Charles Hambro, scion of a famous Jewish banking family. The SOE was established in 1940 to engage in espionage and covert operations behind German lines. Churchill famously declared that the purpose of the SOE was to "set Europe ablaze." During the course of the war, the SOE employed some 13,000 personnel, about 5,000 in the field, and was active throughout Europe and, to a limited extent, in Germany itself.[41] The main focus of SOE activity was occupied France, where some 400 agents worked with French Resistance groups to collect information and organize acts of sabotage against the Germans.[42] The SOE also planned assassinations and kidnappings of German officials and collaborators, but most of these missions appear not to have succeeded.[43] In Poland, another focus of SOE activity, some 600 agents worked with the main anti-Nazi resistance group, the Polish Home Army, in the commission of acts of sabotage and the collection of intelligence. In Czechoslovakia, SOE agents directed the operation that led to the 1942 assassination of SS-Obergruppenführer Reinhard Heydrich.

In Norway, SOE operatives sabotaged the Norwegian heavy water plant that was seen as crucial to any German atomic bomb project. Other SOE operations harassed the Germans in Hungary, Greece, Belgium, and so forth. Unfortunately, many SOE agents in the Netherlands were captured by the Germans, and their supposed radio broadcasts to England were actually made under German supervision. This deception was detected by the SOE's chief cryptographer, Leo Marks, who had a difficult time convincing his superiors that the SOE's operations had been compromised.[44]

Among the most famous of the SOE's many Jewish officers was Vera Atkins (born Vera Rosenberg). Atkins was born in 1908 in Romania, but her mother was a British Jew, and the family emigrated to England before eventually settling in France, where Atkins attended finishing school and the Sorbonne. At the beginning of the war, Atkins was able to return to England and in 1941 joined the SOE, where she was assigned to F Section (France) and given the task of recruiting and training female agents for deployment to occupied France. Between 1941 and 1944, F Section infiltrated thirty-nine female agents into France.[45] Fifteen were captured by the Germans, and twelve of the fifteen were killed. The best known of these was Denise Bloch, a French Jew who had been assigned to work as a courier and to help cut German railway and telephone lines. Bloch was captured by the Germans and killed at Ravensbruck concentration camp.[46]

Because of the circumstances surrounding the loss of agents under her supervision, Atkins became a controversial figure within the SOE. By 1943 the Germans had captured a number of agents and were forcing them to transmit false messages to England. One SOE radio operator in France, Gilbert Norman, who had been captured by the Germans, sought to alert his superiors that he was broadcasting under duress. The Germans, as noted earlier, referred to such an effort to use a captured operator as a *Funkspiel* or, when used against the British, an *Englandspiel*. Norman sought to alert SOE headquarters of the *Englandspiel* by omitting from his transmission the secret security check used to confirm the operator's identity and that he was transmitting freely.[47]

The absence of Norman's security check raised concerns in England. However, Maurice Buckmaster, head of F Section, declared that the omission must have been the result of Norman's carelessness and radioed him, "You have forgotten your double security check. Be more careful next time."[48] It was several months before the SOE confirmed that Norman had indeed been arrested by the Germans and had been attempting to signal London that his transmissions were being made under duress. In the meantime, however, Atkins and Buckmaster had sent a number of new agents to France to join an espionage network that had already been penetrated by the Gestapo. These agents were immediately apprehended and sent to concentration camps.

After the war, Atkins went to Germany to search for all of F Section's missing agents and was able to determine that a total of 117 had been killed.

She also testified at a number of war crimes trials, where she sought punishment for the killers of her agents.[49] Since the war, however, many questions have been raised about Atkins's conduct, in particular, about why Atkins and Buckmaster continued to deploy agents to an espionage network whose penetration by the Germans should have been clear from Norman's transmissions. Perhaps it was a terrible mistake. Some, however, have argued that the SOE sacrificed agents to convince the Germans that British intelligence was unaware that its network had been compromised. This tactic might permit the network's continuing use as an instrument of disinformation. Others have intimated that Atkins, who had relatives in Nazi-occupied Europe, was being blackmailed by the Germans. As is so often the case in the realm of intelligence, the truth is difficult to discern.

Jewish refugees from Axis nations—Germany, Austria, Italy, Hungary, and Romania—were initially considered enemy aliens in England, even though, as Jews, they had little affection for their home governments. Those enemy aliens who expressed a desire to fight were enrolled in the Pioneer Corps (later such enemy aliens were drafted), a noncombatant group assigned mainly to construction duty, loading and unloading supplies, pulling survivors from bombed buildings, and clearing rubble left by German bombs.[50] Some Pioneers were extensively interviewed by Royal Air Force (RAF) intelligence for their knowledge of the locations of German power plants, factories, and airfields that the RAF was attempting to destroy.

The Pioneer Corps was also engaged in the construction of defenses in preparation for the threatened German invasion. The Pioneers dug tank traps, laid mines, and strung miles and miles of barbed wire along possible landing sites. Though noncombatants, the Pioneers worked in areas targeted by the Luftwaffe and suffered casualties from German bombs. In December 1940, for example, five Pioneers were killed by German bombs and buried in London's East Ham Jewish Cemetery.[51] Among the Pioneers were individuals who were, or would become, major figures in European cultural and political life. Pioneers included author Arthur Koestler, newspaper tycoon Robert Maxwell, actor Peter Ustinov, Sigmund Freud's sons Walter and Martin, famous viola player Cecil Aronowitz, tenor Rudolph Jess, pianist Walter Stiasny, actor Nicolai Poliakoff (known as "Coco the Clown"), and many others.[52]

Because Britain granted refuge to only a trickle of Jews from the European continent, the number of Pioneers was small.[53] For those Jews fortunate enough to be allowed to cross the Channel, England was the last hope. Harry Rosney (born Helmut Rosettenstein) wrote, "England, at that hour, was the hope of the world, of freedom and tolerance. We clung to its apron, blessing the day we were allowed to set foot on it, albeit originally on a temporary visa."[54] One well-known Pioneer, Czech Jewish writer Alfred Perles, a long-time friend of Henry Miller, wrote that unlike the English, the Pioneers were all desperate "because they knew from their own experience all the atrocities of which the Nazis, unloosed, were capable. Nearly every one of them had been subject to the cruelty and brutality of the Hitlerites." The English, he said, were apprehensive but had no real idea, as the refugees did, of "the terrible tortures and ordeals in store for them should the Germans be able to get a foothold in these islands."[55]

From among these highly motivated Pioneers, the SOE recruited some of its most determined agents. For example, Walter Freud left the Pioneers to join the SOE in 1943. Freud received parachute, firearms, and other training and was dropped into Italy and later into Austria. After several days in Austria, Freud boldly walked into the mayor's office in the town of Scheifling, declared that he was a member of an advance party of the British army, and ordered the mayor, a prominent Nazi, to take him to the airfield at Zeltweg, some fifteen miles distant.

Knowing that the Germans and Austrians feared nothing more than to be occupied by the Soviet army, Freud told the mayor that he was there to make certain that the airfield would be occupied by the British army rather than the Soviets. The mayor agreed and drove Freud to see the commander of the air base. Freud presented himself as a representative of the British Eighth Army. The German commander also seemed ready to surrender in order to avoid capture by the Russians. After a number of mishaps, however, Freud's brazen effort to single-handedly capture a German airfield failed, but he was able to reach safety behind American lines.[56]

Not all SOE operatives fared as well as Walter Freud. Many, including many Jewish agents, were captured and killed by the Gestapo or in concentration camps. Martin Sugarman has documented the names of more than 1,000 Jews who served in the SOE. Of these individuals, 662 were non-British Jews, and 276 were British citizens. Another 119 were Palestinian Jews.[57] These later individuals, mainly members of the Haganah (Jewish self-defense force) or Palmach (Jewish elite troops), were among the thousands of Palestinian

Jews who volunteered to join the British army to fight the Germans. The fate of many of the 1,000 Jews who served in the SOE is unknown. In addition to those known to have been captured or killed, many simply disappeared in Nazi-occupied lands, and their fate is unknown.

Among the SOE's best known Jewish operatives were the Palestinian Jewish parachutists. In 1942, more than 240 men and women from the Palmach volunteered for training in covert operations. Their mission was to make contact with downed Allied aircrews, to serve as radio operators, and to make contact with partisans in various European countries. The volunteers also hoped to rescue Jews who were then being murdered by the Germans and perhaps help them find a way to reach Palestine. Of the 240 who volunteered, some 119, as noted above, were trained by the SOE, and in 1943, 32 of these volunteers were parachuted into six European countries—9 to Romania, 3 to Hungary, 5 to Slovakia, 10 to Yugoslavia, 3 to Italy, and 2 to Bulgaria. Generally, but not always, the parachutists were sent to countries in which they had been born and where they were native speakers of the local language.[58] Five other Palmach volunteers infiltrated their assigned countries via overland routes.

Several of the parachutists succeeded in accomplishing their missions, making contact with local partisan groups and linking them by radio to London, which sent arms and supplies. Five of the parachutists participated in the October 1944 Slovak uprising aimed at overthrowing the pro-German Slovak People's Party, which had tied Slovakia to the Axis. The uprising was initially successful but was soon quelled by the Germans. Ten parachutists fought alongside Tito's partisans. The Germans, however, captured twelve of the parachutists and executed seven of them. The most famous of those executed was Hannah Szenes, a Hungarian Jew born in Budapest in 1921, who had emigrated to Palestine in 1939 and joined the Haganah. Szenes volunteered for the British army in 1943, joined the SOE, and along with two other Jewish SOE operatives, Yoel Palgi and Peretz Goldstein, parachuted into Yugoslavia, from which the three were expected to make their way to Hungary overland.[59]

The parachutists spent several months with Tito's partisans before making their way toward Hungary. Approaching the Hungarian border, the two men decided that the mission was too dangerous to complete and turned back. Szenes, however, attempted to cross the border and was arrested by the Hungarian police. Szenes was tortured by Hungarian officers and the Gestapo, who repeatedly demanded that she reveal her radio codes to allow the Germans to mount a *Funkspiel* and perhaps lure more SOE operatives to their deaths. Szenes refused and was executed by a German firing squad. Szenes was an accomplished poet, and the circumstances of her death helped give her poetry an international audience. Perhaps her most famous piece is "Ashre Hagafrur," or "Blessed Is the Match," which is performed during Holocaust memorial services throughout the Jewish world:

> Blessed is the match consumed in kindling flame.
> Blessed is the flame that burns in the secret fastness of the heart.
> Blessed is the heart with strength to stop its beating for honor's sake.
> Blessed is the match consumed in kindling flame.

Another of the female Jewish parachutists sent into Nazi-occupied Europe by the SOE was Haviva Reich, who was born in Slovakia in 1914 and, like Szenes, emigrated to Palestine in 1939. Reich enlisted in the Palmach and in 1943 volunteered for the British army and, subsequently, for the SOE. Along with four other SOE agents, Reich was sent to Slovakia in September 1944. Reich and the others helped rescue a number of Allied prisoners of war and downed airmen and sought to create a route through which surviving Jewish children might make their way to Palestine. In October 1944, the parachutists were captured by Ukrainian Waffen SS troops. Reich and one other were subsequently shot, two were killed in a German concentration camp, and one escaped to join a group of Soviet partisans. After the war, Reich's remains, along with those of Hannah Szenes, were disinterred and reburied in Jerusalem.

The SOE, of course, was not the only British intelligence or covert operations group to employ Jewish fighters. For example, a group of German-born Palestinian Jews from the Palmach formed a special intelligence group (SIG) for infiltration behind German lines in North Africa. Refugees from Nazi Germany itself, these individuals were highly motivated to seek some measure of revenge against the Germans.

In 1942, the SIG launched an audacious raid on the Afrika Korps's supply base at Tobruk with the intention of destroying German and Italian fuel-storage facilities and freeing British prisoners of war. If, moreover, the SIG was able to put German coastal artillery out of commission, a larger British force waiting offshore was prepared to land to expand the scope of the attack. Dressed in German uniforms and carrying German identification and weapons, eighty SIG commandos were able to pass through a number of Axis checkpoints and enter the city. There, however, they were discovered before they were able to do much damage. Most were killed or captured, with only a handful of survivors returning to British lines.[60]

Still other Jews recruited by the British army for their language skills were the soldiers of No. 3 Troop of No. 10 Commando. This commando force consisted of soldiers born in Germany and Nazi-occupied Europe.[61] The Jews of No. 3 Troop were mainly former Pioneers and had generally been born in Germany. They were trained as infiltrators and special operators specializing in such matters as concealment, reconnaissance, sabotage, interrogation, and other clandestine and intelligence activities. The 142 Jews of No. 3 Troop engaged in a variety of covert operations before the Normandy invasion, and many fought in Normandy itself. Not surprisingly, given the nature of their assignments, a large percentage of these soldiers was killed, wounded, or captured.[62]

Jews in the OSS

Just as the SOE and other British intelligence and special operations forces recruited Jewish refugees, the American Office of Strategic Services (OSS) sought out a number of Jewish émigrés whose linguistic and cultural backgrounds might make them useful intelligence agents. The OSS was created by executive order in 1942 and authorized to collect intelligence and engage in covert operations. The OSS was prohibited from operating in the Western Hemisphere, which was the province of the FBI, and was prohibited by the military from operating in the Pacific theater.[63] The OSS engaged in a variety of propaganda, intelligence, and covert operations throughout the war, often working with its British counterparts, including the SOE.

During the last year of the war, the OSS made an effort to infiltrate agents into Austria and Germany and, for this purpose, recruited several American Jewish soldiers who were native German speakers and willing to undertake rigorous training and dangerous missions.[64] The best known of these individuals was Corporal Frederick Mayer, an American soldier who had been born in Freiburg, Germany, and emigrated with his family to the United States in 1938. After joining the army in 1941, Mayer was trained by the OSS in covert operations techniques. His training group included a number of other German Jewish refugees.

In 1945, Mayer, now a sergeant, along with another Jewish agent, radio operator Hans Wynberg, and a third man, a disaffected former Wehrmacht officer, Franz Weber, were parachuted into Austria, near Innsbruck, in what was code-named "Operation Greenup." The group's mission was to scout Germany's National Redoubt, which Allied intelligence believed was located somewhere in the Austrian Alps. This redoubt, which actually did not exist, was believed to be a fortress from which Hitler and other Nazi leaders were planning to make their last stand. Once in Austria, Mayer posed as a wounded German officer and was able to secure lodgings in a German officers' barracks near Innsbruck.[65]

From his "fellow officers," Mayer acquired a good deal of valuable information, which Wynberg radioed back to OSS headquarters. Mayer learned that the National Redoubt was a myth but obtained the actual location of the *Führerbunker* in Berlin. Mayer also determined the route of German rail traffic in the Alps and provided information that helped the air force block German rail lines in the Brenner Pass.[66]

Mayer also learned the location of an underground Messerschmitt factory buried deep in the mountains near the town of Kematen.[67] This factory built the ME-262 jet, the world's first operational jet fighter. The ME-262 was much faster than any Allied fighter and in air-to-air combat had established a 5:1 kill ratio over American and British fighters.[68] Very few of these ME-262s had appeared, but Allied air commanders were concerned that the Germans might deploy more and were eager to identify and target the German production facilities.

To obtain access to the factory, Mayer shed his German uniform and disguised himself as a French electrician. With false papers, Mayer was able to join a group of workers reporting for duty at the Messerschmitt plant, where he saw several partially built jet fighters. Mayer also discovered that there was no reason to attempt to bomb the factory. The plant had no parts or raw materials, and its production line had been shut down. As Wynberg's coded radio message informed the OSS, no aircrews would have to be risked in a bombing mission. There would be no more ME-262s.

After several months in Austria, Mayer was betrayed by an informant and captured by the Gestapo. He was severely beaten and tortured but refused to disclose the identities of his team members. Likely to be executed, Mayer hit upon the same tactic employed by his SOE counterpart, Walter Freud: he told the Austrians that he was a high-ranking American officer and that they would be much better off surrendering to him than to the oncoming Soviets. Local Nazi officials agreed, ordered Mayer's release, and surrendered to him.[69] When the American 103rd Infantry Division arrived with orders to attack and seize Innsbruck, the troops were met by Sergeant Mayer, who informed them that he had already captured the city.[70]

In addition to clandestine intelligence and covert operations, the OSS engaged in strategic analysis and evaluation through its Research and Analysis branch (R&A) aimed at understanding the Nazi leadership, the morale of the German civilian population, German goals, and so forth. For this purpose too, the OSS recruited a number of European Jews with language skills and a firsthand understanding of the Germans. During the war, R&A collected 100,000 documents and prepared a variety of reports on such concrete topics as the condition of rail transport on the eastern front as well as more abstract issues, such as possible clues to impending military offensives hidden in Joseph Goebbels's speeches.[71] The more concrete reports, including maps, country handbooks, and regional surveys, were quite useful for strategic planning and military operations.[72]

One rather unorthodox group of OSS analysts consisted of a number of refugee Jewish intellectuals associated with the so-called Frankfurt School of neo-Marxist social theorists. These included such intellectual luminaries as Franz Neumann, Herbert Marcuse, and Otto Kirchheimer. Neumann was recruited by the OSS in 1943 after writing his major study, *Behemoth: The Structure and Practice of National Socialism.*[73] The other two theorists joined soon thereafter and were posted to the Central European Section of R&A. This group was responsible for collecting and analyzing useful information about Nazi Germany from newspaper accounts, radio broadcasts, interviews with prisoners of war, and so forth.

R&A often produced insightful reports that played a role in American planning. For example, Neumann's 1943 report on the morale of the German populace pointed out that in a society like Nazi Germany, American propaganda and psychological warfare were likely to be ineffective so long as the Nazi Party remained in power.[74] The R&A section also advised the U.S. Joint Chiefs of Staff that a popular uprising against Hitler was highly unlikely, though a military coup attempt was possible—an analysis that turned out to be correct.

THE JEWS AND INTELLIGENCE

The two most important Jewish contributions to the intelligence war against Nazi Germany and its Axis partners were in the realms of American cryptanalysis and Soviet espionage. America's SIS, which relied heavily on the talents of Jewish analysts, developed important code-breaking techniques as well as a code machine, SIGABA, that proved invulnerable to Axis cryptologists. The German and other Axis communications decrypted by SIS and by the British shortened the war and contributed to Allied success.

At the same time, Jews in the Soviet intelligence and counterintelligence services learned a great many German secrets while preventing the Germans from learning much about Soviet capabilities and intentions. Soviet intelligence was, in a word, intelligent. Overlapping networks of agents with elaborate cover identities worked for years to make contacts and to collect information. The Red Orchestra, Sissy, Dora, and the others were patient, insidious, and effective. Their Jewish operatives produced intelligence about the Wehrmacht's plans that played an important role in the Soviet military effort.

The same cannot always be said for the British and American agencies, such as the SOE and OSS, which recruited a sizeable number of extraordinarily brave Jewish operatives. Some missions made sense, the destruction of the German heavy water plant, for example. Altogether too often, however, rather than exhibit the patience and planning of the Soviets, these agencies sent teams of operatives into German-occupied territory on intelligence missions or covert operations that seemed to seek immediate results based on weeks rather than years of planning.

In many instances, too, the objectives of these missions seemed hardly worth the lives being risked. Suppose the Jewish parachutists had all succeeded. How would the result have shortened the war? Could the SIG actually have succeeded in its attack on Tobruk, or was this a poorly conceived scheme that cost the lives of many brave soldiers? Unfortunately, the courage of the Jewish troops was not always matched by the intelligence of their commanders. Or perhaps these were troops whose lives were deemed expendable.

5

Partisan Warfare

Resistance movements developed in virtually every nation and territory under German occupation during the war. Many of these movements received support from external sponsors, particularly the Soviet Union, Great Britain, and the United States, which sent arms, supplies, and military advisors to partisans they deemed useful. Western European partisans, for example, received much of their equipment, training, and leadership from Britain's Special Operations Executive (SOE).[1] Resistance groups varied in size and militancy. The Dutch believed in peaceful resistance, a tactic that did not have much success against the Germans. Soviet partisans, on the other hand, relied on bombs and automatic weapons, which, given the nature of their foe, seemed to hold out more promise of success.

Compared to armored divisions and swarms of attack planes, lightly armed partisans would not seem to pose much of a military threat. Even today, when insurgents frequently practice asymmetric warfare against the United States, America knows that its adversaries would prefer to use missiles and tanks if they could afford them. During World War II, though, several factors made the Germans potentially vulnerable to partisan warfare and made the partisan, at least potentially, a useful weapon against the Wehrmacht.

First, German supply lines, especially in the east, were long and fragile. Troops, ammunition, fuel, and so forth had to be moved over long distances on rail lines that could be, and often were, interdicted and disrupted by partisans. Germany depended upon these same rail lines for shipments of such strategic materials as bauxite, nickel, and chrome, also subject to interdiction. Second, when it came to food, the Wehrmacht, especially in the east, had planned to live off the land—that is, German planners counted on being able to feed their troops from local sources in the conquered lands. Partisans, pursuing a scorched-earth policy, could cause serious food problems for the German army. Third, Germany had conquered virtually all of Europe and faced some partisan activity in every conquered country. With the exception of the Soviet partisans, no individual set of guerilla fighters posed a major challenge to the Germans. Cumulatively, however, partisans sapped German strength.

Germany relied, especially in Western Europe, on the help of local police forces to deal with partisans, and especially in France and Holland, these local police were quite helpful.[2] Nevertheless, hundreds of thousands of German military police officers were deployed to maintain security in Europe, especially in the Soviet Union.[3] According to one estimate, as many as 500,000 German soldiers and security personnel were assigned to combat partisans behind German lines in the USSR alone.[4] These deployments were in addition to whatever German military garrisons might also be assigned to each nation, in part for internal and in part for external security. All together, this placed a substantial burden on Germany's limited manpower resources. Thus, as historian Jorgen Haestrup observes, when the Germans needed every man to fight the Soviets in 1943, 380,000 troops were assigned to Norway, 360,000 to Yugoslavia, 65,000 to Holland, and so forth.[5]

The Jews had the most to lose from the German occupation. Accordingly, they could often be found at the forefront of resistance to the Nazis—even though they frequently had to contend with the hostility of their own countrymen as well as the murderous policies of the Germans. Let us examine some of the arenas of partisan warfare in which Jews played a part, beginning with Western Europe and the role of Jews in the French Resistance. We shall not treat the barely perceptible resistance groups in Germany's allies and satellites, the Dutch case where there was mainly passive resistance, or the cases of Norway and Denmark, whose tiny Jewish populations were smuggled to Sweden.

WESTERN EUROPE

Jews and the French Resistance

Americans tend to equate the idea of World War II resistance with the French Resistance, though this may be more a tribute to postwar French literary acumen than to the actual effectiveness of the French Resistance movement. As historians Eric Conan and Henry Rousso remark, the history of the resistance was "spruced up" by French politicians and intellectuals who sought to emphasize French heroism and downplay the extent to which the Vichy regime represented a French historical tradition and the views of many Frenchmen.[6]

Prior to the Normandy invasion, perhaps 200,000 inhabitants of France, about 1 percent of the population, at one time or another played some active role in a resistance organization. Of these individuals, perhaps half were associated with the Francs-tireurs et partisans (FTP), an armed Communist group that began resisting in 1941 when ordered to do so by the Soviets. Between 15 and 20 percent of the active French resistants were Jews.[7] Conversely, about 25 percent of France's Jews took part in the resistance as compared with 1 percent of the overall French population.[8] Jews were even more overrepresented in North Africa, where perhaps a majority of the active anti-Vichy underground fighters were Jews.[9]

In addition to their membership in the general resistance and the Communist resistance, a small number of Jewish resistants were Zionists, members of the Armée juive (Jewish Army), later called the Organization juive de combat (OJC), and others were members of the politically diverse Union de la jeunesse juive and the Milice patriotique juive. The anthem of the general resistance, the "Chant des Partisans," was written by a Jewish novelist, Joseph Kessel.[10] Similarly, the most popular novel in France during the occupation, *La Silence de la mer*, the story of a young French woman who rejects the advances of a German officer, was written by a Hungarian Jewish immigrant, Jean Bruller. Tens of thousands of copies of the novel were produced by underground presses, and more copies were dropped by the Royal Air Force to inspire partisans.[11]

Prior to the war, France was home to about 350,000 Jews, slightly less than 2 percent of the nation's population. Of these, fewer than half were native born. The majority were refugees or fairly recent immigrants from Eastern

Europe. After the June 1940 armistice, three-fifths of France was placed under German control, with the remainder under the nominal authority of the French Vichy government headed by Marshal Henri-Philippe Petain. From London, the previously unknown brigadier general Charles de Gaulle declared that France would continue to resist the Germans, while Petain asserted that France would cooperate with Germany.

Many of those who responded to de Gaulle's call were French Jews, including Jews who had been able to make their way to England and French Jews living in North Africa. In fact, de Gaulle was said to have expressed his "regret and astonishment" that most of those who first joined him in what became the Free French Forces were Jews.[12] These included several members of de Gaulle's general staff, as well as Admiral Louis Kahn, formerly the French navy's chief engineer, who contributed several innovations in antisubmarine warfare to the Allied cause, and quite a few French air force pilots, including future prime minister Pierre Mendes-France, who flew numerous bombing missions over France during the war. After the Allies drove the Germans from North Africa in 1942, French Jews who had been cashiered from the French army in Algeria by the Vichy regime were able to rejoin their units after some conflict with their (formerly) Vichy commanders.

In occupied France, which included Paris, the German military government quickly instituted a series of anti-Jewish decrees—the expropriation of Jewish property, wearing of yellow badges, and so forth—and worked with the French bureaucracy and police to organize the deportation of Jews to the east, where they would be murdered.[13] The French police helpfully compiled a card index of all the Jews of Paris by name, street, occupation, and nationality.[14] In the unoccupied zone, the Vichy government also expropriated Jewish property, prohibited Jews from holding most public offices or engaging in a variety of professions, and instituted a number of other disabilities.

The Vichy government also authorized the internment and deportation of foreign-born Jews, though some Vichy officials sought to thwart efforts by the Germans to deport and murder native-born Jews. Thus, when the Germans demanded 10,000 Jews for deportation in July 1942, the Vichy government agreed to deliver 10,000 foreign-born Jews on the understanding that French Jews would only be deported if not enough foreign Jews could be found.[15] For their part, the Germans were content, at least temporarily, to deport foreign-born Jews. German officials believed that such deportations would be supported by the French populace, which was well known not to like foreigners and would see an opportunity to profit from the property and positions the foreign Jews held.[16] In general the Germans were correct. As Michael Marrus and Robert O. Paxton point out, even French railway crews, who often engaged in minor acts of sabotage directed against the Germans, almost always cooperated in the deportation of foreign-born Jews.[17]

Many native-born French Jews hoped that Vichy would protect them and took heart from such Vichy pronouncements as Admiral François Darlan's remark that "the stateless Jews, who for the past fifteen years have invaded our country, do not interest me. But the others, the good old French Jews, are entitled to all the protection we can give them."[18] At least some of these good old French Jews hoped that they would be protected and that the Germans would be satisfied to take the others. To some extent, this protection was forthcoming. Between 1941 and 1944, about 40 percent of the foreign-born Jews, but only 10 percent of native French Jews, a total of more than 90,000 persons in all, were murdered by the Germans, often with the assistance of French authorities.[19]

In 1942 alone, 38,000 Jews were deported from France's Drancy internment camp to Auschwitz, which the French government officially termed an "unknown destination."[20] Few returned from this unknown place. Given a chance, French officials usually tried to fill German deportation quotas with foreign-born Jews, though it seems unlikely that the native born would have survived much longer if the Germans had not been driven from France in 1944.

As the subjects of the German and Vichy racial laws and the victims of arrests, roundups, internments, and deportations by the French and German police, the Jews had ample reason—indeed, more reason than others—to engage in acts of resistance. Jews were important in the leadership of a variety of resistance groups, including the Communist resistance and more general groups, as well as specifically Jewish groups. The Jewish Army was founded in 1942 in Toulouse by a group of individuals who included Abraham Polonski and David Knout and recruited the first of its some 2,000 fighters from a Torah study group.[21]

During 1942 and 1943, the Jewish Army focused on helping Jews, especially children, escape to Switzerland or cross the Pyrenees into Spain, from where many eventually made their way to Palestine. In 1943, the Jewish

Army began intensive military training in the southern French countryside to prepare to engage in armed struggle against the Germans and collaborators. Renamed the OJC, this group worked in cooperation with other Maquis groups of rural resistants, particularly after the Allied landings, to attack German forces near Lyon, Toulouse, and Grenoble. The OJC also participated in the capture of the German garrison at Castres, where the Jewish fighters were especially pleased to inform the Germans that they were now the prisoners of a group of armed *Juden*.[22]

In the general resistance, Jean-Pierre Levy was the head of the Francs-tireurs, founded in Lyon, to disseminate anti-German and anti-Vichy propaganda and to conduct acts of sabotage. This group became part of the nucleus of de Gaulle's "Secret Army" and of the overall Gaullist organization, the Mouvements unis de résistance (MUR). Levy became the MUR's director of intelligence and security. Daniel Mayer, a Socialist, helped bring about the wartime alliance of various resistance groups under the banner of the Conseil national de la résistance (CNR). Leo Goldenberg, who used the nom de guerre "Leo Hamon," was a leader of the non-Communist Paris resistance and is often credited with negotiating the cease-fire that led to the Germans surrendering Paris in 1944 without a shot being fired. Hamon also organized the destruction of labor ministry files that undermined the German program of compulsory labor in 1944.[23] Gilbert Hirsch-Ollendorf, known as "Gilbert Grandval," was the military head of de Gaulle's French Forces of the Interior (FFI) in Alsace, Lorraine, Champagne, and the Argonne. Raymond Samuel, known as "Raymond Aubrac," was an engineer who specialized in sabotaging bridges and railroads. There were many others.[24]

Perhaps the largest number of Jewish resistants joined the FTP or, if foreign born, the FTP (FTP-MOI), which enrolled immigrant resistants. Immigrants, who included Jews, Poles, Italians, Spaniards, Hungarians, and others who had sought refuge in France during the 1930s, constituted a large element within the resistance, whether through the FTP-MOI or non-Communist forces. The 1939 Stalin-Hitler pact had caused a good deal of dissension and confusion within the French Communist Party, and even after the Germans defeated and occupied France, some party members continued to follow the Soviet line, criticizing the Vichy government but not Nazi Germany.[25] The Germans reciprocated by ignoring the Communists—though the French police continued their prewar operations against them. Many Jewish

Communists found it difficult to refrain from criticizing the Nazis and left the party during this period.

For French Communists, the German invasion of the Soviet Union clarified all former ideological confusion. The party began distributing anti-Nazi tracts, organizing FTP partisan units, and stepping up military training for its militants.[26] The first official act of violence committed by the FTP came in August 1941 when two FTP activists, Pierre Georges and his Jewish accomplice, Robert Brustlein, shot and killed a German naval officer on a metro platform.

This act marked the beginning of the FTP's campaign of violence, which continued until the end of the war. FTP units developed a measure of expertise in bomb making and placed time bombs in a hotel housing Germans, an office hiring workers for the Germans, and the headquarters of the Fascist Parti Populaire Français.[27] The Communist Party was also the first to warn Jews that deportation was a euphemism for murder by poison gas. The Communists told Jews to go into hiding rather than allow themselves to be rounded up by the authorities.

In 1942, thousands of immigrant Jews in Paris were arrested and deported to Auschwitz. This action left hundreds of Jewish teenagers who had hidden from the police wandering the streets and alleys of the city, desperate and seeking revenge. These individuals were recruited by the FTP and became the shock troops of the FTP-MOI, eager to engage in violence and ready to die. For these young Jews, wrote historian Annie Kriegel, herself an MOI member, "Homeland, name, family, house, school, neighborhood, work, everything which provides a point of fixity, and definition of self, had been swallowed up in nothingness. . . . It was to restore these constraints, often in the name of their father who had gone, that so many adolescents feverishly demanded arms."[28]

Historian Susan Zucotti records some of the names: seventeen-year-old Wolf Wajsbrot from Poland, twenty-year-old Leon Goldberg from Lodz, twenty-one-year-old Maurice Fingercwajg from Warsaw.[29] All had seen their parents, brothers, and sisters deported and would never see them again. In December 1942, members of the FTP-MOI's largely Jewish First and Second detachments launched a grenade attack at a truck filled with German soldiers, then threw more grenades at a German restaurant and still more at a group of German soldiers outside a theater.[30] In 1943, a Jewish-led FTP-MOI group threw a bomb into the car of the German commander of Paris, General Ernst von Schaumburg, and assassinated SS General Julius Ritter, head of the German forced-labor program in France.[31]

One Jewish Communist resistant, Abraham Lissner, a leader of the FTP-MOI, recorded 459 military actions by Jewish fighters in Paris alone between March 1942 and November 1943.[32] This included the bombing of workshops engaged in the production of goods for the German army. Some of these were owned by Jews who thought that their efforts would protect them from deportation.[33]

These acts of resistance, of course, led to severe reprisals by the German and French police. FTP and FTP-MOI fighters and organizers were hunted down, tortured, and either shot or sent to Auschwitz. In late 1942 and early 1943, many FTP-MOI fighters were arrested, and by the end of 1943, the entire FTP-MOI leadership in Paris had been captured or killed. Some FTP leaders argued in favor of moving their units to the countryside or to other cities where the police were less vigilant. The Communist Party leadership, however, was determined to continue fighting in the capital to demonstrate its preeminence in the resistance struggle.[34] The result was a continuation of heavy casualties among FTP fighters, particularly among the Jews and foreign Jews of Paris.

While Jews, immigrants, and Communists bore the brunt of the fighting, the ordinary French bided their time until 1943. In that year, the Germans declared that tens, perhaps hundreds, of thousands of additional French workers were to be conscripted to work in German industries, joining the war prisoners and other French workers who had labored in German factories and farms since the armistice. This measure threatened millions of French families and led to an upsurge in recruitment by resistance organizations.[35] The French police reported that 1943 brought an upsurge in partisan attacks on police stations.[36]

In that same year, the government-in-exile encouraged its affiliated forces to step up their sabotage activities in preparation for the Allied landings. Resistance groups responded and set off bombs in factories, fuel-storage depots, and rail yards. Because of acts of sabotage, railway traffic in France dropped by a third in 1944, hampering German troop and supply movements.[37] After the invasion itself, resistance groups derailed German trains, cut communications, and attacked German fuel and ammunition depots. Some resistance units engaged in pitched battles with German forces, though usually without success.

Thus, the main French resistance began when the Normandy invasion made it clear that the German occupation would soon end. To be sure, thousands of French families practiced passive resistance, declining to cooperate with the authorities and sometimes hiding Jews from police roundups. Without this passive French resistance, there is no doubt that many more Jews would have perished.[38] With liberation at hand, hundreds of thousands of the French became enthusiastic resistants under the banner of the FFI. But it must be said that before the Anglo-American invasion, for some of the French, the occupation, as has often been observed, represented one of the great historical eras of Franco-German amity. Indeed, many of the French viewed collaboration with the Germans as a goal to be achieved rather than a crime to be punished.[39]

The extent to which the main resistance groups, other than the aforementioned Jews, immigrants, and Communists, forcefully resisted the Germans, while not insignificant, should not be exaggerated. Prior to the Normandy invasion, there were no pitched battles between resistance fighters and the Wehrmacht or spectacular acts of sabotage that might have forced the Germans to increase the number of troops assigned to policing the French. Indeed, for most of the war years, the German occupation force in France, not including the troops assigned to the Atlantic fortifications (many of whom were anti-Soviet Russians), consisted of about 3,000 civilians and a number of police battalions totaling several thousand men.[40]

For the most part, the Germans found that they could rely on the French police and the paramilitary French Milice to deal with resistants—and to round up Jews for deportation. Until the Allied invasion, these forces were more than adequate for both tasks and showed almost as much enthusiasm as their German colleagues for removing what they deemed to be kikes and Communists from French soil, especially if they were foreign born. Active collaborators probably outnumbered active resisters in France.[41]

Belgium

Outside France, the largest Western European resistance movement arose in Belgium, and, as in the French case, the most militant resistants were Jews, particularly foreign-born Jews who could not count upon any support from

Belgium's government or people.[42] Before the war, approximately 90,000 Jews, constituting about 1 percent of the total population, lived in Belgium. Most of these Jews were foreign born, refugees from Germany or immigrants from Eastern Europe. German forces occupied Belgium in 1940 and quickly promulgated a number of anti-Jewish statutes. Jewish property was confiscated, Jews were barred from the professions, Jewish children were expelled from the schools, Jews were conscripted into forced-labor brigades, Jews were compelled to wear yellow arm bands, and a *Judenrat* (Jewish Council) was established to serve as the conduit for German directives to the Jewish community.

Beginning in 1942, the Germans began deporting Jews to Auschwitz and other death camps. As in France, the Belgian bureaucracy and police, along with local Fascist paramilitaries, helped organize the deportations. And, as in France, some Belgian officials, including Queen Elizabeth, sought to intervene on behalf of native-born Jews. Ultimately, about 40,000 Jews were murdered, including the majority of the foreign-born Jews, as well as some native Belgian Jews.

In response to these developments, several groups of mainly foreign-born Jewish Communists established the Main d'oeuvre immigrée (MOI) led by a group of individuals who had fought in the International Brigades in Spain.[43] A larger Jewish resistance group, the Comité de défense des juifs (CDJ), enrolled both native- and foreign-born Jews. In occasional collaboration with the general Belgian resistance movement, the Resistance Network (RR), the MOI and CDJ engaged in sabotage and violent struggle against the Germans and collaborators. The RR was active throughout the war, engaging in acts of sabotage against the German troop and transport trains that made frequent use of the strategically important Belgian rail system and attempting to rescue the many Allied airmen shot down over Belgium. The MOI and CDJ participated in the RR's general campaign of sabotage and, in addition, specialized in killing informers and collaborators, including officials of the *Judenrat*.

Among the most spectacular of these actions was the sabotage of a train carrying 1,500 Jews to Auschwitz in 1943. A group of CDJ fighters led by George and Alexander Lifshitz stopped the train, freed many of the deportees, and, in an exchange of automatic weapons fire, killed quite a number of German guards.[44] The Lifshitz brothers, along with most other members of the CDJ and MOI leadership, were eventually captured by the Germans and executed. Because of their militancy and high level of anti-German activity, casualties within Belgian resistance groups were reputed to be extremely heavy. However, because of the intensity of the resistance, Belgium, unlike France, was never pacified by the Germans during the war and never became a secure or stable base for German military operations.[45]

Jews had served in the Belgian officer corps before the war—the highest ranking was General Ernest Wiener—and a number of Belgian Jews were able to join the Belgian army-in-exile, which consisted of Belgian colonial forces and Belgian soldiers who had managed to escape the Germans. The Belgian Piron Brigade participated in the Normandy invasion, and the first of its officers to be killed in action was a Jew, Benjamin Pinkus. The defense minister of the Belgian government-in-exile, Camille Gutt, was of Jewish origin.[46]

SOUTHERN AND EASTERN EUROPE

Greece

Before the war, 76,000 Jews lived in Greece, making up nearly 1 percent of the nation's population. Some 55,000 of these Jews were to be found in Salonika, where they constituted 20 percent of the city's residents. The Salonika Jewish community traced its origins to the fifteenth century. Italy invaded Greece in 1940, but with British assistance, the Italians were beaten back. In April 1941, however, the Germans intervened, drove away the British, occupied much of Greece with the Italians, and allowed Bulgaria to annex territory it claimed in northern Greece. Under German rule, Greek Jews were evicted from their homes, their property was expropriated, and many were forced to move into ghettos. Beginning in 1943, the Germans began to deport Jews from Salonika and Thrace. Most were sent to Auschwitz, where more than 60,000 were killed.

Despite the murder of more than three-fourths of the members of Greece's Jewish community, Greek Jews played important roles in the Greek resistance, which vigorously and actively opposed the Nazis. Initial Greek resistance activities were focused on the Bulgarians in the north and quickly suppressed. By the end of 1941, however, the Greek Communist Party had organized the National Liberation Front (EAM) and its military wing, the Greek People's Liberation Army (ELAS).

Along with smaller, non-Communist partisan groups such as the National Republican Greek League (EDES), ELAS launched an armed insurrection in the Greek mountains, committing acts of sabotage and attacking Italian and German garrisons. The most famous act of sabotage conducted by these groups, with the help of the British SOE, was the November 1942 destruction of the Gorgopotamos railway bridge, the main link between northern and southern Greece and an important link in the transport net used to send ammunition to Erwin Rommel's forces in North Africa. The Africa Korps was in fact short of ammunition for several critical weeks as a result of the destruction of the bridge. Even more importantly, in 1943 Greek partisans destroyed chrome, nickel, and bauxite mines upon which German industry was heavily dependent, causing shortages that persisted through the end of the war.[47]

By mid-1943, Greek resistance forces controlled much of the countryside, with Axis troops confined to the major cities and towns. When the Italian government capitulated to the Allies in 1944, a good deal of Italian military equipment was captured by the Greeks. However, large numbers of German troops—eventually as many as 300,000—began entering Greece in anticipation of a possible Allied landing. These troops conducted extensive operations against the Greeks, putting enormous pressure on the resistance movement until the Germans retreated in 1944. In fact, the Allies had hoped that the Germans would send large numbers of troops to Greece, freeing the way for an invasion of Sicily and then Italy. To encourage the Germans to view Greece as a likely invasion site, groups from the British Special Operations Executive and the American Office of Strategic Services had helped the Greek resistance fighters step up their level of activity. In the larger scheme of things, Greek partisans were expendable.

A significant percentage of the officers and leaders of ELAS were Jews, mainly from Salonika.[48] ELAS relied heavily on the educational backgrounds and linguistic skills of its Jewish fighters, drawn from the urban middle class in what, otherwise, was a peasant army. Most of these Jews adopted Greek or nondescript noms de guerre. Thus, Yitzhak Mosheh was Kapetan Kitsos; Daisy Karasso was Kapetanissa Sarika, Louis Cohen was Khronos, David Aharon was Keravnos, Moshe Segora was Toto, and so forth. Many of these resistance fighters died in battle with the Germans or were killed after being captured. The Germans, for their part, lost more than 2,000 soldiers to Greek partisan attacks and were forced to deploy an entire combat division to deal with the Greek partisans.[49]

Yugoslavia

In April 1941, Yugoslavia was invaded by German and Italian forces, and within ten days the Yugoslav army surrendered. The Germans dismembered Yugoslavia, retaining control of Slovenia and most of Serbia, while granting Italy, Hungary, and Bulgaria other portions of Yugoslav territory. Croatia was given independence as a German satellite. The Croatians welcomed German influence, aped German racial laws, and supported the Axis occupation of the remainder of the nation. Outside Croatia, however, resistance emerged to German and Axis rule. Nominally, two resistance groups arose. The first, the Chetniks, were a Serbian royalist and nationalist group seeking to restore the deposed monarchy as well as Serbian preeminence in the Yugoslav confederation. The second, the Partisans, espousing a pan-Yugoslavian ideology, were led by Josip Broz Tito, a Communist and longtime revolutionary supported by the Soviet Union. Tito's Partisans undertook most of the actual fighting against Axis forces, while the Chetniks were ready to collaborate with the Germans and Italians against the Partisans.[50]

While the Chetniks recruited only Serbs, Tito's universalistic ideology allowed the Partisans to recruit fighters from all of Yugoslavia's ethnic groups, including Jews. Between 1941 and 1944, Tito's Partisans grew in strength, at one point numbering several hundred thousand fighters, and came to control large sections of Yugoslavia outside Croatia. German, Italian, and Croatian troops launched a number of major offensives against the Partisans, but these did not succeed in destroying Tito's military forces. Soviet forces and Yugoslav Partisans drove the Germans from Belgrade in October 1944. Following the German retreat, Tito's Partisans defeated the Chetniks and the Croatians in a brief but bloody civil war, and Tito became Yugoslavia's leader.

Prior to the war, fewer than 50,000 Jews lived in Yugoslavia, mainly in the cities of Serbia and Croatia, and more than 60 percent were murdered by the Germans or their Croatian allies. Of those Jews living under German occupation or in Croatia, few survived. However, many Jews were able to make their way to an Italian zone of occupation, where they were relatively safe until the Italian surrender in 1943. By this time, however, the Partisans controlled large swaths of territory where Jews could survive.

Several thousand Jews fought in the Partisan movement. The most prominent was Shmuel Lerer, who called himself "Voja Todorovic." Todorovic was a veteran Communist who had fought in the Spanish Civil War. As commander of the First Partisan Brigade, Todorovic captured the Rajlovac airfield near Sarajevo and destroyed thirty-four German aircraft on the ground. Later, his forces captured the town of Jajce in Bosnia, and Todorovic was promoted to command first the Thirty-ninth Partisan Division and then the Tenth Partisan Strike Force Division, which enjoyed great success against the Germans. After the war, Todorovic was named a general in the Yugoslav army and rose to the third-highest rank in the army. He was also named a National Hero of the Yugoslav Peoples. Todorovic's three brothers, David, Isadore, and Moritz Lerer, also fought as Partisans. Two were killed in action, and one was captured and sent to the Jasnowitz concentration camp in Croatia, where he was murdered.

The Soviet Union

The most important arena of partisan activity during World War II was the German-occupied territory of the Soviet Union. This was true for two reasons. First, German reinforcements and military supplies for the eastern front were mainly carried by rail and truck over vast distances from the west, where they were constantly vulnerable to attack. Even loosely organized partisan groups could attack trains and convoys and delay or prevent soldiers and equipment from reaching the front lines. Telephone and telegraph communications were even more vulnerable to continual disruption by partisan groups.

Second, unlike, say, the American army, which can be completely supplied from its own bases, the World War II–era German army was a traditional force insofar as it was dependent on being able to requisition food and other supplies from the areas it conquered. This practice had been an essential feature of warfare since ancient times. Armies in the field depended on seizing supplies from local granaries in the lands they occupied.[51] According to German planners, as I noted earlier, the 3.5 million soldiers of the Wehrmacht on the eastern front would be fed by commandeering the necessary agricultural produce from Ukrainian, Russian, and other peasants. This plan, though, made the Germans vulnerable to partisans, who, by burning crops and killing livestock, could leave the Wehrmacht short of food.

Soviet partisan activity began soon after the German invasion and increased throughout the war until the Germans had been driven from Soviet territory in 1944. At one time or another, tens of thousands of Soviet citizens drawn from various nationality groups engaged in anti-German partisan activities. A reasonable estimate is that between 20,000 and 30,000 Jews fought as Soviet partisans, some in specifically Jewish units and others in groups of mixed nationality.[52] The actual number may have been higher because Jews in mixed-nationality units often hid their identities.

One leader of Lithuanian partisans, for example, himself Jewish, hid his nationality and told other Jews in his group to hide their own identities.[53] In the Minsk district, a partisan leader who called himself "Nikitin" was actually a former Red Army tank commander named Steingart.[54] Larger partisan groups sometimes recruited Jewish doctors, who were seen as essential to the group's survival. The largest number of specifically Jewish partisans was concentrated in Byelorussia, a republic that contained densely wooded tracts as well as the Pripyat Marshes, ideal terrain for partisan activity. The cities of Byelorussia, particularly Minsk, had also formerly been centers of Jewish life in the USSR.[55]

In the early months of the war, Soviet partisan activity was sporadic and poorly coordinated. The partisans consisted of isolated groups of Soviet troops caught behind the German lines, as well as Communist Party officials and members of the Komsomol who fled into the forests or countryside knowing that they would be killed by the Germans if they were taken prisoner. Very often, these early partisan groups were led by Jewish Communists and soldiers. Some elements of the Soviet population initially supported the Germans, and even those opposed to the Germans did not begin to resist until Soviet military victories in 1942 and 1943 showed that the Germans might actually be defeated. Before that time, the Jews—who had nothing to lose—were the most likely to resist and so were at the forefront of the early resistance movement.[56]

To be sure, even among the Jews, despite rumors of German atrocities in Poland, few had foreseen or believed that the Germans planned to annihilate the entire Jewish population of the occupied zone—something the German *Einsatzgruppen* (special action groups) and *Ordnungspolizei* (order police), along with their Ukrainian auxiliaries, came close to accomplishing within the first few months of the occupation.[57] Surviving Jews hid or fled to the east. But if they could, Jews formed or joined bands of partisans who gradually acquired light weapons with which to defend themselves against the Germans and against roving Ukrainian or even Russian bands who did not much like Jews.

Take, for example, events in Gomel, a small city in Byelorussia captured by the Germans in August 1941. A partisan detachment was created by Communist Party leaders in the forests outside the city. Among the members of this detachment were several Jews, including its commander. These were joined by a number of Red Army stragglers, who also included several Jews who knew they could not surrender to the Germans. The detachment received some training in explosives from a Soviet army intelligence group that also included several Jews who had been dropped behind German lines and proceeded to mine rail lines and derail German trains. The detachment's most successful miner was a Jew from Gomel named Lev Ginzburg, who, I believe, was a distant relative of mine.[58]

These early partisans had few weapons and no supplies and, most importantly, could not count on much in the way of popular support or shelter. Many Soviet citizens greeted the Germans as liberators—or at least as probably better than the Communists—and had little interest in supporting anti-German partisan activities. Initially the Germans saw little reason to pay attention to partisan activities.[59] What the SS sometimes called antipartisan missions during this period were mainly roundups of Jews.

The Germans, of course, soon dispelled any popular notion that they might be benign occupiers. Nazi ideology characterized the Slavic peoples of the USSR as *Untermenschen* fit only to perform slave labor, while German military planning required complete confiscation of the peasants' food and supplies. In the Ukraine, the most anti-Soviet of all the republics, the Germans appointed Erich Koch as *Reichskommisar* (imperial commissioner). In his inaugural speech, Koch declared, "I am known as a brutal dog. . . . Our job is to suck from the Ukraine all the goods we can get hold of. . . . I am expecting from you the utmost severity toward the native population."[60]

When a German official told one of Koch's deputies that 40 million Ukrainians could not simply be annihilated, the deputy replied, "It is our business."[61] German policy inevitably provoked resistance, and by late 1941 and early 1942, partisan activity on the part of Slavs had begun to increase, particularly after the German defeat at Stalingrad punctured the myth of Nazi invincibility.

Stalin distrusted partisans—armed groups not fully under his control. But with the Soviet Union's continued existence in question, in his July 1941 radio appeal to the Soviet people, Stalin called upon all citizens to engage in partisan struggle against the Germans. "Conditions must be made unbearable for the enemy and his collaborators; they must be pursued and annihilated wherever they are."[62] Partisans were asked to swear oaths of loyalty to the Soviet cause and to promise to "work a terrible, merciless, and unrelenting revenge upon the enemy. . . . Blood for blood! Death for death!"[63]

During the course of 1942, the number of active Soviet partisans increased sharply, as did their impact on the Wehrmacht. Increases in both the numbers and effectiveness of the partisans were due in part to the growing number of Soviet army stragglers and escaped prisoners of war who decided to continue fighting. In this case too, the Germans were undermined by their own brutality. Soviet soldiers, as we saw in chapter 2, had been quick to surrender in the early months of the war. However, when troops began to learn of the cruel and inhuman manner in which the Germans treated Soviet prisoners, surrender rates diminished sharply, and even groups of soldiers cut off from their units would continue fighting rather than lay down their guns and turn themselves over to the Germans.

The stragglers and escaped prisoners of war knew how to use weapons, and in some cases entire Soviet infantry units, trapped behind German lines, turned themselves into partisan bands, striking at the Germans whenever possible.[64] The life of the partisan was harsh and often short. The casualty rate for partisans was extremely high. Many were killed by the Germans, some were killed by other partisans, and not a few died of disease. Local peasants, angered by partisans' "economic activities" (theft and extortion), would often inform the Germans, especially if the partisans were Jews or outsiders. One estimate of the annual death rate among Soviet partisans is 42 percent.[65]

As Soviet partisan activity increased, the Germans employed harsh tactics to compel local peasants and villagers to inform them of the presence and location of partisan bands. Typically, the Germans would destroy villages and kill many of their occupants in retaliation for any partisan action in the region. Indeed, Hitler ordered German forces to "spread the kind of terror" that would "make the population lose all interest in insubordination."[66] The Germans ordered that for every German soldier killed by a partisan, between 50 and 100 civilians would be executed.

Responding to this directive, SS troops murdered thousands of civilians along with whatever partisans they managed to capture. The predictable effect of this policy was to completely alienate the civilian population and produce more partisans. By 1942, most Soviet citizens understood that however villainous the Soviet commissars might have been, their cruelty paled in comparison to that of the Germans. As a 1942 Ukrainian joke quoted by historian Kenneth Slepyan put it, "What was Stalin unable to achieve in twenty years that Hitler achieved within one year? That we started to like Soviet rule."[67]

Of course, many Ukrainian partisan groups came to like neither the Soviets nor the Nazis and fought both.[68] And thousands of Ukrainian volunteers served in the German army throughout the war as *Hilfswillige* (non-German volunteers, known as Hiwis, serving in German army units) or *Freiwillige* (members of German army units composed of non-Germans), including the soldiers of the Fourteenth SS Volunteer Division (*Galizien*), which was involved in heavy fighting until the German surrender in 1945. Hitler was initially opposed to this use of Slavic *Untermenschen* in the Wehrmacht, but the enormous German casualties incurred on the Russian front in 1942 and 1943 left the Germans with little choice but to attempt to make use of anti-Soviet Ukrainian and Russian volunteers. While the Ukrainians proved loyal to the Germans, the Russians did not. When sent to France in 1944, the mainly Russian and Byelorussian Thirtieth SS Division mutinied, killed its German officers, and defected to the Allies.

Initially, the Soviet military had paid little attention to partisans, but by mid-1942, as partisan action intensified, Soviet military planners began to realize their potential. In May 1942, Soviet military headquarters (Stavka) created the Central Staff of the Partisan Movement under the supervision of Byelorussian party secretary Panteleimon Ponomarenko to coordinate and support partisan activities. From this point forward, Soviet military planners sought to integrate partisan activity into their overall effort. Arms and supplies were channeled to partisan units. Partisans were regularly employed to disrupt German communication and supply lines and to destroy critical elements of the German's military infrastructure, such as bridges, airfields, rail yards, and fuel and supply terminals.[69]

Stalin directed Ponomarenko to formalize and codify these ideas, and the result was People's Commissariat of Defense (NKO) Order 189, "On the Tasks of the Partisan Movement." NKO 189 declared that partisans operating behind the German's lines had a critical role to play in the destruction of the German army.[70] Partisans were directed to attack German communications lines and infrastructure. Partisans were to prevent German forces from acquiring local grain and other food supplies by seizing or destroying them to prevent foodstuffs from falling into German hands. Partisans were to assassinate German officials and Soviet collaborators.[71] Partisans were to engage in propaganda and recruitment activities among local villagers.

The partisan movement, moreover, was to become an "all-peoples movement." In other words, all elements of the Soviet population in occupied areas were expected to participate in and cooperate with partisan activities. Partisans drawn from different nationality groups were further directed to fight the Germans, not one another. This aspect of NKO 189 was very important to Jewish partisans, as well as to members of other minority nationalities, who often had been the victims of violence at the hands of xenophobic fellow partisans. After NKO 189, partisan violence against Jews and others was prohibited. Partisan leaders were specifically directed to provide arms and supplies to unarmed Jews who had sought refuge in the forests. Partisans were also told to offer refuge to any remaining Jews in ghettos and, if possible, to add them to their detachments.[72]

Jews soon constituted the third-largest nationality group among the Soviet partisans, behind only the far more numerous Russians and Ukrainians. The Ukrainians, it is worth noting, were nationalists and could not precisely be called Soviet partisans. Ukrainian partisan groups professing allegiance to Stepan Bandera's Organization of Ukrainian Nationalists (OUN) were vehemently anti-Soviet and sometimes willing to cooperate with the Germans against the Soviets. The OUN was also vehemently anti-Semitic and responsible for the murder of many Jews. Curiously, Bandera himself had a number of Jewish associates who participated in his movement.[73]

The universalistic implications of NKO 189 were sometimes ignored by loosely disciplined partisan bands, but in its wake, Jews in the occupied territories noticed a general improvement in their treatment by other partisan groups. One Byelorussian commissar prohibited partisans from using anti-Semitic expressions, and another reminded partisans that their duty to save the lives of Soviet citizens extended to Jews.[74] Anti-Semitic actions by partisans became subject to punishment. One Ukrainian partisan leader, for example, was executed for, among other crimes, killing five Jews.[75] Jewish partisan units also reported an improvement in their relations with non-Jewish partisans.[76]

Jewish survivors of the German *Einsatzgruppen* (special action groups) were hidden throughout the occupied Soviet Union, but the main concentrations, according to historian Yitzhak Arad, were in the forests around Minsk, in the swamps of western Byelorussia, in the Rudniki Forest of southeastern Lithuania, and in the forests of western Ukraine. These were large areas of dense forests and rugged terrain that had been near enough to large Jewish ghettos to allow at least a small number of Jewish survivors and escapees to reach them and to seek some measure of shelter from the Germans. As was the case in other regions, partisan activity in the forests around Minsk began in 1941 and consisted initially of scattered resistance by Communist Party and Komsomol members, along with Soviet army stragglers. These were joined by groups of Jews from the Minsk ghetto underground, many of whom had also served in the Soviet army.[77]

In 1942, two Jewish underground groups, commanded by Israel Lapidot and Nahum Feldman, also left the Minsk ghetto for the forests, where they were joined by non-Jewish partisans. Lapidot's unit was constituted by the underground Communist Party organization as an element of the Second Minsk Partisan Brigade. It attacked police stations, mined railroad tracks, and destroyed bridges until the Red Army drove the Germans from Byelorussia in 1944.[78] Feldman's unit, for its part, became affiliated with several other Jewish and non-Jewish partisan groups as part of the Frunze Brigade, which included a Jewish partisan commander named Ziskin, former Minsk Jewish underground leader Hersh Smolar, and hundreds of other Jews who had fled the Minsk ghetto. All told, as many as 2,000 Jewish partisans were active in the Minsk region between 1941 and 1944.

A second area in which Jewish partisans were active consisted of the Kozyany and Naroch forests of western Byelorussia. Several hundred Jews, many living in family camps, took shelter in these forests in 1942. These individuals were barely armed and were refugees more than partisans. They had all they could do to defend themselves against armed bands of bandits and partisans and could hardly take part in any attacks on the Germans. At the end of 1942 and beginning of 1943, however, the Soviet Central Staff of the Partisan Movement gradually asserted its authority in the region. Several disciplined partisan groups entered the forest and recruited and armed Jews from among the refugees and recruited a number of armed fighters from the Vilna (Vilnius) ghetto.

These reconstituted partisan groups fought the Germans as well as Polish nationalist partisans in the region. An armed Jewish unit calling itself "Revenge" was established in August 1943. Later that same year, however, the Soviet government decided that the presence of Jewish partisans in the region was causing disaffection on the part of local peasants. Some of the Jewish partisans were disarmed, and others were integrated into non-Jewish units. These took part in heavy fighting against the Germans in late 1943 and early 1944, as well as in numerous acts of sabotage against the German rail system.[79]

The third major region of Jewish partisan activity was the Rudniki Forest near Vilna in Lithuania and the nearby Nacha Forest on the border between Lithuania and Byelorussia. Jewish partisans entered the Rudniki Forest in 1943 after escaping from the Vilna ghetto. The first group was led by Nathan Ring, a former ghetto police officer who was later executed by the Soviets for his previous collaboration with the Germans. The second group, led by Abba Kovner and Chyena Borowska, was able to flee Vilna just before the Germans "liquidated" the ghetto in September 1943. After some disputes, Kovner took command of both groups, which grew with the arrival of Jewish escapees from labor camps in Vilna.[80]

The Central Staff of the Partisan Movement in the region was represented by Genrikas Zimanas, a Jew whose nom de guerre was "Jurgis." In October 1943, Zimanas took charge of all Soviet partisan groups in southern Lithuania. Zimanas was concerned that the large number of Jewish partisans in the Rudniki Forest would inflame the already decidedly anti-Semitic sentiments of the local Lithuanian peasants and so decided to dispatch some of the Jewish partisans from Rudniki to the Nacha Forest. Subsequently, Zimanas disbanded the purely Jewish units and distributed their fighters among multinational units commanded by Russians and Lithuanians. The Central Staff viewed purely Jewish units as a continuing irritant to the local population, which would be more likely to support partisans led by members of their own nationality.

The best-known groups of Jewish partisans, including the group led by Tuvia Bielski and made famous in the film *Defiance*, operated in a fourth region, the Naliboki and Lipichany forests of western Byelorussia. Jews from a number of towns and villages in the region began to hide in these forests in 1942.

These included the Bielski family, whose camp eventually included 1,200 Jews. Another significant Jewish partisan group was commanded by Shalom Zorin. This group consisted mainly of refugees from the Minsk ghetto and, like the Bielski camp, after 1943 operated under the authority of the Soviet Central Staff. Both Zorin and Bielski resisted efforts to disperse their partisans among multinational units. And, indeed, the commanders of many of the multinational units did not welcome Jews and were happy to send their Jewish partisans to Zorin or Bielski.

A third Jewish unit in the region was commanded by Dr. Yehezkel Atlas and consisted mainly of Jews who had escaped from the Derchin ghetto in 1942.[81] These were later joined by Jews from Dyatlovo commanded by Hirsch Kaplinski. Along with other Soviet partisans, the Bielski and Zorin units fought not only against the Germans but also against Polish nationalist partisans who opposed both the Germans and Soviets. In Poland, for this reason, Bielski is considered a murderer, and the film *Defiance* was generally boycotted by Polish audiences. Bielski managed to survive the war and lived in New York City until his death in 1987.

Resistance in the Ghettos and Camps

As suggested above, most Jewish partisans were individuals or families who had managed to escape from one of the many urban ghettos established by the Germans, often just before these were liquidated and the Jews sent to death camps. For Jews in the ghettos, the decision to resist or to attempt to escape and flee to the forests was a difficult one. To begin with, the Germans liquidated ghettos in increments, claiming the deportees were being "resettled." At each step, the risks of escape or resistance seemed greater than the risk of doing nothing. Indeed, it was initially difficult for most Jews to believe that the Germans actually intended to kill them all. Resistance brought savage retaliation, while passivity seemed to hold out some hope of survival. Often the ghetto *Judenrat* would take this position and discourage escape or resistance. By the time Jews realized the truth and resisted, it was too late. "The public wants the enemy to pay dearly," said Warsaw ghetto diarist Dr. Emanuel Ringelblum. "We will attack him with knives, with sticks, with bullets. We will not allow him to stage a roundup, to seize people in the streets, because now everybody knows that every labor camp spells only death. Now we must resist. Old and young alike must oppose the enemy."[82] But by the time this sentiment prevailed, resistance was no longer possible.

The idea of flight was further complicated by the fact that escape was a possibility only open to the young, for whom it meant abandoning family members. Also, the Jews generally lived in the cities and towns of the USSR. To most, the forests represented an alien environment in which survival seemed highly unlikely. Some saw their options as death in the ghetto or death in the forest and preferred the former.[83] As a result, Jews who might have had some chance to escape usually waited until it was too late and the Germans had begun their final liquidation of the ghetto. At this point, after a brief and futile uprising, a handful of desperate survivors would attempt to make their way into the forests.

One important example of this phenomenon is the case of the Minsk ghetto. Minsk was the capital of Byelorussia and a long-standing center of Jewish life. In 1941, after overrunning the region, the Germans established a ghetto for the Jews of Minsk and surrounding towns. Altogether about 75,000 Jews were herded into the Minsk ghetto. Communist activists among the Jews soon organized an underground resistance movement led, as noted above, by Hersh Smolar and Nahum Feldman, both of whom had prior experience organizing underground forces.[84]

Smolar and Feldman recruited a number of printers who operated an underground press, which disseminated information and propaganda in the ghetto. Another underground group was organized by Mikhail Gebelev, a Communist Party member and experienced propagandist. Gebelev's group was able to steal a radio and a typewriter, listen to Soviet news broadcasts, and type leaflets for distribution in the ghetto.[85]

Smolar and Feldman secured the cooperation of the *Judenrat* and ghetto police and sought to make common cause with non-Jewish Communist underground groups operating in Minsk outside the ghetto, as well as with partisan groups in the forests near the city.[86] Through these contacts, the ghetto underground was able to smuggle Jews into the forests. Most Jews of the Minsk ghetto, however, believed that they were more likely to survive if they simply remained in the ghetto and avoided trouble, and they had no interest in escaping to the uncertainties of life in the forests.

The Germans became aware of the Jewish underground and in 1942 began arresting its leaders and members in preparation for the liquidation of the ghetto. As the Germans became harsher in their treatment of the ghetto's Jews, more were willing to risk escape to the forests, particularly after a bloody *Aktion* on the day of Purim in 1942.[87] Smolar and Feldman were able to organize the escape of approximately 2,000 Jews, many of whom became partisans operating in the forests around Minsk. Several Jewish partisan groups were led by Jewish former Red Army officers, such as Semyon Ganzenko, a former first lieutenant.[88] During the course of 1943, another 8,000 Jews fled the ghetto. By this time partisan units had come under the control of the Soviet government and were receiving arms from the Soviet army. Many of these Jews received weapons and were conscripted into partisan units.

Similar events took place in the Vilna ghetto as well as the ghettos established in Kaunas (Kovno ghetto), Riga, Grodno, Pinsk, and throughout the German-occupied territories of the Soviet Union. Ghetto undergrounds, generally without weapons or resources, organized to fight the Germans. When there was no further possibility of resistance, a handful of survivors made their way to the forests, where some were able to obtain weapons and join or organize partisan units.

Jews from the Kovno ghetto, for example, joined the "Death to the Occupier" Soviet partisan battalion in the Rudniki Forest, though many members of the Kovno Jewish underground chose to remain in the ghetto with their families—and perished with them.[89] Armed resistance took place even in the small ghettos when the Jews knew their situation was hopeless. For example, in July 1942 the Jews of Nesvizh, a small city in Byelorussia, were able to steal a few weapons and prepare Molotov cocktails so that when a force of Germans and Lithuanians arrived to liquidate the ghetto, the Jews were reportedly able to kill or wound forty of them before the surviving Jews escaped to the forests.[90] Similar events took place in Kleck, Lakhva, Kremenets, Tuchin, Lyakhovichi, and Braslav. Jews fought, most died, and the survivors joined the partisans.[91]

The Effectiveness of Soviet Partisan Warfare

Soviet partisans fought the Germans from 1941 until 1944, when the last elements of the Wehrmacht were driven from the USSR. How effective were they? According to Soviet sources, partisans in Byelorussia killed 500,000 Germans, while partisans in the Ukraine killed 460,000 Germans and damaged or destroyed 5,000 locomotives, 50,000 railway cars, and 15,000 German automobiles.[92] These numbers, especially the German casualty figures, are obviously greatly exaggerated. However, numbers given by the Germans themselves are impressive.

In November 1943, German chief of operations General Alfred Jodl estimated that during three months in 1943, Soviet partisans had set off nearly 6,000 explosions along the railway lines on which the Wehrmacht depended. These, he acknowledged, had a significant effect on military operations.[93] In his testimony at the Nuremberg Trials, General Erich Manstein said that in 1944, during a seven-hour period, partisans carried out 1,000 acts of sabotage on roads and railways in his sector alone.[94] More recent estimates suggest that during the course of the war, Soviet partisans killed between 35,000 and 50,000 German soldiers and local collaborators in the occupied territories, while about 100,000 German soldiers, or 4 percent of the German army, were employed in antipartisan activities in the USSR.[95] Other estimates put the number of German troops involved in antipartisan efforts in the Soviet Union at 250,000 at a time when German frontline forces were understrength by nearly 750,000 troops.[96]

Whatever the precise numbers, there can be little doubt that Soviet partisan activity posed an important challenge to the Germans. Even Hitler declared, "If the repression of bandits in the east, as well as in the Balkans, is not pursued by the most brutal means, the forces at our disposal will, before long, be insufficient to exterminate this plague."[97] Because of their extremely long supply lines and poor logistical planning, the German army on the Soviet front was extremely vulnerable to partisan attack.

During the period prior to the invasion of the USSR and in the early years of the war itself, German planners had consistently underestimated the army's need for fuel, food, ammunition, spare parts, and other supplies and greatly overestimated the capacity of the German supply services to deliver these to the front lines.[98] As a result the vaunted German army was constantly lurching from fuel crisis to food crisis to ammunition crisis as it moved forward into the USSR.

Army Group North, for example, had been assigned the task of seizing Leningrad in 1941 but was forced to halt outside the city because it ran out of ammunition.[99] One reason that Army Group Center pulled back from the gates of Moscow was lack of fuel and ammunition. The German army simply did not have enough trains or trucks or even horses to supply a huge army, fighting a determined foe, over vast distances.

Even the main reason that the Germans lacked winter clothing in 1941–1942 was a shortage of trains and trucks with which to bring the clothing to the troops in the front lines.[100] Supplies remained a critical problem throughout the war in the east. Given the Germans' always tenuous supply situation, Soviet partisan attacks on German trains, trucks, and communication lines were extremely damaging to the Wehrmacht. Seeking to more fully exploit this German weakness, in 1943, Stavka ordered Soviet partisan units to focus on what was called the "Rail Campaign."[101] They were to concentrate on trains, railroad bridges, and tracks in an effort to destroy the Wehrmacht's logistical capabilities. This campaign, in which thousands of Jewish partisans participated, resulted in considerable disruption of German rail transport and helped set the stage for the Soviet army's successful attacks upon the Germans in 1943 and 1944.[102]

Data collected for one Jewish partisan group are suggestive of the impact of the Soviet partisans and the Jews in particular. Between 1943 and 1944, the "Avenger" group, consisting of escapees from the Vilnius ghetto and led by Abba Kovner, mentioned above, kept records of its activities. In this brief period, the Avengers reported having sabotaged 5 bridges, destroying 7 locomotives, 33 railroad cars, and 315 telephone and telegraph poles and dismantling 188 miles of railway tracks. The Avengers also estimated that they killed or wounded 212 enemy soldiers, mainly Lithuanian or Ukrainian auxiliaries.[103] In absolute terms, these numbers may appear small, but multiplied by several hundred Jewish or heavily Jewish partisan groups—there were twenty-two such groups in the Vilna area alone—the disruption of the always tenuous German supply lines began to become a serious matter for the Wehrmacht.

The Polish Resistance

German supply and communication lines were also vulnerable to interdiction by the Polish resistance, which was one of the largest resistance groups in Nazi-occupied Europe. The main Polish resistance group, the Home Army (Armia Krajowa, or AK), was formed in 1939 after the Germans and Soviets invaded, divided, and occupied Poland. Both occupying powers were brutal. The Germans viewed Poles as useful slave laborers and conscripted tens of thousands for this purpose, while the Soviets systematically murdered or deported thousands of Polish officials, military officers, intellectuals, and others deemed capable of fomenting nationalist resistance.[104]

The AK initially engaged in armed resistance against both German and Soviet occupation forces. After the Soviet retreat in 1941, though, the AK organized numerous acts of sabotage, assassination, and armed violence against the Germans and their allies and auxiliaries. Poland was a major rail center, and many German supply trains en route to the eastern front originated in or passed through Polish territory, creating possibilities for sabotage.

Perhaps even more importantly, a good deal of German military industry was located along both sides of the Polish-German border, including the territory annexed from Poland, and relied heavily on conscripted Polish laborers and Jewish slave laborers generally also drawn from Poland. The German rocket-development facilities at Peenemunde, for example, were only several miles from the Polish border and relied on conscript and slave labor. These facilities were actually moved further into Poland after Peenemunde was bombed by the British in 1943.

The location and Polish labor force of many German military industries, like the rail system, invited sabotage by the AK. Between 1941 and 1944, according to Polish sources, the AK and other Polish resistance groups damaged 25,000 pieces of railway equipment, derailed 732 trains, and damaged or destroyed more than 4,000 German army vehicles. During this same period, Polish workers in German factories were said to have engaged in extensive sabotage of German weapons and military equipment, including building faults into thousands of artillery shells, missiles, aircraft engines, artillery pieces, and pieces of electronic equipment.[105] The German governor-general of occupied Poland declared that from 1943 on, great numbers of ammunition depots were destroyed by saboteurs, that trains on several railways could only pass at special times under heavy guard, and that railway sabotage in 1944 increased to more than ten explosions each day.[106]

Many AK fighters perished during the war, particularly in 1944, when the AK launched a revolt in Warsaw, believing that the Soviet army, by that time only twenty miles from the city, would join forces with the Poles to crush the Germans. Unfortunately, the Soviet army failed to arrive, and the Germans killed or captured a large segment of the AK's military force. Poles believe that the Soviets deliberately allowed the Germans to defeat the AK in order to ease the way for postwar Soviet domination of Poland. The Soviet government claimed (and the current Russian government maintains) that its forces were exhausted and very nearly out of fuel and ammunition and thus unable to attack Warsaw.

Prior to the war, slightly more than 3.3 million Jews lived in Poland, mainly in the cities and larger towns. In 1940 and 1941, Jews were forced into a number of large urban ghettos, most importantly in Warsaw, Cracow, Lubin, Lvov, and Lodz. From these ghettos, Jews were deported to death camps at Treblinka, Chelmno, Belzec, and elsewhere. Between 1942 and 1944, the Germans murdered approximately 3 million of Poland's Jews. Underground Jewish resistance organizations arose within the major ghettos, most notably the Jewish Fighting Organization (ZOB) in Warsaw and the Jewish Military League (ZZW), which established underground cells in several cities. The ZOB was established by a coalition of Zionist youth groups, while the ZZW was formed mainly by Jewish former officers of the defeated Polish army, most notably David Apfelbaum.

The ZZW formed close ties to the AK, which supplied the ZZW with weapons and ammunition.[107] The ZZW had over 300 armed members in Warsaw and hundreds of other fighters deployed throughout Poland.[108] Through its contacts with the AK, the ZZW was also able to help small numbers of Jews escape the ghettos and go into hiding or join resistance forces, though, to be sure, a sizeable number of anti-Semitic elements within the AK, particularly in a smaller group sometimes affiliated with the AK, the National Armed Forces (NSZ), were indifferent to the murder of Jews.[109] ZOB fighters engaged in acts of sabotage and the assassination of German officials in Cracow and in Bialystok.[110]

Several hundred ZZW and ZOB fighters, joined by some non-Jewish members of the AK, launched the Warsaw Ghetto Uprising of January 1943 to resist efforts by the Germans to liquidate the ghetto and deport its remaining Jews to the Treblinka extermination camp.[111] When deportation from the ghetto began in July 1942, the *Judenrat* reassured Jews that they were being resettled as forced laborers. Within several months, however, the AK brought information to the ZZW that the "resettled" Jews had actually been murdered by the Germans. By this time, more than 250,000 Jews from Warsaw had been killed at Treblinka.

When the Germans came in January to deport the last of the ghetto's occupants, they were met by gunfire and homemade Molotov cocktails and forced to withdraw. ZZW fighters led by Apfelbaum and ZOB fighters led by Mordechaj Anielewicz took control of the ghetto and in some instances executed Jews they believed to have collaborated with the Germans.

In April and May 1943, 2,000 German troops, commanded by SS Officer Jürgen Stroop, attacked the ghetto, systematically setting fire to buildings that harbored resistance fighters.[112] This tactic gradually forced the defenders into an ever-smaller space. The heaviest fighting took place around the ZZW's stronghold at Murkowski Square, where a Polish flag and the ZZW's banner could be seen from the streets of Warsaw outside the ghetto.[113] The Germans regarded the flags as entirely too visible symbols of resistance and their capture as "a matter of great political and moral importance."[114] At the end of April, the flags were gone, and all the ZZW's leaders dead. The ZOB's leaders were killed soon thereafter.

During the course of the uprising, as many as 15,000 Jews died, and 50,000 others were deported to Treblinka, where they were murdered. The precise number of German casualties is disputed but may have numbered 300. Several dozen ZZW, ZOB, and AK fighters escaped though sewers and tunnels. A number of the Jews formed Jewish partisan units or joined existing units. Jewish partisan commanders included Samuel Jegier, Chil Grynszpan, and Mieczyslaw Gruber. A Jew using the nom de guerre "Szymek" commanded a unit of Polish partisans, and a Jewish veterinarian named Dr. Mieczyslaw Skotnicki commanded a mixed Polish-Jewish unit.[115]

Jews also revolted in the Lvov, Czestochowa, Bedzin, and Bialystok ghettos.[116] Resistance groups in the Bialystok ghetto managed to acquire several dozen rifles and pistols and, with these, along with Molotov cocktails, held off the Germans and Ukrainian auxiliaries for nearly two weeks when they came to liquidate the ghetto.[117] As in the case of Warsaw, survivors sought to make their way to the forests to join partisan units.

There was no resistance in the Lodz ghetto, Poland's second largest, where the *Judenrat* led by Hannah Arendt's bête noire, Chaim Rumkowski, enforced cooperation with the Germans. Rumkowski was convinced that cooperation would save at least some Jews. The Lodz ghetto indeed survived a year longer than its counterpart in Warsaw. In 1944, however, the Germans decided to liquidate Lodz and sent its remaining 70,000 Jews, including Rumkowski, to Auschwitz, where all but 877 were murdered.[118]

A number of Jewish fighters, including those who escaped from Warsaw and the other ghettos, often using assumed names and carrying "Aryan" papers issued by the AK, fought in AK units or in partisan detachments affiliated with the Communist Party. According to historian Michael Borwicz, quite a number of Jewish fighters using assumed names were killed in battle by the Germans during the abortive Polish revolt of 1944.[119]

Jewish partisan detachments are said to have numbered twenty-eight with another thirteen mixed detachments in which Jews constituted at least one-third of the fighters. Most operated in the heavily forested region near Lubin, where a Jewish unit, formed by Grynszpan, Gruber, Leon Kassman, Alexander Skotnicki, and others, engaged in acts of sabotage and assassination, as well as a number of pitched battles with the Germans, throughout the war.[120] At least 1,000 Jews who had been in hiding in Warsaw fought in the 1944 Warsaw revolt. These included members of the AK, ZOB, and ZZW, as well as a large group of freed prisoners from the Gesiowka concentration camp.[121]

Thousands of Jews, in addition, volunteered in 1941 for what came to be known as "Anders's Army." This army consisted of Polish prisoners of war held by the Soviets since their invasion of Poland in 1939. After the Germans invaded the USSR, Stalin authorized the release of Polish prisoners and the formation of a Polish military force under the nominal authority of the Polish government-in-exile. This force was commanded by General Wladyslaw Anders and eventually consisted of more than 40,000 soldiers, of whom a large number were Jews. Anders's Army was sent to the Middle East to support the Anglo-Soviet invasion of Iran, came under British command, and was transported through Iran, Iraq, and Palestine. In Palestine, 4,000 of Anders's Jewish soldiers received the general's permission to leave the force and join Jewish settlements in the region. These veterans, who included future Israeli prime minister Menachem Begin, became the nucleus of the future Israeli Defense Force.[122]

Czechoslovakia

In 1939, under pressure from the Germans, Slovakia seceded from Czechoslovakia and declared itself an independent state. Germany then entered the remainder of the country and declared the Czech provinces of Bohemia and Moravia a Reich protectorate in which ethnic Germans would become German citizens, while Czechs would become protectorate citizens. Slovakia, a nominally independent state, was required to cooperate with Germany, to provide the German army with access as it mobilized for the attack on the USSR, and, later, to provide troops to assist the German army.

Encouraged by the Czech government-in-exile, led by Edvard Benes and headquartered in London, some resistance groups arose both in the protectorate and in Slovakia, but resistance was minimal. Even acts of sabotage, which could have been important, given Bohemia's significance to the German armaments industry, were minor and scattered. Workers, for example, at the huge Skoda armaments works in Pilsen were generally cooperative.[123] Skoda continued producing enormous quantities of German munitions until near the end of the war, when it was heavily damaged by American bombers. With the exception of brutal German retaliation for the 1942 assassination of Reich security chief Reinhard Heydrich by Czech dissidents and the British SOE, the German occupation of the protectorate was relatively light-handed and did not generate the sort of popular anger produced by the German occupation of, say, Poland or the USSR.

Slovakia, for its part, was an independent state allied with Germany, and with the exception of small groups of partisans sponsored by the USSR, there was little resistance to the regime. However, by 1944 Slovaks saw that Germany's days were numbered. With the Soviet army approaching Slovakia's border, elements of the Slovak army, supported by groups of civilians, attempted to change sides in what has come to be known as the Slovak National Uprising. This uprising was crushed by the Germans, but small numbers of dissident soldiers and others fled to the mountains until the Soviet army pushed the Germans out of Slovakia in 1945.

A small number of Jewish Zionists and Communists were active in the Slovak resistance. The Slovak Communist Party, which included many Jews, created an underground resistance movement soon after the German invasion of the USSR. Subsequently, the Zionist Socialist youth movement Hashomer Hatsair established contact with this movement. Some Jews joined the Communist resistance, while others joined resistance groups loyal to the former Czechoslovakia.[124] In 1941–1942, Jews in Slovak labor camps began to collect arms and prepare to defend themselves.

During the national uprising, former Jewish soldiers rejoined their units and fought as officers and soldiers in the regular army. Others fought as irregulars, with a total of perhaps 2,500 Jews taking part in the fighting. A group of several hundred armed Jewish escapees from the Novaky labor camp fought against the Germans and subsequently joined partisan groups in the mountains after the uprising's collapse. In addition, the Soviets dispatched an airborne brigade, identified as the Second Czechoslovak Brigade, composed of Czechs and Slovaks and including a large number of Jews, to take part in the fighting.[125] After the uprising was defeated, many fighters fled into the Tatra Mountains and continued resisting as partisans. Several partisan commanders and many of the physicians who joined partisan bands were Jews.[126] More than 250,000 Jews had lived in Czechoslovakia before the war, and more than 80 percent were murdered by the Germans.

DID THE PARTISANS MATTER?

Partisan warfare did not defeat the Germans but it did hasten their defeat. Across Europe, partisans killed tens of thousands of German troops—50,000 or more, according to German sources.[127] This number does not take into account German auxiliaries such as Ukrainians and Croats or German officials and collaborators executed by resistance fighters. Partisans also interdicted German supplies, cut communications, interfered with troop movements, and otherwise made things more difficult for the Germans. After the Normandy invasion, even the previously quiescent French cut roads and rail lines and organized hit-and-run attacks that slowed German troop formations on their way to the beachheads. For example, the powerful Second SS Panzer Division lost only thirty-five men but was delayed ten days by sporadic French ambushes on its way to the front.[128] By the time it arrived, it was too late to have much effect upon the Allied advance.

Jews were among the most vehement of the resistance fighters. In the Soviet Union, Belgium, France, even Greece and Yugoslavia, Jews led partisan units, fought, and died. In Norway and Denmark the non-Jewish resistance helped the Jews to escape to safety in Sweden. In the Netherlands there was virtually no resistance, but every other occupied nation in Europe had its Jewish resistance fighters. This was so even in the death camps, where resistance had a moral, if not a military, significance.

6

Aftermath and Afterward

From Tragedy to Farce

By the summer of 1945, Hitler was dead and the war in Europe had come to an end. Rather than ask why the Jews failed to resist, we might reasonably ask whether the Allies would have won without the Jews. Jewish engineers and factory managers designed and built the weapons upon which the Soviet army depended. Jews helped prepare America to fight, and Jewish scientists built America's atomic bomb. Jewish spies and cryptanalysts gave the Allies advance notice of Germany's military plans. Jewish partisans helped interdict Germany's fragile supply lines. Perhaps we can never know if the Allies would have defeated Hitler without the Jews. But we can say that the Allies did not defeat Hitler without the Jews.

At the very least, without its Jewish scientists, weapons engineers, transport experts, and production supervisors, the USSR could well have seen its military capabilities destroyed by the initial German onslaught and might never have been able to launch its successful counterstrokes—efforts that ultimately depended more on the Soviet Union's superb weapons and revived manufacturing capabilities than its superior manpower. And as to the United States, America's Jewish atomic scientists gave the United States an ace in the hole, a weapon that precluded America's defeat and would have destroyed Nazi Germany if it had been needed. Some might wish to quibble about the extent of the Jewish contribution to other elements of the Allied war effort, but had Germany not surrendered in the summer of 1945, a weapon designed mainly by Jewish scientists would have ended the war in Europe as it did the war in Japan.

Whatever their success, the Jews were hardly in a position to celebrate. The war's aftermath did not fully end the tragedy of the Nazi period. Six million Jews were dead, and several hundred thousand survivors sat in displaced persons camps because they were unwelcome everywhere, including the United States, Great Britain, and the Commonwealth nations. One Canadian government official is said to have responded to proposals to allow more Jewish immigrants to enter the country by declaring, "None is too many!"[1] Britain would neither admit Jews nor allow them to emigrate to Palestine. Most Jewish refugees wanted to come to the United States, but America would not liberalize its restrictive immigration policy.[2] Instead, the Harry S. Truman administration pressed the British to admit 100,000 Jewish refugees to Palestine and subsequently worked to bring about the creation of the State of Israel, in part to house the refugees it did not want.[3]

Some Nazis, to be sure, were punished. Those Germans who found themselves in Soviet hands suffered mightily, the less guilty along with the more guilty. As to the others, the Allies organized a series of military tribunals to hold Nazi leaders accountable for their conduct. The best known of these tribunals were the 1945–1946 Nuremberg Trials. Of course, several of the major Nazi leaders, such as Heinrich Himmler, Joseph Goebbels, and Adolf Hitler himself, had committed suicide at the end of the war. However, hundreds of other important officials were in Allied custody, along with many lesser figures. The most important of the imprisoned Nazi leaders, including Hermann Goering and several senior military officers, were charged with war crimes and crimes against humanity. A few were ultimately sentenced to the gallows. Several lesser officials of the Nazi regime, including a handful of concentration camp personnel, corporate chieftains who had abused slave laborers, and physicians who had engaged in medical experiments on concentration camp prisoners, were sentenced, some to death, in subsequent trials.

In point of fact, the Nuremberg and other tribunals were designed more to legitimate the outcome of the war than to secure justice for the victims of Nazism.[4] Many tens of thousands of Germans and their Ukrainian, Lithuanian, Croatian, and other auxiliaries had been willing participants in the most heinous crimes of the Nazi era, serving as concentration camp guards, as members of SS *Einsatzgruppen* or *Ordnungspolizei* battalions in the east, and as agents of the SS, the SD (Sicherheitsdienst, German civilian intelligence agency), and the Gestapo.[5] Not only were most of these individuals unmolested after the war, but some, including a number of infamous Gestapo and SS officers, such as Klaus Barbie, were recruited by American and other intelligence agencies, which saw them as potentially useful Cold War assets.[6]

Nazi scientists, some of whom had overseen or perpetrated acts of barbarism, were brought to the United States to work in America's space program.[7] The Vatican and the International Red Cross, for their own reasons, helped a number of Nazis.[8] The Canadians would not accept Jewish refugees before, during, or in the immediate aftermath of the war. Canada did, however, admit most of the members of the Ukrainian Waffen SS Galizien Division, a unit implicated in a number of atrocities, as "farm laborers."[9] Thus, a small number of high-ranking Nazis were, with great fanfare, tried and punished in order to affirm the criminality of the Nazi regime and the moral superiority of the victorious Allies. Thousands of other Nazis, among them the perpetrators of vicious and brutal acts, were ignored or put to work for those same Allies.

In both the Soviet Union and the United States, moreover, despite the fact that they had contributed mightily to each nation's war effort, soon after the war Jews found themselves under political attack. In the Soviet Union, the government was confronted with an upsurge of popular anti-Semitism, most notably in areas that had been occupied by the Germans. The inhabitants of these areas, who had often cooperated with the Nazis, feared that Jews might return and seek restoration of their homes, property, and positions. Nationalist movements, especially in the Ukraine and Lithuania, sought to exploit this popular anti-Semitism to attack the Soviet regime.[10]

Stalin, who disliked and distrusted the Jews, responded to the nationalist threat by embarking on a new anti-Semitic campaign of his own, which was dubbed a campaign against "cosmopolitans." The Soviet press began to impugn the loyalty of these cosmopolitans and to suggest that they might betray the socialist motherland. A number of the leading figures of the wartime Jewish Anti-Fascist Committee (JAFC) were accused of plotting to transform the Crimea into a Zionist republic to serve as a base for American imperialism. Shlomo Mikhoels, head of the JAFC and director of the Moscow State Yiddish Theater, was murdered by the KGB in January 1948. Many of the Jewish heroes of the war were purged. For example, General Isaak Zaltzman, the "tank king" whose T-34s did so much to win the war, was removed from his position, stripped of his party membership, and given a factory job as a day laborer.

Zaltzman was perhaps fortunate—many others were simply liquidated. By the early 1950s, Jews had been effectively barred from the Soviet foreign service, from foreign-trade institutes, from positions of military command, and from senior positions in the bureaucracy, as well as from positions of leadership within the party itself. The positions formerly held by Jews were given not only to Russians but also to members of minority nationality groups as part of the regime's effort to curb nationalist opposition and expand its political base.

Because Jews constituted the best-educated and most talented group in the Soviet populace, the regime could not completely dispense with their services in the professions, in scientific research, or in the civil service. The government, however, relied upon a policy of intimidation to check Jewish influence. This was one motive behind the arrest of some of the Soviet Union's leading Jewish physicians in 1953. In the case of the so-called doctors' plot, a number of Moscow physicians were charged with conspiring with American intelligence services to destroy the Soviet leadership. Hundreds of other Jewish doctors throughout the USSR were dismissed from their posts. The accused physicians were saved from execution only by Stalin's sudden death.[11]

Even after Stalin left the scene, the Soviet regime continued its efforts to placate the nation's various nationality groups by increasing their representation in the civil service, the professions, and institutions of higher education. This was often accomplished at the expense of Jews, who were progressively relegated to ever more marginal positions. By the 1960s, Jews exercised little power in the Soviet Union. During the 1970s it became possible for Jews to leave the USSR, and in two great waves during the 1970s and 1990s, more than 1 million emigrated to Israel and a smaller number to the United States.

American Jews also came under attack after the war. If America's Jews thought that anti-Semitism had been ended by the defeat of Nazi Germany, they soon discovered that they were mistaken. Not long after America's victory over Germany and Japan, a struggle for control of the Democratic Party led to the reemergence of an anti-Semitic discourse in the national political arena. Southern and conservative Democrats saw Franklin Roosevelt's death as an opportunity to reassert their own power within the Democratic Party at the expense of the labor leaders and liberal intellectuals who had become important political figures in the Roosevelt administration. Conservative and Southern Democrats were able to seize control of the House Un-American Activities Committee (HUAC), originally established to investigate Nazis, and use it to investigate and smear their foes in the liberal and labor union wings of the Democratic Party by identifying them with communism.

Many of those accused of Communist sympathies were Jews. Some had indeed been involved with Socialist or even Communist groups in the 1930s, while others were simply victims of the fact that HUAC investigators knew that the Gentile public would be only too ready to believe charges of communism leveled at Jews. Often HUAC hearings seemed designed mainly to embarrass prominent Jews, especially those who had anglicized their names or otherwise disguised their ethnic identities.

For example, during HUAC's probe of alleged Communist infiltration of the motion picture industry, Mississippi congressman John Rankin seemed to take great delight in revealing that several Hollywood stars with American-sounding names who had signed a petition attacking HUAC were actually Jews. One signature on the petition was June Havoc. "We found out," said Rankin, "that her real name is June Hovick." "There is one who calls himself Edward G. Robinson," Rankin intoned. "His real name is Emmanuel Goldenberg." Jewish writers and producers who had cooperated with the Roosevelt administration's to make anti-Nazi films in the late 1930s were now declared by HUAC investigators to have been "prematurely anti-Fascist" and, hence, possibly Communists.[12]

Jews responded to these attacks by distancing themselves from Communists or anyone with leftist sympathies and disciplining leftists in their own ranks. Jewish film producers, for example, fired and blacklisted writers, actors, and producers known to have leftist views, and a variety of Jewish organizations, such as the American Jewish Committee (AJC), and organizations in which Jews were influential, such as the American Civil Liberties Union (ACLU), cooperated vigorously with government investigators in order to demonstrate the Jewish community's loyalty to America and aversion to communism. Throughout the late 1940s and early 1950s, the ACLU took great pains to assert that no free-speech issues were at stake in the conviction of individuals for teaching or advocating communism, and the AJC mounted a major public relations campaign to demonstrate that Jews were 100 percent American.

The effort of the Jewish community to combat postwar anti-Semitism was bolstered by a renewal of the prewar alliance between Jews and the Eastern Protestant establishment. As they had in the 1930s, Jews and Northeastern Protestants found themselves facing a common set of enemies. Like the Jews, segments of the Protestant establishment came under attack in the postwar period, nominally for having been too tolerant of the Communist threat to America's security.

The name most commonly associated with this charge is that of Senator Joseph McCarthy, and the term "McCarthyism" has indeed become a synonym for political inquisition or witch hunt. In general, the McCarthyites represented Midwestern Republicans and so-called national capital—that is, small business as well as domestic manufacturing industries whose orientation was the American rather than the world market. The major animus of this wing of the GOP, led by Senator Robert Taft of Ohio, was directed toward its Eastern establishment rivals within the Republican Party—rivals who, in the Taft wing's view, had betrayed Republicanism by cooperating with the New Deal.

Because the upper-class, high Episcopalian foes of the Midwesterners could not plausibly be identified with Jews, the McCarthyites had no particular use for anti-Semitism as a political weapon. Indeed, several of McCarthy's most important aides, such as Roy Cohn and David Schine, were themselves Jews. McCarthy's targets, instead, included such pillars of the Protestant establishment as Secretary of State Dean Acheson. McCarthy characterized the secretary as the leader of the treasonous "Acheson Gang," which had sheltered the spy Alger Hiss and had sold out American interests to the Soviet Union at the postwar Yalta Conference.

After Senator Taft's defeat at the 1952 Republican National Convention and Dwight D. Eisenhower's victory in the general election, the Eastern establishment closed ranks against McCarthy and its other right-wing opponents and, seeking political partners, allied itself once again with the Jewish community, which was also eager to bring an end to the anti-Communist campaign. Using the institutions in which one or both groups were influential—the media, foundations, universities, courts, and public interest groups—Protestant and Jewish opponents of the various anti-Communist crusaders joined forces to charge them with violating civil liberties and "chilling" free speech.

Major news organizations such as CBS, an institution owned by Jews and staffed by distinguished-looking Protestants like Edward R. Murrow, whose March 1954 "See It Now" broadcast was instrumental in discrediting McCarthy, played an important role. The ACLU, whose executive board was a Jewish-Protestant alliance, began to vigorously defend the victims of HUAC and the Hollywood blacklists, as well as individuals who had been prosecuted for refusing to take loyalty oaths. The Ford Foundation, an establishment bastion, sponsored books and articles defending civil liberties and made awards to individuals who had fought against the anti-Communist crusaders.[13]

The Jewish-Protestant alliance also used its influence over the national media to deprive its opponents, especially anti-Semites, of access to print pages and airtime, while at the same time securing and publicizing information that eventually sent a number of anti-Communist crusaders, including one-time HUAC chairman J. Parnell Thomas, to prison for financial and other misdeeds. Together, Jews and Eastern establishment Protestants were sufficiently powerful to declare that anti-Semitic commentary and charges that members of either group had Communist ties "smacked of McCarthyism" and automatically should be seen as beyond the pale of the politically permissible. From the late 1950s on, conservatives who sought to maintain a modicum of respectability avoided the least hint of anti-Semitism in their literature and broadcasts. The late William Buckley is an example of a prominent conservative author and pundit who warned his colleagues on the political right to eschew anti-Semitic commentary.

THE REST OF THE STORY

The travails of the Jews, of course, did not end with the events of the 1950s any more than they concluded with the death of Hitler. The postwar European settlement of the "Jewish problem" led so inexorably to a new series of difficulties for the Jews that I feel compelled to tell what the late newscaster Paul Harvey called "the rest of the story."

The rest of the story is the gradual rise of a new anti-Semitism in both Europe and America. This new anti-Semitism, often cloaked as anti-Zionism, does not pose an existential threat, à la Hitler, to the world's Jews. Yet, combined with Muslim anti-Semitism, more than a shadow of a threat to at least the 6 million Jews of Israel has begun to form. Ironically, many of these Israeli

Jews descend from Europe's surviving Jewish community, and the threat they face follows directly from the travails of their parents and grandparents.

Many in Europe and the Arab world, and even some in America, currently claim to see in the creation of Israel an example of Jewish greed and aggression. In actuality, Israel's founding was very much the result of the West's postwar unwillingness to accept Jewish refugees. Governments that felt that even one Jewish refugee was too many had to find someplace to resettle several hundred thousand Jews. Since it might have been considered unseemly, at the very least, to reopen the German resettlement facilities at Auschwitz or Treblinka that had so effectively resettled Jews to the next world, the Jewish refugees had to be sent somewhere in this world. To the Americans and eventually even to the British, a State of Israel seemed the least undesirable alternative. Within two decades of Israel's creation, though, the reasons for its existence were forgotten or had became irrelevant, and new configurations of political forces gave rise to a renewed European anti-Semitic discourse taking the form of anti-Zionism. Though most pronounced in Europe, this discourse has made its way across the Atlantic to America.

August Bebel, one of the founders of Germany's Social Democratic Party, viewed the susceptibility of German workers to the anti-Semitic propaganda that was commonplace in nineteenth-century Europe as a dangerous source of division within the Socialist movement. Indeed, he saw agitation against the Jews as a snare designed to lure workers into alliances with reactionary forces in German society. Hence, Bebel famously referred to anti-Semitism as the "socialism of fools." The anti-Semitic discourse that has developed in recent years might be called the liberalism of fools and perhaps exemplifies history's insistence on repeating itself as farce.

Expressions of antipathy to Jews on the part of some left liberals produce divisions within the progressive political camp and align portions of the liberal community with strange and unsavory bedfellows, such as the Saudi royal family, European Fascists, and American "white nationalists," whose own agendas are hardly liberal or progressive. The European Left loudly proclaims its anti-Zionism by denouncing Israel as a racist and apartheid state and calling for boycotts of Israeli products, citizens, and ideas. With less fanfare, European leftists engage in "an anti-Jewish discourse" at dinner parties and university seminars and in the media.[14] In the United States, left-liberal anti-Zionists are joined by prominent African Americans, who, like their white compatriots, sometimes conflate anti-Zionism and anti-Semitism. How else shall we interpret Professor Cornel West's description of Harvard's Jewish former president, Larry Summers, as the "Ariel Sharon of higher education."[15]

Many left liberals who are fond of denouncing Israel and Zionism, of course, deny that they are anti-Semites and claim to be driven by nothing more than a moral commitment to ending what they see as the brutality and mendacity of the Israelis—a nation they say threatens the peace of the entire world.[16] Many seem to agree with the former French ambassador to the Court of St. James, Daniel Bernard, who opined that the world's troubles were all because of "that shitty little country Israel."[17] And perhaps some even agree with London's former mayor, Ken Livingston, who advocates going to Israel to kill Israeli soldiers, or, for that matter, with Oxford poet Tom Paulin, who says that "Jews from Brooklyn" who have settled in the West Bank "are Nazis, racists. . . . They should be shot dead."[18]

It is certainly logically possible to possess separate and distinct attitudes toward the State of Israel and the Jewish people and, perhaps, even to like Jews while simultaneously believing that Israel constitutes the chief threat to world peace today. It is difficult to fully understand, however, why anyone without at least a bit of antipathy toward Jews would choose to focus his or her special moral outrage on the Jewish state. Israel, to be sure, is neither inhabited nor governed by saints. Its policies, like those of many other regimes, often merit and properly receive severe criticism.[19] Yet, many on the political left appear to single out Israeli policy while paying little or no attention to regimes that, on the surface at least, seem considerably more repressive and even racist.

Why not rail against the brutality of the North Koreans or the Chinese or the Burmese, or the tyrannical policies of Israel's Arab and Iranian neighbors, or the racism that is evident in the treatment meted out to Italy's Roma or dark-skinned immigrants in Scandinavia or Koreans in Japan or black Christians in the Sudan? These observations are not meant to excuse the Israelis for their misdeeds but rather to ask why some in the progressive camp focus all their wrath on Israel when there might appear to be so many other potential targets for censure.

The Israelis, of course, are also accused of the particular crime of pursuing an ongoing policy of stealing Arab land. And unfortunately some in Israel seem to regard the continuing expropriation and settlement of Arab land as some sort of divine mission.[20] On the political left, though, it is often asserted that the very existence of the State of Israel represents an illegitimate theft of Arab land. Progressive British scholar and frequent leader of anti-Israel boycotts, Jacqueline Rose, for example, echoes the Arab view that the creation of Israel in 1948 was a tragedy or catastrophe (*al nakba* in Arabic).[21]

Certainly, one can make this argument. Indeed, Arabs and Jews, and possibly others as well, have historic, religious, and legal land claims in the Middle East that merit attention. Yet why single out Jewish claims to the land of Israel as particularly lacking in legitimacy? There is no square inch of earth on the planet whose rightful ownership cannot be contested on one or another ground. It hardly needs to be said that the United States occupies millions of square miles of territory stolen from the Native Americans, as well as land taken by force from the Mexicans, whose Spanish forebears had previously stolen it from Native Americans. The ancestors of the modern-day Europeans stole their land too. But since these land thefts occurred long ago, the rightful ownership of Western European territory is only occasionally contested these days. In the case of America, the original landowners were largely exterminated by the European settlers and so are not in a position to press their claims with much vigor.

The main difference between the Israelis and other contemporary landowners might seem to be that Israel has only existed as a state for a few decades. Israel, moreover, unlike the United States and others, failed to launch a sustained campaign of annihilation against the previous landowners, who therefore remain quite able to vocally and violently assert their irredentist claims. Should Israel, however, deserve relegation to the status of a pariah for having been insufficiently murderous?

Those nations currently occupying lands whose previous inhabitants they exterminated might seem more blameworthy than those who did not pursue a genocidal program. The point here is not to absolve Israel from reproach but rather to question why many in the left-liberal camp seem to regard Israel as meriting uniquely harsh criticism and even ostracism from a community of nations whose members are not a particularly scrupulous group. One suspects that at least some who declare that Israel and the Zionists are the world's chief villains might have begun with attitudes about Jews that colored their perceptions.

Again, in principle it is possible to become anti-Zionist without first being an anti-Semite. But even those for whom anti-Zionism begins as something other than a politically correct form of anti-Semitism can find it difficult to remain vehemently opposed to Israel for very long without developing at least a measure of hostility toward Israel's supporters—namely, the American and handful of remaining European Jews with whom anti-Zionists constantly clash. In the political arena it is difficult to maintain a strong commitment to an anti-Zionist discourse without becoming a bit of an anti-Semite. Indeed, those who regularly clash with the Jews and perhaps learn to view the Jews as their foes may come to regard the enemies of the Jews as their friends. This process may explain the "green/brown" alliances that have sprung up in Europe between progressives and neo-Nazis who find common ground on the Jewish question.[22]

Such alliances have also arisen in the United States. A case in point is a recent article in the left-liberal newsletter *Counterpunch,* claiming that Israel makes a practice of capturing Palestinians in order to harvest their organs for transplantation.[23] Is this merely an anti-Zionist screed? Well, not exactly. The article's author, Alison Weir, founder of the anti-Israel organization If Americans Knew and veteran of many battles against Israel and its supporters in America, intimates that this alleged Israeli practice is derived directly from the ancient Jewish tradition of murdering Gentiles to obtain their blood for ritual purposes.

And to whom does a contemporary progressive turn for help in understanding and reinventing this hoary blood libel? Weir purports to rely, among other sources, on the writings of one "Israel Shamir," whose Internet postings under the title "Bloodcurdling Libel" explain that a small group of medieval Jews actually did engage in the ritual murder of Christians.[24] Interestingly, this Israel Shamir is neither a biblical scholar nor a historian. The name Shamir, as it turns out, is one of the many pseudonyms employed by a shadowy European neo-Nazi based in Sweden.[25] Anti-Zionism in this case becomes difficult to distinguish from anti-Semitism and, as Bebel might have predicted, leads a left-liberal activist to find common ground with a Nazi.

What accounts for the anti-Semitism of the political Left? For the most part, Jews are themselves politically liberal—many are left liberals—and associate anti-Semitism with their traditional enemies on the political right, not their compatriots in the progressive camp. But whether the source is left-wing or right-wing, Jews have a tendency to ascribe anti-Semitism to irrationality, scapegoating, and what some call "enduring myths" about the Jewish people. And certainly, like other ethnic and racial prejudices, anti-Semitism seems to involve a substantial element of mythology and irrationality. Take, for example, some of the claims propagated by the Arab media and apparently believed throughout the Muslim world. According to the Egyptian and Jordanian press, Israel distributes drug-laced chewing gum and candy designed to make women sexually corrupt and to kill children; Israel deliberately infects Palestinian children with the HIV virus; Israel poisons Palestinians with uranium and nerve gas; Jews use the blood of Gentiles to make matzos for Passover; the 9-11 terrorist attacks were perpetrated by Jews, not Arabs; and so forth.[26] Some of these claims have gained traction in the West, as well as with many Europeans and some Americans prepared to believe the most outlandish tales about the Jews.

In general terms, at least, the origin of ethnic prejudice is hardly difficult to explain. Whatever its social, psychological, economic, or even evolutionary basis, suspicion of strangers is the norm in all societies, while acceptance of outsiders is unusual and generally ephemeral. Certainly, everywhere that Jews have lived, their social and religious marginality—their position "outside society," as Hannah Arendt put it—has sooner or later exposed Jews to suspicion, hostility, and discrimination.

Even in multiethnic societies, Jews have usually been the most successful and visible, hence the most exposed, outsiders. In America, Jews currently appear to be accepted by the larger community. Nevertheless, at least in part by their own choosing, American Jews continue to maintain a significant and visible measure of communal identity and distinctiveness in religious, cultural, and political matters, staunchly resisting full assimilation into American society. This marginality, in turn, leaves Jews more vulnerable to attack than more fully assimilated American ethnic groups.

For example, during the 2008–2009 global economic crisis, the news media paid no attention to the precise ethnic or religious backgrounds of the mainly non-Jewish top executives of such institutions as Countrywide, Beazer Homes, Fannie Mae, and Merrill Lynch, whose practices contributed to the debacle. No one found it useful to point out, for instance, that Angelo Mozilo, former CEO of Countrywide Financial Corp., an institution that became notorious for its predatory lending practices, is of Italian descent. At the same time, however, the religious identifications of Jewish executives like Bernard Madoff were frequently noted by the media, especially the new online media, where tirades against the Jews have become a staple. But even the old media were not totally oblivious to the Semitic countenances of several of the corporate villains. In an October 2008 *Saturday Night Live* skit, for example, actors portraying Marion and Herb Sandler, former owners of Golden West Financial Corp., were presented as greedy and boorish New York Jews. A caption on the screen labeled the Sandlers as "people who should be shot."

Given this media attention to the misdeeds of Jewish businesspeople, it is hardly surprising that one recent survey found that many Americans—32 percent of Democrats and 18 percent of Republicans—blamed "the Jews" for the financial crisis.[27] Europeans are even more likely to see the Jews as especially blameworthy in the fiscal realm. A 2009 survey found that 31 percent of Europeans believed that Jews made the financial crisis possible, and 41 percent thought Jews had too much power over the world's financial markets.[28]

These general considerations, of course, do not explain why, at this particular time, a particular political stratum has chosen to adopt the rhetoric of anti-Semitism. As I have argued elsewhere, where anti-Semitism becomes an important feature of political discourse, more is usually involved than simple malice toward the Jews.[29] A reservoir of anti-Jewish sentiment is a necessary but insufficient condition for the emergence of an anti-Semitic politics. In the political arena, principles and rhetoric are tools and weapons that are seldom brandished unless they serve some set of political interests. Generally, an anti-Semitic politics develops only when some congeries of political forces finds it expedient to make use of whatever latent anti-Semitism might be available for mobilization.

In the case of the current anti-Semitic rhetoric of the liberal Left, three sets of progressive forces have found reason to attack Israel and the Jews. These are European leftists, American leftists, and black radicals in the United States. For each of these groups, an anti-Semitic discourse has a slightly different political purpose, though there is considerable overlap in the anti-Semitic rhetoric of the three. A fourth anti-Zionist group that seems to parrot some of the anti-Semitic rhetoric of the first three consists, perhaps improbably, of politically progressive Jews in America, Europe, and even Israel itself. These

Jews appear to find it in their own political interest to join the attack on the evil Zionist entity.

THE EUROPEAN LEFT AND ANTI-SEMITISM

The anti-Semitism of the European Left is generally more extreme, more widespread, and easier to explain than the anti-Semitic and anti-Zionist rhetoric of the other political forces mentioned above. To put the matter simply, the anti-Semitism of the European Left is rooted in demographic and electoral considerations, namely, the presence of more than 15 million—possibly as many as 20 million—Muslims in Western Europe and the high probability that this population will increase substantially during the next decade.[30] The Jewish population of Western Europe, by contrast, is only about 1 million and is declining.

Between the creation of the Jewish state in 1948 and the 1967 Six-Day War, European Socialists generally maintained close ties to Israel, whose Labor governments they found congenial and whose generally Socialist policies they admired. Indeed, during this era, many European leftists spent summers in Israel working on kibbutzim.[31] How better to demonstrate one's commitment to the principle of collectivization than to spend a few months working on a collective farm. The European Left's enchantment with life on the kibbutz, however, diminished during the early 1970s, when Israel aligned its security policies with those of the United States and, from the Left's perspective, became a satellite of the American imperialists.

In the view of the European Left, matters grew even worse after 1977, when the new Likud Party came to power in Israel, for the next fifteen years replacing the Israeli Labor Party with a conservative government that looked to the American Republicans rather than European Socialists for inspiration and support. And, of course, Israel's continuing occupation of the territories seized during the 1967 war and periodic military actions against the Palestinians and Lebanese continually angered and offended European leftists. These international and partisan shifts brought about a cooling of the relationship between Israel and European leftists and paved the way for subsequent events triggered by massive Arab immigration to Western Europe.

Beginning in the 1970s, millions of Muslims migrated from the Middle East and North Africa to France, Germany, England, Spain, the Netherlands, and other European countries. Initially, these immigrants were recruited to fill Western Europe's acute labor shortages. Subsequently, illegals, political refugees, and the children of immigrants added to Europe's Muslim population. Today, more than 5 millions Muslims live in France; roughly 3 million reside in Germany; 1.6 million live in Britain; and Spain and the Netherlands each host approximately 1 million.[32] Smaller Muslim communities are found in the remaining nations of Western Europe.

For European Socialists and other leftists, this ongoing influx of mainly poor Muslims has seemed to offer an enormous political opportunity. On the basis of economic interest, as well as lack of ties to bourgeois European society, these growing Muslim communities have appeared to represent an important new electoral base for parties of the Left. Properly organized and mobilized, hundreds of thousands, even millions, of Muslim adherents and voters might greatly enhance the political strength of Socialist and other progressive parties. Accordingly, Socialist and other progressive groups have championed immigrant rights, the rights of asylum seekers, and the quick provision of the full benefits of the European welfare state to new arrivals.

The Left has also stood firmly against anti-Muslim sentiment resulting from the terrorist activities of some Muslims. After the London tube bombings on July 7, 2005, for example, left-wing former mayor Ken Livingston addressed a huge throng of Londoners in Trafalgar Square and told them they should not start looking for "who to blame and who to hate."[33] The result of these efforts is that the overwhelming majority of Muslim voters favor the Socialists and other progressive European parties.

The problem faced by the European Left, however, in seeking to take advantage of the political opportunity seemingly offered by millions of poor Muslims is that the values and beliefs of this potential Muslim mass base are often at odds with many of the Left's most deeply held values—women's rights, gay rights, abortion rights, opposition to the death penalty, and separation of church and state. Even the matter of animal rights divides elements of the Left from the Muslim community; witness the near riot that took place in the Italian town of Luino when animal rights activists sought to prevent local Muslims from carrying out a ritual slaughter of rams and lambs for an annual Islamic feast. The ritual requires the animals to be bled to death after their throats are slit, a practice that the defenders of animal rights found barbaric and outrageous.[34] Efforts by progressive politicians to appease Muslims on such matters as homosexuality, female circumcision, the wearing of veils in schools, and so forth tend to alienate moderate-liberal European voters, who have shown an increasing inclination to support conservative parties that favor limits on further immigration and restrictions on the ability of Muslims to practice their religious customs in public spaces, as exemplified by Switzerland's November 2009 constitutional referendum, which enacted a prohibition on the construction of minarets.

At the same time, many Muslim leaders—especially the more radical— have not been particularly anxious to submit to the leadership of, or even to make common cause with, secular leftist politicians. In Britain, for example, some radical Islamists refused to participate in demonstrations against the wars in Iraq and Afghanistan that had been organized by the secular Left. Radical Islamists believed that Marxists and other secular radicals were seeking to lure young Muslims into their fold and away from their own Islamic organizations. Radical Islamists urged young Muslims not to listen to "atheist Marxists" but, instead, to fight under a religious banner.[35]

To win the support of Europe's Muslims, progressives have made an effort to tolerate Muslim religious views and practices that might appear completely inconsistent with a secular leftist orientation. In Britain, for example, some leftist feminists have taken up the cause of the right of Muslim women to wear the *hijab*. And in Germany the feminist leader of the Green Party denounced as "immoral" a Baden-Wuttenberg state requirement that applicants for citizenship answer questions about their personal views. One of these allegedly immoral questions was, "Where do you stand on the statement that a wife should obey her husband and that he can hit her if she fails to do so?"[36]

On the hard Left, the expression of support for Muslim cultural and religious values is now seen as a properly Leninist strategy to be adopted by vanguard parties in order to draw the most progressive elements of the Muslim working class into the struggle against capitalism and imperialism. In this effort, acceptance of Muslim culture is a "litmus test of the capacity of revolutionaries to relate to the working class as it is, as opposed to what it was 30 years ago or in books that we have read."[37]

Of course, among the most prominent values espoused by Europe's Muslims is hatred of Israel and Jews. Throughout the Muslim world, anti-Israel and anti-Jewish oratory, newspaper and magazine articles, and radio and television broadcasts are commonplace. The *Protocols of the Elders of Zion*, which purports to unmask the secret Jewish plan for world domination, is discussed and believed by millions of Muslims and is even referenced in the Palestinian Hamas Covenant of 1988.[38] Hamas also accuses the Jews of launching the French and Russian revolutions and the two world wars to promote Zionist objectives. In 2002, the *Protocols* was made into a forty-one-part television series for Egyptian TV and then sold to seventeen other Islamic television stations.[39] A similar series, produced by Syrian television in 2003, presents a close-up of the ritual murder of a Christian boy by two Jews.[40]

In a similar vein, Sheikh Husayn Fadlallah, who provided the spiritual inspiration for Lebanon's Hezbollah movement, often declared that Israel was the expression of the corrupt, treacherous, and aggressive Jewish personality.[41] Or take the views of former Syrian defense minister Mustafa Tlass, whose book *The Matzo of Zion* is known throughout the Arab world. According to Tlass, "The Jew can kill and take your blood in order to make his Zionist bread. Here opens a page more ugly than the crime itself: the religious beliefs of the Jews and the perversions they contain, which draw their orientation from a dark hate toward all humankind and all religions."[42]

Following the 9-11 terrorist attacks in the United States, substantial segments of the Arab media declared that the destruction of the World Trade Center had been the work of the Jews. For example, the Syrian ambassador to Iran declared, "The Israelis have been involved in these incidents and no Jewish employee was present in the World Trade Center building on the day."[43] The Jews had allegedly received a secret directive from Israeli intelligence services warning them not to report for work.[44] This claim is widely believed in the Arab world. Indeed, a Middle Eastern graduate student at my own university once assured me that the story of the "4,000 Jews" who stayed home from work on September 11, 2001, was well known to be true.

The steady diet of anti-Semitic propaganda in the Muslim media both reflects and reinforces hatred of the Jews, which is more or less universal in the Muslim Middle East. American audiences were treated to an example of the scope of Muslim anti-Jewish feeling when television host Greta Van Susteren famously broadcast a clip from Saudi state television in which a young Saudi child was asked what she thought of Jews. The three-year-old had presumably never met a Jew but was certainly able to parrot what she had been taught:

Van Susteren: Tonight, a disturbing message of hate from a source barely out of diapers, a three-year-old Muslim girl.

[Begin video clip.]

Basmallah, toddler: Allah's mercy and blessing upon you.

Doaa 'Amer, IQRAA-TV host: What's your name?

Basmallah: Basmallah.

'Amer: Basmallah, how old are you?

Basmallah: Three and a half.

'Amer: Are you a Muslim?

Basmallah: Yes.

'Amer: Basmallah, are you familiar with the Jews?

Basmallah: Yes.

'Amer: Do you like them?

Basmallah: No.

'Amer: Why don't you like them?

Basmallah: Because.

'Amer: Because they are what?

Basmallah: They're apes and pigs.

'Amer: Because they are apes and pigs. Who said they are so?

Basmallah: Our God.

'Amer: Where did he say this?

Basmallah: In the Koran.

[End video clip.]

Van Susteren: It was part of an interview conducted by a Muslim women's magazine seen on Saudi Arabian television.[45]

Muslims living in Europe generally harbor anti-Jewish attitudes not so different from those manifested by their coreligionists in the Middle East. And, of course, if they forget to hate Jews, they can easily be reminded in their mosques and by the hundreds of Islamist websites that can be viewed anywhere in the world. Muslim viewers in Europe can also watch Hamas and Hezbollah television, both filled with anti-Semitic content and exhortations to violence against the Jews, over satellite television providers such as Saudi Arabia's Arabsat and Egypt's Nilesat.[46]

In the Muslim nations of the Middle East, of course, there are virtually no Jews, so anti-Semitism is limited to the level of rhetoric. Western Europe, however, hosts about 1 million Jews—living mainly in France and England—along with synagogues and other Jewish institutions. As a result, Europe's Muslims are able to act out their hatreds by attacking Jews. Thousands of incidents of anti-Jewish violence, mainly perpetrated by young Muslims, have taken place in France, England, and other European countries during the past several years.[47] In Germany, Muslim demonstrators chant, "Hamas, Hamas, Jews to the gas." In France, Muslims have attacked Jewish schools, firebombed synagogues, and stoned buses carrying Jewish schoolchildren. Throughout Europe, Jews have been attacked and beaten.[48] Reluctant to point the finger of guilt at Muslims when reporting incidents of anti-Jewish violence, the European press usually limits itself to noting that Muslims are "overrepresented" among the perpetrators.[49]

To segments of the European Left, Muslim hatred of the Jews represents a political opportunity rather than a moral problem. Opposition to Israel and the Jews is a vehicle through which European leftists can reach out to the Muslim community without much political risk. European liberals who might be worried about Muslim treatment of women and apparent disdain for animal rights have little use for Israel and, with the exception of the continent's few remaining Jews, little interest in the fate of the Jews. Indeed, levels of traditional European anti-Semitism—amounting to a lingering disdain—remain fairly high in Europe despite the murder of most of the Jews a couple of generations earlier.[50]

These political considerations are the backdrop for the anti-Semitic discourse of the European Left. Anti-Semitic rhetoric, participation in protests, demands for boycotts of Israel, and the like are a risk-free way of expressing solidarity with, and reaching for the support of, the millions of Muslims who now claim European citizenship or residence. Hence, in the demonstrations against Israel and the Jews that are usually organized in Europe in response to almost any incident of violence pitting Israel against the Arabs in the Middle East, the Left is very much in evidence. In Belgium, these include the Belgian Socialist Party and the Belgian Green Party. In Germany, an official of the Free Democratic Party declared that Palestinian violence against Jews was appropriate. He said, "I would resist too, and use force to do so . . . not just in my country but in the aggressor's country as well."[51] In France, anti-Zionist demonstrations would not be complete without the participation of various trade union officials, the Revolutionary Communist League, the Greens, the French Communist Party, and the Human Rights League.[52]

Three elements of this progressive political outreach to Europe's Muslims are particularly worth noting. The first is a new form of Holocaust denial. Jews usually cite the Holocaust as a major moral and political justification for the creation of the State of Israel. In truth, no country would grant admission to the remnants of Europe's Jewish communities. But because Jews cite the Holocaust as a justification for Israel's creation, some Muslims, including the leaders of Iran and several Arab states, profess to believe that the Holocaust was invented or exaggerated by the Jews. Europe's leftists, of course, know very well that the Holocaust occurred but, in an effort to express solidarity with Muslims, have sought to use the imagery of the Holocaust against its Jewish victims.

Thus, in the leftist media, the Star of David is redrawn to resemble a Nazi swastika, Israeli soldiers are portrayed as goose-stepping Nazis, and the Palestinians are presented as the true victims of terror and repression. Israeli leaders are often said to be worse than Hitler. Israel is accused of conducting a "holocaust" against the Palestinians.[53] Oxford poet Tom Paulin compares Zionists to the Nazi SS, and Belgian Simon-Pierre Nothomb tells newspaper readers that the West Bank is dotted with concentration camps.[54] Of course, the extreme Left takes these matters just a bit further, with some prepared to defend such Holocaust deniers as Robert Faurisson, who declares that the Holocaust is a historical lie designed to benefit the State of Israel at the expense of the Palestinian people.[55]

The second noteworthy aspect of the Left's effort to build bridges to Muslims is what might be called the Judaization of the antiglobalism campaign.[56] To many progressives, the loud and sometimes violent campaign conducted against the World Trade Organization, World Bank, International Monetary Fund, and other global economic institutions has always represented a form of outreach to the Third World, which is allegedly victimized by these agents of Western economic imperialism. In recent years, the European Left, focusing its outreach on Muslims, has reframed the issue of globalization to emphasize the role of Jews in international banking and international financial institutions. Such names as Summers, Greenspan, Wolfensohn, Fischer, Bernanke, and so forth are cited by the opponents of globalization to intimate to Muslims that financial globalization is part of the long-standing Zionist conspiracy to take control of the world. French antiglobalization activist José Bové explains that Israel is conspiring with the World Bank to integrate the Middle East into globalized production in order to exploit Palestinian labor.[57] To draw attention from this plot, the Israelis, according to Bové, have instigated anti-Semitic violence in France and other European countries. "The Israeli government and its secret services have an interest in creating a certain psychosis, in making believe that there is a climate of anti-Semitism in France, in order to distract attention from what they are doing."[58]

Muslims easily accept these ideas. Former Malaysian prime minister Mahathir Mohamad once complained that "Jews determine our currency levels and bring about the collapse of our economy." The 2008–2009 global financial crisis provided additional fuel for this view. Hamas spokesman Fawzi Barhum, for example, blamed the "Jewish lobby" for the crisis. He said this lobby "controls the U.S. elections and defines the foreign policy of any new administration in a manner that allows it to retain control of the American government and economy." For his part, Iranian president Mahmoud Ahmadinejad declared that the Jews dominate financial and monetary centers "in a deceitful, complex and furtive manner."[59] The notion that Jews use globalization to seize control of the world economy, of course, also resonates with the ideas of the Far Right and occasionally produces the green/brown alliances mentioned above. Neo-Nazis are eager to help their leftist compatriots shut down what they call the "Jew World Order WTO."

The third interesting element of the European Left's courtship of Muslims is the role of progressive intellectuals. Progressive political parties and factions see Muslims as potential supporters. Some left-wing intellectuals are active in the political arena or, at the very least, are eager to further what they see as anti-imperialist, anticapitalist, or Third World causes. Others, though—particularly the university-based intellectuals who sign petitions to boycott Israeli universities, or men and women of letters like Tom Paulin, or the late Portuguese novelist and Nobel laureate José Saramago, who accuses the Jews of committing crimes "comparable to Auschwitz"—seem to find anti-Semitism intellectually titillating, an opportunity to be radically chic and to say what for so long could not be said. Some German intellectuals in particular welcome the opportunity to accuse the Jews of perpetrating another Holocaust—a view that helps them overcome their own nation's past. For these individuals, anti-Semitism seems more emotionally satisfying than politically useful. They themselves, however, are useful. The radically chic Saramagos and Paulins and so forth provide the ideas and imagery that others can use to further their political goals.

ANTI-SEMITISM AND THE AMERICAN LEFT

Progressive forces in the United States are not oblivious to the possibility of building political alliances with America's Muslims, whom they view as a potentially radical and anti-imperialist force. And, as in Europe, one outgrowth of this effort has been an anti-Zionist and anti-Semitic discourse. As we shall see, however, the possibility of forging new political alliances is not the only factor leading America's left liberals to express hostility toward Israel and the Jews.

The Muslim-Progressive Alliance

America's Muslim community is much smaller, more prosperous, and politically more conservative than Europe's.[60] Nevertheless, as the events of the past several years have indicated, some among America's Muslims are drawn to radical political activity. Moreover, radical religious and educational leaders, often funded by Saudi Arabia, have had some success convincing younger Muslims, including Muslim college students, to identify with their coreligionists in the Middle East and to regard Zionists and Jews as their mortal foes.

The precise number is disputed, but roughly 3 million Muslims of Middle Eastern background are estimated to live in the United States, with the heaviest concentrations in California, New York, Illinois, and New Jersey. Muslims in the United States have established a number of political organizations, such as the Council on American-Islamic Relations (CAIR), the Muslim Public Affairs Council, and the Muslim Students' Association (MSA). These and other Muslim groups work to create a positive public image for the Muslim community and to promote Muslim interests in the political arena. CAIR and MSA, in particular, are active on college and university campuses, where they have built alliances with a number of left-liberal and radical groups that together endeavor to promote what they call the global "BDS" agenda. The acronym stands for international boycott, divestment, and sanctions against Israel.

At a number of schools, particularly in California, CAIR, MSA, and their secular campus activist allies, including the Workers' Student Alliance and the Radical Student Union, regularly sponsor anti-Zionist and anti-Semitic activities, such as the annual celebration of "Israel Apartheid Week," a name coined in reference to Israel's allegedly racist policies. Apartheid Week, initially launched at the University of Toronto, takes place every March to coincide with the annual anniversary of the Arab's 1948 defeat and the formation of the State of Israel. For its 2009 Apartheid Week campus presentations, the MSA unveiled several colorful new posters. One featured an image of a hooked-nose Hasidic Jew with a Star of David pointing a bazooka at an Arab carrying a slingshot. Another showed an Israeli helicopter with a swastika on top dropping a bomb on a baby bottle.[61]

Generally, Apartheid Week and similar events feature speakers who denounce Israel and its supporters in the United States. One popular speaker is Abdul Malik Ali, imam of an Oakland, California, mosque. Ali is fond of declaring that the 9-11 terrorist attacks were staged by the Israelis "to give an excuse to wage war against Muslims around the world."[62] Another popular speaker is Affad Shaikh, civil rights coordinator of CAIR's Los Angeles office. Shaikh calls for an end to interfaith gatherings and in his blog has posted, "DEATH TO ALL JUICE," which we can assume is not a reference to beverages containing citrus fruit. Speaking at the University of California, San Diego (UCSD), Shaikh compared the school favorably to the University of California, Irvine, a campus noted for the prevalence of anti-Semitic activities, where he had often spoken in the past. "It is critical that UCSD get credit," Shaikh declared. "UCI is not half as anti-Semitic as UCSD."[63]

A number of America's best-known left liberals and radicals have been eager to demonstrate their solidarity with the Muslim community. Some have participated regularly in Israel Apartheid Week events and endeavored to promote other aspects of the BDS agenda. One popular Apartheid Week speaker is Ward Churchill, who explains that Jewish writers have paid a great deal of attention to the European Holocaust in order to construct a "conceptual screen" behind which to hide Israel's ongoing genocide of the Palestinian people.[64]

Other popular Apartheid Week speakers include left-liberal anti-Zionist Jews such as Norman Finkelstein and Ilan Pappe. In addition to those who speak or lead panels at Apartheid Week events, other progressives wait in reserve to denounce critics of Apartheid Week, whom they declare are intent on promoting racism and curbing free speech. Among the most outspoken of these individuals is Canadian Jewish anti-Zionist Michael Neumann, a left-liberal philosophy professor at Trent University, who once declared, "If an effective strategy for promoting [the Palestinian cause] means that some truths about the Jews don't come to light, I don't care. If an effective strategy means encouraging reasonable anti-Semitism, or reasonable hostility to Jews, I also don't care. If it means encouraging vicious racist anti-Semitism, or the destruction of the State of Israel, I still don't care."[65]

Another expression of the effort by left-liberal activists to forge a relationship with Muslims is the campaign to encourage America's colleges and universities—and occasionally other institutions as well—to divest their holdings in companies linked to the State of Israel. Patterned on the campaign to isolate South Africa in the 1960s, the anti-Israel divestment was launched at the University of California, Berkeley, by a coalition of left-liberal and Muslim groups, including the Students for Justice in Palestine and the San Francisco chapter of the American-Arab Anti-Discrimination Committee.

The movement spread from Berkeley to a number of other college campuses, including Harvard, MIT, Yale, and Michigan, where local coalitions of Muslims and left liberals organized under the umbrella of the Palestine Solidarity Movement (PSM). PSM advocates nonviolent action to encourage awareness of the Palestine issue but declines to condemn acts of terrorism against Israelis. At PSM's 2002 conference at the University of Michigan, delegates reportedly chanted, "Kill the Jews!"[66]

PSM efforts on a number of campuses touched off considerable controversy, with Harvard's former president Larry Summers denouncing calls for divestment as "anti-Semitic in their effect if not their intent."[67] The presidents and trustees of a number of schools explicitly rejected the idea of divestment, while most university administrators simply ignored the campaign. Thus far, PSM has claimed only one success. In February 2009, Hampshire College sold its shares in a mutual fund with ties to Israel. College administrators, however, deny that this sale was prompted by any political motivation and say that the school owns shares in several Israeli firms.

The failure of the divestment campaign to influence university administrators and trustees led anti-Israel activists to organize a new effort aimed mainly at college and university faculty members. This endeavor is the U.S. Campaign for the Academic and Cultural Boycott of Israel (USACBI). Organized in 2009 by a group of California professors, USACBI calls upon American academics to sever all ties with Israeli universities. The USACBI's advisory board includes a number of Muslim academics, such as Hamid Dabashi, professor of Iranian studies at Columbia, as well as a number of non-Muslim, left-liberal academics, such as David Lloyd of the University of Southern California and James Petras of Binghamton University, a professor whose published work often attacks Israel and "Jewish power" in the United States.

As the foregoing examples suggest, efforts to build alliances between progressive political forces and Muslims in the United States mainly, albeit not exclusively, take place in and around university campuses. This particular locus is important for both groups. To begin with, the political Left is far stronger on campus than it is virtually anywhere else in American society. Unlike its European counterparts, the American Left has little presence in the party system, the trade unions, or local and national governments. The American Left's main bastions are a number of public-interest and political-advocacy groups, a small number of church groups, some segments of the media, and a great many college and university campuses where, particularly in the humanities and social sciences, Republicans and conservatives have virtually no presence and even professors who are merely liberal Democrats run the risk of being labeled dangerous reactionaries. Known conservatives are very unlikely to be offered positions at America's top schools.

At the same time, college campuses are also useful political venues for Muslim organizations like CAIR and MSA. A number of schools enroll sizeable contingents of Muslim students, including thousands from the Middle East itself. Saudi Arabia alone sends more than 10,000 students to the United States every year. These students are easily mobilized to participate in anti-Zionist rallies and protests, to disrupt Jewish events, to shout down pro-Israeli speakers, and to urge their non-Muslim classmates to take a harsher view of Israel and a more positive view of the Arab cause. In this way, the Muslim-progressive campus alliance, though limited in scope, has the potential to breed long-term consequences. In the meantime, its main consequence has been a growth in anti-Semitic rhetoric as well as some anti-Semitic violence on several of America's campuses.[68]

Anti-Semitism and Anti-Imperialism

Coalition politics is not the only source of the American Left's anti-Zionist rhetoric. Some on the left also find an anti-Zionist or anti-Semitic discourse to be a useful instrument with which to attack the legitimacy of U.S. foreign policy by unmasking the Zionist cabal that has hijacked America's policy-making processes. A posture of anti-Zionism allows progressives to claim the patriotic high ground usually occupied by their opponents in foreign policy debates.

Since the Cold War, progressive forces in the United States have denounced American foreign policy as overly aggressive and an expression of America's imperialist designs. Progressives, of course, strongly opposed U.S. military endeavors in Korea, Indo-China, the Persian Gulf, Afghanistan, and elsewhere. Left liberals generally asserted that America was needlessly squandering its blood and treasure, alienating much of the world, and pursuing an agenda defined by defense contractors, multinational corporations, and politicians seeking to divert the public's attention from America's own social inequalities.

The progressive critique of American foreign policy was not without a measure of validity. Several of America's military ventures were ill advised, to say the least. Nevertheless, opponents of American military interventions typically found themselves charged with lacking patriotism and with demonstrating undue solicitude for the nation's foreign foes. Often, progressives were advised to love America—"or leave it!" And even when the public at large eventually tired of a particular war, the original left-liberal naysayers were seldom given credit for their prescience. Instead, their patriotism remained in question. Progressives were placed in a particularly precarious political position after the 9-11 terrorist attacks that sparked American military campaigns in Afghanistan and Iraq. From the perspective of the Left, the George W. Bush administration had seized an opportunity to launch two wars designed mainly to expand American hegemony in the Middle East and to ensure privileged American access to Middle Eastern oil supplies. However valid, this argument and the accompanying political refrain, "No blood for oil," was seen as unpatriotic outside the left-liberal camp and only increased the political isolation of the American Left.

This backdrop helps to explain a second important element of the American Left's anti-Semitic discourse. This is the charge that American foreign policy—especially American military campaigns in the Middle East—is the product of an effort by American Jews, led by the Israel lobby and a cabal of "neoconservative" Jewish officials, to promote Israeli goals at the expense of the United States. The great political value of this accusation, from the Left's perspective, is that it allows progressives—usually impugned for lack of patriotism—to present themselves as the true defenders of American interests. A similar argument had, of course, been made during the 1990s by right-wing anti-Semites like paleoconservative commentator Pat Buchanan, who famously called Congress "Israeli-occupied territory."

In some respects, the Left's embrace of Buchananism seems peculiar. Buchanan more or less consistently argues that foreign policy should be based upon the national interest. America's liberal Left, on the other hand, usually favors a foreign policy tied firmly to principle and morality rather than naked self-interest. Nevertheless the notion of Jewish conspirators shedding American blood to serve Israeli purposes has become an important element of the progressive critique of American foreign policy, especially since the 2007 publication of John Mearsheimer and Stephen Walt's well-known book *The Israel Lobby and U.S. Foreign Policy*, which gave the imprimatur of a University of Chicago professor and a Harvard professor to an argument that had previously been made by less prominent scholars.[69]

Like its counterpart in Europe, the American Left initially became disenchanted with Israel during the early 1970s, when Israeli security policies were aligned with those of the United States. The Left's antipathy for Israel was increased by the Jewish state's ongoing occupation of territories captured in the 1967 war and the emergence of the conservative Likud bloc, which displaced Labor as Israel's dominant political force. From the 1970s onward, American progressives, including some Jewish left liberals, frequently attacked Israel as an aggressive agent of American imperialism, a brutal occupying power, and perpetrator of what were declared to be racist policies toward Arab residents of the occupied territories and Israel proper.

These criticisms intensified in response to what was deemed harsh Israeli suppression of the first and second Palestinian intifadas during the 1980s and early 2000s, as well as various Israeli military operations against Fatah, Hamas, and Hezbollah militias. Israel's elaborate security wall, designed to inhibit Palestinian suicide bombers from reaching their targets in Israeli cities, was dubbed an "apartheid fence" and, for progressives, became a symbol of Israeli racism. Progressives were generally unmoved by the Israeli government's assertions that it had a duty to protect its citizens from terrorists, suicide bombers, and rocket attacks.

Historically, the mainstream U.S. media were generally sympathetic to Israel and, in their coverage of both the 1967 and 1973 Middle East wars, presented Israel as a victim of Arab aggression. During the 1970s and 1980s, however, more liberal periodicals such as the *New York Times* began to cover the Middle East from a more "balanced" perspective, presenting Israel and its Arab foes as more or less equally blameworthy for what was often characterized as a self-perpetuating cycle of violence, especially pitting Israelis against Palestinians in a struggle for possession of land to which both had a claim.

Gradually, with the help of their American supporters, the Palestinians learned to improve their own media image at the expense of the Israelis. Israel had always benefited from casting itself as a David standing up to Arab Goliaths. The Palestinians learned how to reframe this story so as to present themselves as a defenseless people victimized by a brutal Israeli military occupation. Making use of this new media frame, Palestinians were, for example, able to convince large segments of the American and international press that a 2002 battle in the Palestinian town of Jenin, which had resulted in the deaths of fifty-two Palestinians and twenty-three Israelis, had been a "massacre" in which hundreds, perhaps thousands, of Palestinian civilians had been butchered.[70]

In a similar vein, in June 2010, Palestinians staged an effort to undermine Israel's blockade of Gaza by dispatching a ragtag flotilla of vessels crewed by Palestinians and their various supporters to bring supplies to the Hamas-controlled enclave. The goal of the flotilla was to provoke an Israeli military response, which could be broadcast to the world as another example of Israel's barbarism. The Israelis understood the Palestinian strategy but were determined to maintain their blockade. When Israeli commandos armed mainly with nonlethal weapons boarded the vessels, they were attacked by individuals wielding clubs and knives. In the ensuing melee, several Israelis were injured and a number of Palestinians killed and injured. As expected, liberal opinion throughout Europe condemned Israel, and the incident led to violent anti-Israel demonstrations and boycotts in France and elsewhere.[71]

After September 2001, any sympathy for the Arab cause that might have emerged in the United States was tempered by outrage over the murder of thousands of American civilians by Arab terrorists. In response to the attack, the Bush administration launched major military campaigns against the Taliban regime in Afghanistan and Saddam Hussein's government in Iraq. Both wars were initially popular. As is often the case, however, the public soon tired of the costs and casualties inevitably associated with military operations. The Bush administration came under fire for having underestimated (the president might have said "misunderestimated") the difficulties involved in simultaneously suppressing major insurgencies in two nations. At the same time, critics questioned the Bush administration's explanation for having launched an invasion of Iraq in the first place. Bush had asserted that the Iraqi regime was developing weapons of mass destruction (WMDs) that would pose a danger to the United States. American forces searched every nook and cranny in Iraq for these WMDs, but to no avail. The weapons had never existed, and the entire story appeared to have been fabricated by the administration to provide a pretext for the American invasion.

This revelation offered progressives an opportunity to provide their own Judeocentric explanation for the invasion of Iraq and, indeed, for American policy in the Middle East more generally. In a host of books and articles, published mainly during Bush's second term, progressives as well as a number of Muslim authors (and a number of right-wing anti-Semites) pointed to the prominence of Jewish neoconservatives in the Bush administration. The list included government officials like Paul Wolfowitz, Richard Perle, Elliott Abrams, Kenneth Adelman, Douglas Feith, and Lewis Libby, as well as journalists like William Kristol and Charles Krauthammer and a number of academics and pundits.

Progressives borrowed from the Buchananite Right the notion that these "neocons," working closely with the pro-Israel lobby in Washington, were able to gain control over U.S. foreign policy. The result, as Mearsheimer and Walt put it, was the emergence of a foreign policy that "was a significant source of anti-Americanism in the Middle East and a source of tension with key strategic allies."[72] Mearsheimer and Walt go on to suggest that the neocons and Israel lobby bore much of the responsibility for the war in Iraq, "a strategic disaster for the United States."[73]

Other progressives assert that Jews continue to conspire to lead the United States into wars in the Middle East. For example, leftist sociologist James Petras, author of a number of anti-Zionist tracts, writes, "The American Jewish lobby [has led] a large-scale, intensive, and partially successful campaign to demonize Iran and Syria." At the top of the Jewish lobby's agenda, according to Petras, is "a new war against Iran on behalf of Israel."[74]

It is certainly true that the Israel lobby and many, if not all, neocons have been concerned with Israel's security and are hostile to the radical Muslim regimes of the Middle East, which they continue to view as threats to American military and economic interests. Nevertheless, attributing responsibility for America's actions in the Middle East to the machinations of Jewish lobbyists, pundits, and officials seems somewhat far-fetched. At the very least, this line of argument appears to give insufficient weight to the brute fact that the key policy makers behind the Iraq debacle were named George W. Bush, Dick Cheney, and Donald Rumsfeld—not a Yid among them. And while Bush may have been too easily influenced by Cheney and Rumsfeld, these two worthies had far, far too much confidence in their own abilities and were not sufficiently influenced by anyone.[75]

Nevertheless, attacking the Jewish neocons and the Israel lobby provides left liberals with a patriotic critique of American foreign policy. Rather than rail against U.S. militarism and imperialism and thereby commit themselves to political isolation, groups on the left can attack the Jews for hijacking American foreign policy and committing the nation to an imperialist agenda designed to serve Israel's interests. Elaboration of this anti-Semitic thesis has become a cottage industry in recent years, with left-wing and some right-wing authors vying with one another, in an ersatz green/brown competition, to develop ever more lurid titles. My personal favorite is *The Host and the Parasite: How Israel's Fifth Column Consumed America.*[76]

This left-liberal discourse, to be sure, has thus far failed to produce any general increase in anti-Semitic attitudes in the American populace, where anti-Semitic views have varied within a narrow 12 to 15 percent range for a number of years. However, the notion of Israel as a malign influence seems to have seeped from the left-liberal fringe into the general consciousness of the Democratic Party. Recent surveys indicate that while 75 percent of Republicans believe Israel is an ally of the United States, only 55 percent of Democrats agree.[77] In addition, more than half the Democrats surveyed in 2009 express equal levels of sympathy for Israel and the Palestinians—a substantial shift from previous surveys.[78] It is certainly possible to be suspicious of Israel without being in the least bit anti-Semitic, but, again, one attitude tends to give rise to the other.

Black Anti-Semitism

A second source of anti-Semitic discourse on the American political left is America's black community. In recent years, a number of African American politicians and public figures have made anti-Semitic comments and speeches. One notable example is former U.S. representative from Georgia and 2008 Green Party presidential candidate Cynthia McKinney. When McKinney was defeated for reelection in 2002, her father, a veteran Georgia state legislator, declared that the "J-E-W-S" were to blame. When McKinney lost another race in 2006, the head of her security detail confronted a reporter whom he took to be Jewish. "Put on your yarmulke and celebrate," he told the reporter. In 2008, McKinney was taken into custody by the Israeli navy as she took part in an attempt to penetrate the naval blockade of the Gaza Strip. McKinney called Israel's activities in Gaza "full-scale, outright genocide."[79]

Jews are often outraged and surprised by this sort of rhetoric on the part of blacks because the Jewish community recalls the important role it played only a few decades ago in the civil rights movement. During the 1950s and 1960s, Jews were prominent in most, if not all, of the nation's major civil rights organizations. Stanley Levinson, a Jewish attorney, was Dr. Martin Luther King Jr.'s chief adviser. Kivie Kaplan, a retired Jewish businessman from Boston, served as president of the National Association for the Advancement of Colored People (NAACP) and was also one of Dr. King's major fund-raisers and financial contributors. Attorney Jack Greenberg headed the NAACP Legal Defense Fund after the late Supreme Court justice Thurgood Marshall was named to the Second Circuit Court of Appeals by President Lyndon Johnson. At the same time, Jewish intellectuals and the journals of opinion they controlled spoke out forcefully on issues of civil rights, Jews contributed most of the funds available to civil rights groups, and Jewish organizations such as the American Jewish Committee and the Anti-Defamation League provided financial, legal, and organizational support for civil rights groups.

Its involvement in the struggle for black civil rights, to be sure, involved a measure of self-interest on the part of the Jewish community. Jewish organizations recognized that the civil rights movement's goal of outlawing discrimination in such areas as education and employment would serve the desire of Jews for fuller inclusion in American society. By supporting African Americans in the battle for civil rights, Jews were fighting to demolish the barriers that stood in their own way as well.[80] But interest was not everything. Jews also had a strong moral commitment to the civil rights cause. Indeed, some Jews risked their lives as well as their resources in the struggle. More than half the lawyers who made their services available to civil rights demonstrators in the South were Jews. A majority of the whites who accepted the danger of service as "freedom riders" were Jews, as were nearly two-thirds of the whites who went into the South during the violent "Freedom Summer" of 1964. These, of course, included Michael Schwermer and Andrew Goodman, who, along with their black colleague James Chaney, were murdered by racist thugs in Mississippi.

This alliance between blacks and Jews has not entirely evaporated. In 2008, for example, a majority of the whites in Democratic presidential candidate Barack Obama's inner circle were Jews, as were a number of President Obama's key appointees. Nevertheless, relations between blacks and Jews have deteriorated significantly in recent years. Most surveys indicate that African Americans are generally the most anti-Semitic segment of the American-born populace, with about 28 percent of black respondents—more than double the national average—indicating some measure of antipathy toward Jews. Black anti-Semitism predates the emergence of a sizeable contingent of Muslims within the black community, though this development certainly has not reduced anti-Jewish feeling among blacks.

A number of prominent African American political and intellectual figures commonly voice anti-Israel and anti-Jewish views and accuse Jews of conspiring against blacks. Louis Farrakhan, Jesse Jackson, and Al Sharpton have all frequently made use of coarse, anti-Semitic language. And while Barack Obama has courted Jewish support, his former pastor, Jeremiah Wright, has been a vociferous critic of Israel. Wright apparently blames the Jews for Obama's reluctance to maintain his formerly close ties with the minister. In a recent interview, Wright said, "Them Jews ain't going to let him [Obama] talk to me. . . . He's got to do what politicians do. And the Jewish vote, the AIPAC vote that's controlling him, that will not let him send representation to the Darfur Review Conference, that's talking this craziness on Israel because they're Zionists, they will not let him talk to somebody who calls a spade what it is. Ethnic cleansing is going on in Gaza—the ethnic cleansing of the Zionists is a sin and a crime against humanity."[81]

The existence of a substantial reservoir of anti-Semitic sentiment in the black community may encourage black political figures to believe that anti-Semitic comments will find a receptive audience among their constituents. At the same time, the anti-Semitic rhetoric of black public figures almost certainly serves to legitimate and encourage hostility toward Jews within the larger African American community.

What motivates some black public figures to engage in an anti-Semitic discourse? Ironically, today's black anti-Semitism is, in part, an unforeseen outgrowth of the success of the civil rights alliance between blacks and Jews. The civil rights movement brought about the enfranchisement of millions of African Americans who previously had been denied the right to vote. Voting rights greatly enhanced the importance of African Americans in American political life and, particularly, in the Democratic Party coalition, which became heavily dependent upon black electoral support.

The increased political weight of African Americans, in turn, encouraged members of the black political stratum to seek greater influence, more significant political offices, and a larger share of the public expenditures controlled by the Democrats. In many instances this effort led to conflicts with other groups in the Democratic coalition. Blacks came to be especially resentful that Jews, a much smaller group, seemed to hold more prominent positions and to exercise more power within the Democratic Party than African Americans. As recently as 2000, for example, some black Democrats were angered when Al Gore chose a Jew, Connecticut senator Joseph Lieberman, as his vice presidential running mate rather than an African American as many had hoped. Lee Alcorn, president of the Dallas NAACP chapter, said he opposed "any kind of partnership between the Jews at that kind of level because we know that their interest primarily has to do with, you know, money and these kinds of things."[82] The chairman of the *Amsterdam News*, Wilbert Tatum, suggested the only reason Gore had chosen Lieberman was that "Jews from all over the world will be sending bundles of money."[83]

The development of an anti-Semitic discourse in the African American community is also related to the emergence of several cohorts of ambitious young African American politicians, eager to supplant existing black notables and assume leadership positions. Those, like Barack Obama or Massachusetts governor Deval Patrick, who aspired to national leadership developed an inclusive rhetoric and were careful to maintain good relations with the existing political establishment. On the other hand, younger political notables who sought primarily to gain prominence within the black community believed that anti-Semitic, or in some cases anti-Zionist, rhetoric could be a useful weapon against the members of that establishment. In a variety of different contexts, insurgent forces within the African American community charged that incumbent leaders were the paid puppets of whites—of Jews in particular. Precisely because established black leaders had worked closely with Jews in the civil rights movement and often were dependent upon Jewish funding, they were quite vulnerable to this charge.

The first major black politician to successfully use this tactic was Malcolm X. Malcolm denounced established black politicians who had been allied with and dependent upon white support as collaborators who had sold out the black community. Since the most prominent white allies of black causes were usually Jews, Malcolm's rhetoric often contained anti-Semitic or anti-Zionist references. In this way, Malcolm underscored the difference between himself and the "kept" black politicians, especially black members of Congress who received financial and other forms of assistance from Jewish organizations and, in exchange, gave their support to Israel and other Jewish causes. Thus, Malcolm accused the Jews of sapping "the very life blood of the so-called Negroes to maintain the state of Israel." In another speech, Malcolm dismissed a question about the Holocaust by criticizing those who became "wet-eyed over a bunch of Jews who brought it on themselves."[84] The same tactic was adopted by Malcolm's successor, Louis Farrakhan, who achieved considerable notoriety by referring to Judaism as a "gutter religion." When established black leaders sought to repudiate such comments or to remind blacks of the support Jews had given to the civil rights movement, they in effect provided ammunition for their more radical foes—buttressing charges that they had sold out to whites. Later, based on the same political calculus, Jesse Jackson and his protégé Al Sharpton made use of anti-Semitic slurs in their own bids for prominence in the black community. And today, a number of black political figures, like Cynthia McKinney, continue to make use of anti-Semitic rhetoric to demonstrate their racial bona fides. Others, like Maryland's Donna Edwards, make a major point of criticizing Israel, though they eschew more overt anti-Semitism.

Still one more role played by black anti-Semitism is in support of efforts by African Americans to forge alliances and coalitions with other groups that may have their own reasons for supporting expressions of antipathy for Jews. Some African Americans have, for instance, sought ties with groups in Africa and the Middle East, and some, like Cynthia McKinney, have received considerable funding from Muslim groups in the United States. Identification with Third World forces allows American blacks to see themselves as participants in a worldwide struggle against oppression. Most Third World participants in this struggle, of course, are strongly opposed to Israel; hence, anti-Zionism can be an important element of Third World solidarity for African Americans, as it is for Western European Socialists. Hence, delegations of American blacks often attend international conferences where racism, imperialism, and Zionism are condemned. African American participants are expected to give their support to these resolutions and usually do so with enthusiasm. In 2009, the Congressional Black Caucus (CBC) was sharply critical of the Obama administration for boycotting the second UN Conference on racism. At the previous conference in 2001, delegates had voted to declare Zionism a form of racism. The 2009 conference, featuring a keynote address in which Iran's president, Mahmoud Ahmadinejad, declared that the Holocaust was merely a pretext for Israeli aggression, also focused on the alleged crimes of the Jewish state. Cynthia McKinney was especially outraged that the United States would not be participating. McKinney had led the CBC in demanding American participation at the 2001 conference, having been forced to go "toe to toe" with the Anti-Defamation League and Jewish members of Congress.[85]

An anti-Semitic discourse has also helped radical and left-liberal blacks achieve a more prominent position on the American Left. Through the 1960s, blacks were a subordinate group on the left, especially within the Communist Party, which was dominated by Jewish intellectuals. Harold Cruse, a black Communist, described this situation in his well-known 1967 work, *The Crisis of the Negro Intellectual*. Jewish Communists, said Cruse, always sought to ensure their complete political and ideological power over their black allies. Jews sought to dominate the field of "Negro studies" and made sure that

Jews always held the top Communist Party posts in the black community.[86] Through a posture of anti-Semitism, blacks simultaneously link themselves to non-Jewish leftists, most of whom are anti-Zionist, if not anti-Semitic, while intimidating Jewish leftists who are, in effect, accused of being insufficiently militant in their support for Third World causes—perhaps even of being closet Zionists. As we shall see below, attempting to disprove this implicit or explicit charge is one reason that some Jewish leftists have become vehemently and outspokenly anti-Zionist.

Thus, left-liberal blacks add their voices to the anti-Semitic discourse of the contemporary Left. Jews find black anti-Semitism particularly galling in view of the contribution made by the Jewish community to the civil rights cause not so very long ago. Politics, however, is about interests, not gratitude. And some black public figures are likely to continue to find that anti-Semitic rhetoric serves their political interests.

Jewish Anti-Zionism and Anti-Semitism

A final important source of anti-Semitic discourse on the political Left consists of European, American, and even Israeli Jews whose criticism of Israel and those Jews who support Israel has become so vehement as to constitute a form of Jewish anti-Semitism. At first blush, the notion of Jewish anti-Semitism may seem somewhat problematic. Indeed, a recent essay by Indiana University English professor Alvin Rosenfeld accusing a number of prominent Jewish intellectuals of promoting anti-Semitism generated considerable controversy.[87]

Yet, just as there are Americans who appear to hate their country enough to take up arms against it—the "American Taliban," to take one recent example—there have always been Jews who, for whatever reason, reject their own community in favor of some other religious or social identification. Within the Jewish community, such individuals are often castigated as "self-hating Jews," a term that seems to suggest a psychological aberration. Often cited as an exemplar of a deeply disturbed, self-hating Jew is Otto Weininger, a young, turn-of-the-century, Viennese Jewish intellectual. Weininger converted to Christianity in 1902 and in 1903 published a book titled *Sex and Character*, in which he characterized Judaism as a cowardly, feminine religion that lives as a parasite on its masculine host nations.[88] Weininger killed himself soon after his book's publication but was later praised by Adolf Hitler as "the one decent

Jew."[89] Psychological explanations might also be useful in understanding the behavior of various American neo-Nazis, such as Davis Wolfgang Hawke, aka Andy Greenbaum, who have turned out to be Jewish.[90]

Yet understanding the vehement anti-Zionism of a number of left-liberal Jewish intellectuals and political activists—prominent examples might include Jacqueline Rose, Noam Chomsky, Michael Neumann, the late Tony Judt, Ilan Pappe, and Norman Finkelstein—or even the outright anti-Semitism of a Gilad Atzmon does not require an effort to demonstrate that these individuals are lunatics. Indeed, referring to such persons as self-hating Jews is usually no more than an effort to dismiss their views as the products of some form of mental aberration.

In fact, the anti-Zionism shading into anti-Semitism of segments of the Jewish Left is a choice rather than an aberration and is related to Israel's place in the international system. Between 1948 and the 1967 war, Israel was a small and beleaguered Socialist country whose chief international sponsor was France. Israel's Arab foes during these decades were feudal monarchies and military dictatorships that trumpeted quasi-Fascist ideologies. Most Jewish leftists had no difficulty reconciling their political orientation with a favorable view of Israel. During the late 1960s and early 1970s, however, Israel's international position was transformed. Israel became a regional superpower, an occupying power no less, led by a succession of conservative governments whose security policies were aligned with those of the United States. At the same time, several of the Arab states, along with the Palestinians, aligned themselves with radical states and liberation movements in the Third World and labeled the Israelis imperialists, brutal occupiers, and racists.[91]

These changes in Israel's place in the world have made it increasingly difficult to be both pro-Israel and a member in good standing of the left-liberal community. Intellectuals and activists have felt compelled to make choices. For some left liberals, identification with the Jewish community and with Israel outweighed any attachment to the political Left. A number of today's neoconservatives, such as Norman Podhoretz, began their movement from the Socialist camp to the Democratic Party because of Soviet anti-Semitism, then became Republicans when they lost confidence in the Democratic Party's security policies, including its willingness to defend Israel.[92] Other Jewish leftists and liberals continue to resist the pressure to choose or have sought to carve out an increasingly shaky middle ground where they can be both politically Left and pro-Israel. Some of these individuals are represented by such organizations as Americans for Peace Now or J Street and periodicals such as *Tikkun*, which are sharply critical of Israeli policies but generally supportive of Israel's existence as a nation.

A third group of Jewish left liberals has decided that protecting its bona fides on the political left is too important to be risked by offering any support at all to Israel. To some extent this decision reflects a particular moral and political commitment, but social factors are at work as well. A pro-Israel stance means alienating friends and associates in the progressive community. On some elite university campuses, even failing to be sufficiently opposed to Israel may lead to a professor being labeled a "right winger" and ostracized from polite academic society. Accordingly, as Edward Alexander has observed, some left-liberal Jewish intellectuals express a sense of embarrassment or even shame at the idea that they might be identified with Israel.[93] Thus, Jacqueline Rose writes of her shame at Israeli actions.[94] Similarly, the late NYU history professor Tony Judt declared that because of Israel, "non-Israeli Jews feel themselves exposed to criticism and vulnerable to attack for things they didn't do. . . . The behavior of a self-described Jewish state affects the way everyone else looks at Jews."[95] Some progressive Jewish intellectuals have gone so far as to publicly renounce their "right of return" to Israel, hoping this will help their friends and colleagues avoid confusing them with the Zionists.

In their books, articles, speeches, and other presentations, these anti-Zionist Jews have little to say that is different from the utterances of other anti-Zionist progressives. One group, exemplified by Ilan Pappe, asserts that from its very founding the State of Israel was committed to a program of "ethnic cleansing."[96] A group led by Noam Chomsky views Israel as an agent of U.S. imperialism.[97] Another group, exemplified by Michael Neumann, accuses Israel of practicing genocidal policies against the Palestinians.[98] Still another group, exemplified by Norman Finkelstein, declares that the Holocaust, if not exactly a myth, is exaggerated and misused by Zionists as a justification for the existence of the State of Israel.[99]

These Jewish progressives add little to the substance of the discussion. What they say is said by others as well—Gentile progressives and Muslims in particular. The particular contribution of the Jewish anti-Zionists is political rather than intellectual. When Muslims or Gentiles denounce Israel, their motives might be suspect and their assertions taken with a grain of salt. The

Muslim might simply be advocating for Palestine, and the Gentile might perhaps harbor some ill will toward Jews. When Jews denounce Israel, they claim
a special status as truth tellers. Some begin their denunciations by citing their
own childhood Torah study or work on a kibbutz or parents who survived the
Holocaust. Judith Butler, for example, cites her own Jewish upbringing as the
source of her moral authority to absolve the other progressive anti-Zionists
of the charge of anti-Semitism.[100] When individuals such as these denounce
Israel, the casual listener is more likely to assume them to be credible. No
wonder America's most media-savvy Nazi, David Duke, found much to
praise in the work and courage of Chomsky, Finkelstein, and the others.[101] A
clever fellow, Duke recognized a group of kindred spirits who, in their own
way, were working to promote his cause.

And suppose the Jewish anti-Zionists won. Suppose Israel was erased from
the map. Would the Muslim and other anti-Zionist—but not anti-Semitic—
friends of the anti-Israel Jews love and respect them for their efforts? My
suspicion is that what was often said in Yiddish to Chaim Rumkowski and
other members of the various *Judenräte* would apply here as well: *Es vet gornit
helfen* (It won't help at all).

Notes

1: INTRODUCTION: THE PROBLEM OF JEWISH RESISTANCE

1. Raul Hilberg, *The Destruction of the European Jews* (New York: Holmes and Meier, 1985), 293–95.

2. Reuben Ainsztein, *Jewish Resistance in Nazi-Occupied Eastern Europe* (London: Elek Books, 1974), chs. 6, 7, and 8.

3. Hannah Arendt, *Eichmann in Jerusalem: A Report on the Banality of Evil*, rev. ed. (New York: Penguin, 1963), ch. 7.

4. Arendt, *Eichmann in Jerusalem*, 117.

5. Quoted in Peter Liberman, *Does Conquest Pay? The Exploitation of Occupied Industrial Societies* (Princeton, NJ: Princeton University Press, 1996), 49.

6. Robert O. Paxton, *Vichy France: Old Guard and New Order, 1940–1944* (New York: Alfred A. Knopf, 1972), 294–95.

7. Martin Sugarman, *Fighting Back: British Jewry's Military Contribution in the Second World War* (London: Valentine Mitchell, 2010).

8. Tore Gjelsvik, *Norwegian Resistance, 1940–45* (Toronto: University of Toronto Press, 1979). Also Leni Yahil, *The Rescue of Danish Jewry* (Philadelphia: Jewish Publication Society, 1969).

9. Alan S. Milward, "The Economic and Strategic Effectiveness of Resistance," in *Resistance in Europe, 1939–1945*, ed. Stephen Hawes and Ralph White (London: Allen Lane, 1975), 197.

2: THE SOVIET UNION: THE WAR OF THE ENGINEERS

1. Benjamin Pinkus, *The Jews of the Soviet Union* (Cambridge: Cambridge University Press, 1988), ch. 1.

2. John D. Klier and Shlomo Lambroza, eds., *Pogroms: Anti-Jewish Violence in Modern Russian History* (Cambridge: Cambridge University Press, 1992).

3. Pinkus, *Jews of the Soviet Union*, ch. 1.

4. Yuri Slezkine, *The Jewish Century* (Princeton, NJ: Princeton University Press, 2004), 222.

5. Slekzine, *Jewish Century*, 224–25.

6. Slekzine, *Jewish Century*, 226.

7. Louis Rapoport, *Stalin's War against the Jews* (New York: Free Press, 1990), 61–97.

8. Leonard Schapiro, "The Birth of the Red Army," in *The Red Army*, ed. B. H. Liddell Hart (New York: Harcourt, Brace and Company, 1956), 24–32.

9. David M. Glantz and Jonathan House, *When Titans Clashed* (Lawrence: University Press of Kansas, 1995), 6.

10. Glantz and House, *When Titans Clashed*, 8.

11. Glantz and House, *When Titans Clashed*, 9.

12. David R. Stone, *Hammer and Rifle: The Militarization of the Soviet Union, 1926–1933* (Lawrence: University Press of Kansas, 2000), ch. 1.

13. Rapoport, *Stalin's War against the Jews*, 54.

14. Pinkus, *Jews of the Soviet Union*, 145–209.

15. Leonard Schapiro, "The Great Purge," in Liddell Hart, *Red Army*, 66–67.

16. David M. Glantz, *Stumbling Colossus: The Red Army on the Eve of World War* (Lawrence: University Press of Kansas, 1998), 27–28.

17. Glantz and House, *When Titans Clashed*, 11.

18. Schapiro, "Great Purge," 69.

19. Mary R. Habeck, *Storm of Steel: The Development of Armor Doctrine in Germany and the Soviet Union, 1919–1939* (Ithaca, NY: Cornell University Press, 2003), 262–63.

20. Habeck, *Storm of Steel*, 276.

21. Glantz and House, *When Titans Clashed*, 37.

22. Quoted in Glantz, *Stumbling Colossus*, 31.

23. M. R. Elliott, "Soviet Military Collaborators during World War II," in *Ukraine during World War II*, ed. Y. Boshyk (London: Edmonton, 1986), 92–96.

24. Walter S. Dunn Jr., *Hitler's Nemesis: The Red Army, 1930–1945* (Westport, CT: Praeger, 1994), 5.

25. Richard Overy, *Russia's War: A History of the Soviet Effort, 1941–1945* (New York: Penguin, 1998), 118.

26. Mark Lincoln Chadwin, *The Warhawks: American Interventionists before Pearl Harbor* (Chapel Hill: University of North Carolina Press, 1968).

27. Yitzhak Arad, *In the Shadow of the Red Banner: Soviet Jews in the War against Nazi Germany* (Jerusalem: Gefen, 2010), 1.

28. Arno Lustiger, *Stalin and the Jews* (New York: Enigma Books, 2003), 137.

29. Arad, *In the Shadow*, 2.

30. Catherine Merridale, *Ivan's War: Life and Death in the Red Army, 1939–1945* (New York: Metropolitan Books, 2006), 288–89.

31. Alexander Solzhenitsyn, *Two Hundred Years Together* (Moscow: Vagrius, 2008).

32. Rachel Bayvel, "Tales of Tank City," *Jewish Studies Quarterly*, no. 198 (summer 2005).

33. Lustiger, *Stalin and the Jews*, 138.

34. Gershon Shapiro, *Under Fire* (Jerusalem: Yad Vashem, 1988).

35. Arad, *In the Shadow*, 116.

36. Alexander Werth, *Russia at War, 1941–1945* (New York: E. P. Dutton, 1964), 212–13.

37. Dunn, *Hitler's Nemesis*, 6.

38. Merridale, *Ivan's War*, 288.

39. Merridale, *Ivan's War*, 298.

40. Yuriy Rubin, "Jews of the Former Soviet Union Fought for Freedom," *Jewish Independent*, May 9, 2003.

41. Arad, *In the Shadow*, 6.

42. Shapiro, *Under Fire*, 277.

43. Arad, *In the Shadow*, 99.

44. Arad, *In the Shadow*, 100.

45. Dunn, *Hitler's Nemesis*, 4.

46. Dunn, *Hitler's Nemesis*, 115.

47. Quoted in Arad, *In the Shadow*, 137.

48. Werth, *Russia at War*, 216.

49. Overy, *Russia's War*, 170.

50. Arad, *In the Shadow*, 138.

51. Arad, *In the Shadow*, 139.

52. Overy, *Russia's War*, 170.

53. Overy, *Russia's War*, 155–56.

54. Dunn, *Hitler's Nemesis*, 6–7.

55. Dunn, *Hitler's Nemesis*, 110.

56. Glantz and House, *When Titans Clashed*, 51.

57. Heinz Guderian, *Panzer Leader* (New York: Da Capo Press, 1996), 162.

58. Lennart Samuelson, *Tankograd: The Formation of a Soviet Company Town: Cheliabinsk, 1900s–1950s* (New York: Palgrave Macmillan, 2011), 148–49.

59. Samuelson, *Tankograd*, 203.

60. Samuelson, *Tankograd*, 199.

61. Glantz, *Stumbling Colossus*, 191.

62. John T. Greenwood, "The Aviation Industry, 1917–97," in *Russian Aviation and Air Power in the 20th Century*, ed. Robin Higham, John T. Greenwood, and Von Hardesty (London: Frank Cass, 1998), ch. 6.

63. Glantz, *Stumbling Colossus*, 201.

64. Overy, *Russia's War*, 155.

65. Arad, *In the Shadow*, 141.

66. Dmitriy Khazanov and Aleksander Medved, *La-5/7 vs Fw-190: Eastern Front 1942–45* (Oxford, UK: Osprey Publishing, 2011), 35–36.

67. Von Hardesty, *Red Phoenix: The Rise of Soviet Air Power, 1941–1945* (Washington, DC: Smithsonian Books, 1982), 178–79.

68. Arad, *In the Shadow*, 141.

69. Hardesty, *Red Phoenix*, 170.

70. R. A. Belyakov and J. Marmain, *MiG: Fifty Years of Secret Aircraft Design* (Annapolis, MD: Naval Institute Press, 1994), 29.

71. Tom Alison and Von Hardesty, "Aviation and the Transformation of Combined-Arms Warfare," in Higham, Greenwood, and Hardesty, *Russian Aviation and Air Power in the 20th Century*, 102.

72. Hardesty, *Red Phoenix*, 176.

73. David Glantz and Harold M. Orenstein, *The Battle for Kursk, 1943* (London: Frank Cass, 1999), 260.

74. Alison and Hardesty, "Aviation," 102.

75. Hardesty, *Red Phoenix*, 176.

76. Hardesty, *Red Phoenix*, 98.

77. Belyakov and Marmain, *MiG*, 20–31.

78. Overy, *Russia's War*, 155.

79. Arad, *In the Shadow*, 150.

80. Arad, *In the Shadow*, 151.

81. Bayvel, "Tales of Tank City."

82. Bayvel, "Tales of Tank City."

83. Matthew Hughes and Chris Mann, *Inside Hitler's Germany: Life under the Third Reich* (Dulles, VA: Brassey's, 2000), 144.

84. Dunn, *Hitler's Nemesis*, 5–6.

85. Roger R. Reese, *Why Stalin's Soldiers Fought: The Red Army's Military Effectiveness in World War II* (Lawrence: University Press of Kansas, 2011), 161.

86. Overy, *Russia's War*, 159–60.

87. Overy, *Russia's War*, 161.

88. Reese, *Why Stalin's Soldiers Fought*, 177.

89. Werth, *Russia at War*, 410–12.

90. Amnon Sella, *The Value of Human Life in Soviet Warfare* (New York: Routledge, 1992), 153.

91. Roger Reese, *The Soviet Military Experience: A History of the Soviet Army, 1917–1991* (New York: Routledge, 2000).

92. Overy, *Russia's War*, 162.

93. Jay Leyda, *Kino: A History of the Russian and Soviet Film*, 3rd ed. (Princeton, NJ: Princeton University Press, 1983), 379.

94. Leyda, *Kino*, 377.

95. Peter Kenez, *Cinema and Soviet Society: From the Revolution to the Death of Stalin* (London: I. B. Tauris, 2009), 177.

96. Quoted in Merridale, *Ivan's War*, 183.

97. Overy, *Russia's War*, 138. See also Shimon Redlich, *War, Holocaust and Stalinism: A Documented History of the Jewish Anti-Fascist Committee in the USSR* (Luxembourg: Harwood Academic Publishers, 1995).

3: THE UNITED STATES: THE ANTI-NAZI COALITION

1. Marcia Graham Synott, *The Half-Opened Door: Discrimination and Admissions at Harvard, Yale and Princeton, 1900–1970* (Westport, CT: Greenwood, 1979). Also Marcia Graham Synott, "Anti-Semitism and American Universities: Did Quotas Follow the Jews?," in *Anti-Semitism in American History*, ed. David Gerber (Urbana: University of Illinois Press, 1986), 233–71.

2. Discussed in E. Digby Baltzell, *The Protestant Establishment: Aristocracy and Caste in America* (New Haven, CT: Yale University Press, 1987).

3. Geoffrey C. Ward, *A First-Class Temperament: The Emergence of Franklin Roosevelt* (New York: Harper, 1989), 254.

4. Steven Fraser, *Labor Will Rule: Sidney Hillman and the Rise of American Labor* (New York: Free Press, 1991).

5. Samuel Hand, *Counsel and Advise: A Political Biography of Samuel I. Rosenman* (New York: Garland, 1979).

6. Robert Shogan, *Prelude to Catastrophe: FDR's Jews and the Menace of Naziism* (Chicago: Ivan Dee, 2010).

7. Michael Parrish, *Felix Frankfurter and His Times* (New York: Free Press, 1982). Also Joseph Lash, *Dealers and Dreamers* (New York: Doubleday, 1988).

8. Jerold Auerbach, *Unequal Justice: Lawyers and Social Change in Modern America* (New York: Oxford, 1976), ch. 6.

9. Wayne S. Cole, *America First: The Battle against Intervention, 1940–1941* (Madison: University of Wisconsin Press, 1953).

10. Mark Lincoln Chadwin, *The Warhawks: American Interventionists before Pearl Harbor* (Chapel Hill: University of North Carolina Press, 1968).

11. Chadwin, *Warhawks*, 93.

12. Chadwin, *Warhawks*, 90.

13. Hadley Cantril, *The Human Dimension: Experience in Policy Research* (New Brunswick, NJ: Rutgers University Press, 1967).

14. Chadwin, *Warhawks*, 199.

15. British Security Coordination, *The Secret History of British Intelligence in the Americas, 1940–45* (New York: Fromm International, 1999), 79.

16. Chadwin, *Warhawks*, 215.

17. British Security Coordination, *Secret History*, 80–85.

18. British Security Coordination, *Secret History*, 74–75.

19. Liva Baker, *Felix Frankfurter* (New York: Coward-McCann, 1969), 240–41.

20. Arnold Forster, *Square One: A Memoir* (New York: Donald Fine, 1988), ch. 1.

21. Forster, *Square One*, 57–59.

22. Naomi W. Cohen, *Not Free to Desist: The American Jewish Committee, 1906–1966* (Philadelphia: Jewish Publication Society of America, 1972), ch. 9.

23. Cohen, *Not Free*, ch. 9.

24. Neal Gabler, *An Empire of Their Own: How the Jews Invented Hollywood* (New York: Crown, 1988).

25. Clayton R. Koppes and Gregory D. Black, *Hollywood Goes to War: How Politics, Profits and Propaganda Shaped World War II Movies* (Berkeley: University of California Press, 1990), 22.

26. Koppes and Black, *Hollywood*, 23.

27. Koppes and Black, *Hollywood*, 27.

28. Susan A. Brewer, *Why America Fights: Patriotism and War Propaganda from the Philippines to Iraq* (New York: Oxford University Press, 2009), 92.

29. Koppes and Black, *Hollywood*, chs. 1-3.

30. Ruth Sarles, *A Story of America First* (Westport, CT: Praeger, 2003), ch. 4.

31. George Q. Flynn, *The Draft, 1840-1973* (Lawrence: University Press of Kansas, 1993), ch. 2. Also J. Garry Clifford and Samuel R. Spencer Jr., *The First Peacetime Draft* (Lawrence: University Press of Kansas, 1986).

32. Warren F. Kimball, *The Most Unsordid Act: Lend-Lease, 1939-1941* (Baltimore: Johns Hopkins University Press, 1969), 153.

33. Chadwin, *Warhawks*, 155.

34. Alan P. Dobson, *US Wartime Aid to Britain, 1940-1946* (London: Croom Helm, 1986).

35. Edward R. Stettinius Jr., *Lend-Lease: Weapon for Victory* (New York: MacMillan, 1944), ch. 8.

36. Samuel Eliot Morrison, *The Battles of the Atlantic, September 1939-May 1943* (Annapolis, MD: Naval Institute Press, 1947), ch. 5.

37. John Baylis, *Anglo-American Defense Relations, 1939-1984: The Special Relationship* (New York: St. Martin's Press, 1981), 8.

38. George C. Herring Jr., *Aid to Russia, 1941-1946* (New York: Columbia University Press, 1973), 7.

39. Chadwin, *Warhawks*, 242-49.

40. Chadwin, *Warhawks*, 244.

41. Robert H. Jones, *The Roads to Russia: United States Lend-Lease to the Soviet Union* (Norman: University of Oklahoma Press, 1969), 55.

42. Herring, *Aid to Russia*, 22.

43. Stettinius, *Lend-Lease*, 209.

44. Chadwin, *Warhawks*, 210.

45. Gabler, *An Empire*, 344.

46. Chadwin, *Warhawks*, 215–19.

47. Howard J. Leavitt, *Semper Chai: The Jewish Experience in the U.S. Marine Corps* (New York: Xlibris, 2002), ch. 8.

48. Joseph Bendersky, *The Jewish Threat: Anti-Semitic Politics of the U.S. Army* (New York: Basic Books, 2000), 295.

49. Deborah Dash Moore, *G.I. Jews: How World War II Changed a Generation* (Cambridge, MA: Harvard University Press, 2004), 167.

50. I. Kaufman, *American Jews in World War II*, vol. 1 (New York: Dial Press, 1947), ch. 16.

51. Robert Boven, *Most Decorated Soldier in World War II: Matt Urban* (New York: Trafford, 2006).

52. The 756th Tank Battalion, "Medal of Honor Citation for 2nd Lt. Raymond Zussman," http://www.756tank.com/MOHzussman.htm.

53. Steven L. Ossad and Don Marsh, *Major General Maurice Rose: World War II's Greatest Forgotten Commander* (New York: Taylor, 2006).

54. 100th Bomb Group (Heavy), "Lt. Col. Robert 'Rosie' Rosenthal Awards and Citations," http://www.100thbg.com/mainpages/history/history5/rosie_medals.htm.

55. Ossad and Marsh, *General Maurice Rose*, 75.

56. Steven A. Bank, Kirk J. Stark, and Joseph J. Thorndike, *War and Taxes* (Washington, DC: Urban Institute Press, 2008), 84.

57. PBS, "Report to the Secretary on the Acquiescence of This Government in the Murder of the Jews, Initialed by Randolph Paul for the Foreign Funds Control Unit of the Treasury Department, January 13, 1944," http://www.pbs.org/wgbh/amex/holocaust/filmmore/reference/primary/somereport.htm.

58. Milton Friedman and Rose Friedman, *Two Lucky People* (Chicago: University of Chicago Press, 1998), 123.

59. W. Elliot Brownlee, *Federal Taxation in America: A Short History*, 2nd ed. (New York: Cambridge University Press, 2004), 87.

60. Brownlee, *Federal Taxation*, 108–9.

61. Bank, Stark, and Thorndike, *War and Taxes*, 90–92.

62. Bank, Stark, and Thorndike, *War and Taxes*, 98.

63. Carolyn Jones, "Mass-Based Income Taxation: Creating a Taxpaying Culture, 1940–1952," in *Funding the Modern American State, 1941–1995: The Rise and Fall of the Era of Easy Finance*, ed. W. Elliott Brownlee (New York: Cambridge University Press, 1996), 107–8.

64. Bank, Stark, and Thorndike, *War and Taxes*, 100.

65. Bank, Stark, and Thorndike, *War and Taxes*, 95.

66. Charlotte Twight, "Evolution of Federal Income Tax Withholding: The Machinery of Institutional Change," *Cato Journal* 4, no. 3 (winter 1995): 384.

67. Hugh Rockoff, "The United States: From Ploughshares to Swords," in *The Economics of World War II*, ed. Mark Harrison (Cambridge: Cambridge University Press, 1998), 108.

68. John Bush Jones, *The Songs That Fought the War: Popular Music and the Home Front, 1939–1945* (Waltham, MA: Brandeis University Press, 2006).

69. Christopher P. Lehman, *The Colored Cartoon* (Amherst: University of Massachusetts Press, 1973).

70. Lawrence R. Samuel, *Pledging Allegiance: American Identity and the Bond Drive of World War II* (Washington, DC: Smithsonian Institution Press, 1997), 101.

71. Samuel, *Pledging Allegiance*, 101.

72. Koppes and Black, *Hollywood*, 59.

73. Allan M. Winkler, *The Politics of Propaganda: The Office of War Information, 1942–1945* (New Haven, CT: Yale University Press, 1978), 56.

74. Winkler, *Politics of Propaganda*, 61.

75. Koppes and Black, *Hollywood*, 66.

76. Brewer, *Why America Fights*, 113.

77. Koppes and Black, *Hollywood*, 103.

78. Bosley Crowther, "Movie Review: The World at War (1942)," *New York Times*, September 4, 1942, http://movies.nytimes.com/movie/review?res=9900E3D91E3CE3 3BBC4C53DFBF668389659EDE.

79. Adam J. Berinsky, *In Time of War: Understanding American Public Opinion from World War II to Iraq* (Chicago: University of Chicago Press, 2009).

80. Richard Rhodes, *Hedy's Folly: The Life and Breakthrough Inventions of Hedy Lamarr, the Most Beautiful Woman in the World* (New York: Doubleday, 2011).

81. Richard Rhodes, *The Making of the Atomic Bomb* (New York: Simon & Schuster, 1986), 185.

82. Quoted in Rhodes, *Making of the Atomic Bomb*, 415.

83. Quoted in Rhodes, *Making of the Atomic Bomb*, 445.

4: JEWISH INTELLIGENCE

1. Hervie Haufler, *Codebreakers' Victory: How the Allied Cryptographers Won World War II* (New York: New American Library, 2003), 7.

2. Bartholomew Lee, *Radio Spies—Episodes in the Ether Wars*, unpublished manuscript, TVRadioFilmTheatre.com, 2002, http://www.trft.org/TRFTPix/ spies9eR2006.pdf.

3. Haufler, *Codebreakers' Victory*, 12.

4. Lee, *Radio Spies*, 37.

5. Stephen Budiansky, *Battle of Wits: The Complete Story of Codebreaking in World War II* (New York: Touchstone, 2002), 229.

6. Haufler, *Codebreakers' Victory*, 18.

7. Budiansky, *Battle of Wits*, 54.

8. E. H. Hinsley and Alan Stripp, eds., *Codebreakers: The Inside Story of Bletchley Park* (Oxford: Oxford University Press, 1993).

9. Stuart Milner-Barry, "Hut 6: Early Days," in Hinsley and Stripp, *Codebreakers*, 91.

10. Hinsley and Stripp, *Codebreakers*, ch. 1.

11. Martin Sugarman, *Fighting Back: British Jewry's Military Contribution in the Second World War* (London: Valentine Mitchell, 2010), ch. 6.

12. Budiansky, *Battle of Wits*, 313.

13. Budiansky, *Battle of Wits*, 315.

14. Sugarman, *Fighting Back*, 115.

15. Budiansky, *Battle of Wits*, 288.

16. Rolf Noskwith, "Hut 8 and Naval Enigma, Part II," in Hinsley and Stripp, *Codebreakers*, 121.

17. Budiansky, *Battle of Wits*, 294.

18. Leo Marks, *Between Silk and Cyanide: A Codemaker's War, 1941–1945* (New York: Touchstone, 2000).

19. Elliot Carlson, *Joe Rochefort's War* (Annapolis, MD: Naval Institute Press, 2011).

20. Budiansky, *Battle of Wits*, 24.

21. CNN, "Wealthy Eccentrics," http://money.cnn.com/galleries/2007/fortune/0702/gallery.rich_eccentrics.fortune/5.html.

22. Haufler, *Codebreakers' Victory*, 112.

23. Budiansky, *Battle of Wits*, 33.

24. Budiansky, *Battle of Wits*, 211.

25. Haufler, *Codebreakers' Victory*, 130.

26. V. E. Tarrant, *The Red Orchestra: The Soviet Spy Network inside Nazi Europe* (London: Cassell, 1995), 120.

27. Tarrant, *Red Orchestra*, 121.

28. Jewish Virtual Library, "Leopold Trepper," *Encyclopedia Judaica*, http://www.jewishvirtuallibrary.org/jsource/judaica/ejud_0002_0020_0_20028.html.

29. Tarrant, *Red Orchestra*, 125.

30. Yitzhak Arad, *In the Shadow of the Red Banner: Soviet Jews in the War against Nazi Germany* (Jerusalem: Gefen, 2010), 110.

31. Tarrant, *Red Orchestra*, 131.

32. Robert Stephan, *Stalin's Secret War: Soviet Counterintelligence against the Nazis, 1941-1945* (Lawrence: University Press of Kansas, 2004), 113-14.

33. David M. Glantz, *The Role of Intelligence in Soviet Military Strategy in World War II* (Novato, CA: Presidio, 1990).

34. Stephan, *Stalin's Secret War*, 113.

35. Tarrant, *Red Orchestra*, 156-57.

36. Tarrant, *Red Orchestra*, 166.

37. Arad, *In the Shadow*, 112.

38. Stephan, *Stalin's Secret War*, ch. 3.

39. Stephan, *Stalin's Secret War*, 57.

40. Stephan, *Stalin's Secret War*, 58.

41. William J. MacKenzie, *The Secret History of SOE: The Special Operations Executive, 1940-1945* (London: St. Ermins, 2002).

42. M. R. D. Foot, *SOE in France: An Account of the Work of the British Special Operations Executive in France, 1940-1944*, 2nd ed. (London: Frank Cass, 2004).

43. Terry Crowdy, *SOE Agent: Churchill's Secret Warriors* (Oxford, UK: Osprey, 2008).

44. Marks, *Between Silk and Cyanide*.

45. Sugarman, *Fighting Back*, 304.

46. E. H. Cookridge, *Inside SOE* (London: Arthur Barker, 1966).

47. Sarah Helm, *A Life in Secrets: Vera Atkins and the Missing Agents of WWII* (New York: Random House, 2005), 36.

48. Helm, *Life in Secrets*, 57.

49. Helm, *Life in Secrets*, 318-30.

50. Helen Fry, *The King's Most Loyal Enemy Aliens* (London: Sutton Publishing, 2007), 18.

51. Fry, *King's Most Loyal Enemy Aliens*, 18.

52. Fry, *King's Most Loyal Enemy Aliens*, 13.

53. Bernard Wasserstein, *Britain and the Jews of Europe, 1939–1945* (New York: Oxford University Press, 1988).

54. Fry, *King's Most Loyal Enemy Aliens*, 4.

55. Quoted in Fry, *King's Most Loyal Enemy Aliens*, 3.

56. Fry, *King's Most Loyal Enemy Aliens*, 101–2.

57. Sugarman, *Fighting Back*, 286–87.

58. Judith Tydor Baumel-Schwartz, *The World War II Parachutists and the Making of Israeli Collective Memory* (Madison: University of Wisconsin Press, 2010).

59. Peter Hay, *Ordinary Heroes: Chana Szenes and the Dream of Zion* (New York: Putnam's, 1986).

60. Sugarman, *Fighting Back*, ch. 8.

61. Ian Dear, *Ten Commando* (London: Pen and Sword Press, 2011).

62. Sugarman, *Fighting Back*, ch. 13.

63. Eugene Liptak, *Office of Strategic Services, 1942–45* (Oxford, UK: Osprey Publishing, 2009).

64. Patrick K. O'Donnell, *They Dared Return: The True Story of Jewish Spies behind the Lines in Nazi Germany* (New York: Da Capo Press, 2009).

65. Tom Moon, *The Grim and Savage Game: The OSS and the Beginning of U.S. Covert Operations* (New York: Da Capo, 2000), 277.

66. Liptak, *Office of Strategic Services*, 37.

67. O'Donnell, *They Dared Return*, 92.

68. O'Donnell, *They Dared Return*, 93.

69. O'Donnell, *They Dared Return*, ch. 26.

70. Moon, *Grim and Savage Game*, 276.

71. Barry M. Katz, *Foreign Intelligence: Research and Analysis in the Office of Strategic Services, 1942–1945* (Cambridge, MA: Harvard University Press, 1989), 18.

72. Moon, *Grim and Savage Game*, 17.

73. Franz Neumann, *Behemoth* (New York: Oxford University Press, 1944).

74. Moon, *Grim and Savage Game*, 38.

5: PARTISAN WARFARE

1. M. R. D. Foot, *S.O.E. in France: An Account of the Work of the British Special Operations Executive in France, 1940–44*, rev. ed. (London: Her Majesty's Stationary Office, 1968), 442.

2. Hsi-Huey Liang, *The Rise of Modern Police and the European State System from Metternich to the Second World War* (Cambridge: Cambridge University Press, 1988), 299.

3. Peter Liberman, *Does Conquest Pay? The Exploitation of Occupied Industrial Societies* (Princeton, NJ: Princeton University Press, 1996), 47.

4. Martin K. Sorge, *The Other Price of Hitler's War: German Military and Civilian Losses Resulting from World War II* (New York: Greenwood Press, 1986), 57.

5. Jorgen Haestrup, *European Resistance Movements, 1939–1945: A Complete History* (Westport, CT: Meckler Publishing, 1981), 463.

6. Eric Conan and Henry Rousso, *Vichy: An Ever-Present Past* (Hanover, NH: University Press of New England, 1998).

7. Yuri Suhl, ed., *They Fought Back: The Story of the Jewish Resistance in Nazi Europe* (New York: Shocken, 1975), 285.

8. Paul Webster, *Petain's Crime: The Full Story of French Collaboration in the Holocaust* (Chicago: Ivan Dee, 1991), 143.

9. Webster, *Petain's Crime*, 155.

10. Webster, *Petain's Crime*, 146.

11. Webster, *Petain's Crime*, 146.

12. Lucien Steinberg, "The Participation of Jews in the Allied Armies," in *Jewish Resistance during the Holocaust*, ed. Meir Grubsztein (Jerusalem: Yad Vashem, 1971), 385.

13. François Hollande, "The Crime Committed in France by France," *New York Review*, September 27, 2012, 40–41.

14. Lucy S. Dawidowicz, *The War against the Jews, 1933–1945* (New York: Holt, Rinehart & Winston, 1945), 362.

15. Robert O. Paxton, *Vichy France: Old Guard and New Order, 1940–1944* (New York: Alfred A. Knopf, 1972), 182.

16. Milton Dank, *The French against the French: Collaboration and Resistance* (Philadelphia: Lippincott, 1974), 225.

17. Michael Marrus and Robert O. Paxton, *Vichy France and the Jews* (New York: Basic Books, 1981), 331.

18. Renée Poznanski, *Jews in France during World War II* (Boston: Brandeis University Press, 2001), 364.

19. Dawidowicz, *War against the Jews,* 363.

20. Poznanski, *Jews in France,* 286.

21. Julian Jackson, *France: The Dark Years, 1940–1944* (New York: Oxford University Press, 2003).

22. Susan Zuccotti, *The Holocaust, the French and the Jews* (New York: Basic Books, 1993), 275.

23. Olivier Wieviorka, "France," in *Resistance in Western Europe,* ed. Bob Moore (Oxford, UK: Berg Publishing, 2000), 142.

24. Zucotti, *Holocaust,* 266.

25. John F. Sweets, *The Politics of Resistance in France, 1940–1944* (DeKalb: Northern Illinois University Press, 1976), ch. 4.

26. Webster, *Petain's Crime,* 151.

27. Poznanski, *Jews in France,* 351.

28. Jackson, *France,* 569.

29. Zucotti, *Holocaust,* 269.

30. Zucotti, *Holocaust,* 270.

31. Zucotti, *Holocaust,* 270.

32. Cited in Zucotti, *Holocaust,* 270.

33. Anny Latour, *The Jewish Resistance in France, 1940–1944* (New York: Holocaust Library, 1980), 179.

34. Poznanski, *Jews in France*, 354.

35. Wieviorka, "France," 134.

36. Marrus and Paxton, *Vichy France*, 322.

37. Wieviorka, "France," 135.

38. Zucotti, *Holocaust*, 285–89.

39. Paxton, *Vichy France*, ch. 1.

40. Marrus and Paxton, *Vichy France*, 241.

41. Christopher Lloyd, *Collaboration and Resistance in Occupied France: Representing Treason and Sacrifice* (London: Palgrave Macmillan, 2003), ch. 1.

42. Jacob Gutfreind, "The Jewish Resistance Movement in Belgium," in Suhl, *They Fought Back*, 304–11.

43. Peter Lagrou, "Belgium," in Moore, *Resistance in Western Europe*, 47.

44. Gutfreind, "Jewish Resistance Movement," 310.

45. Jorgen Haestrup, *European Resistance Movements*.

46. Steinberg, "Participation of Jews," 388.

47. John L. Hondros, *Occupation and Resistance: The Greek Agony, 1941–44* (New York: Pella, 1983).

48. Steven Bowman, *Jewish Resistance in Wartime Greece* (Edgware, Middlesex, UK: Vallentine Mitchell, 2006), 4.

49. Hondros, *Occupation and Resistance*, 153–62.

50. Ronald H. Bailey, *Partisans and Guerillas* (Alexandria, VA: Time-Life, 1980), 80.

51. Martin Van Creveld, *Supplying War: Logistics from Wallenstein to Patton*, 2nd ed. (New York: Cambridge University Press, 2004), ch. 5.

52. Reuben Ainsztein, *Jewish Resistance in Nazi-Occupied Eastern Europe* (London: Elek Books, 1974), 394.

53. Kenneth Slepyan, *Stalin's Guerillas: Soviet Partisans in World War II* (Lawrence: University Press of Kansas, 2006), 211.

54. Yitzhak Arad, *In the Shadow of the Red Banner: Soviet Jews in the War against Nazi Germany* (Jerusalem: Gefen, 2010), 269.

55. Arad, *In the Shadow*, 343.

56. Ainsztein, *Jewish Resistance*, 281.

57. Shalom Cholavsky, "Jewish Partisans—Objective and Subjective Difficulties," in *Jewish Resistance during the Holocaust*, ed. Meir Grubsztein, 326.

58. Ainsztein, *Jewish Resistance*, 284.

59. Slepyan, *Stalin's Guerillas*, 32–33.

60. Richard Overy, *Russia's War: A History of the Soviet Effort, 1941–1945* (New York: Penguin, 1998), 133.

61. Overy, *Russia's War*, 133.

62. Overy, *Russia's War*, 143.

63. Overy, *Russia's War*, 143.

64. Slepyan, *Stalin's Guerillas*, 37–38.

65. Sara Shner-Nishmit, *The 51st Company: The Story of the Jewish Partisan Group from the Slonim Ghetto* (Tel Aviv: Lohamei Hagataot and Misrad Habitahon, 1990).

66. Overy, *Russia's War*, 144.

67. Slepyan, *Stalin's Guerillas*, 39.

68. Overy, *Russia's War*, 149.

69. Slepyan, *Stalin's Guerillas*, 47.

70. Slepyan, *Stalin's Guerillas*, 48.

71. Slepyan, *Stalin's Guerillas*, 48.

72. Slepyan, *Stalin's Guerillas*, 209.

73. Philip Friedman, "Ukrainian-Jewish Relations during the Nazi Occupation," in *Roads to Extinction: Essays on the Holocaust*, ed. Philip Friedman (Philadelphia: Jewish Publication Society, 1980), 188.

74. Slepyan, *Stalin's Guerillas*, 210.

75. Slepyan, *Stalin's Guerillas*, 210.

76. Nechama Tec, *Defiance* (New York: Oxford University Press, 2008), 109.

77. Arad, *In the Shadow*, 267.

78. Arad, *In the Shadow*, 268.

79. Arad, *In the Shadow*, 283.

80. Arad, *In the Shadow*, 284.

81. Arad, *In the Shadow*, 306.

82. Joseph Kermish, "The Place of Ghetto Revolts in the Struggle against the Occupier," in *Jewish Resistance during the Holocaust*, ed. Meir Grubsztein, 271.

83. Cholavsky, "Jewish Partisans," 331.

84. Barbara Epstein, *The Minsk Ghetto, 1941–1943: Jewish Resistance and Soviet Internationalism* (Berkeley: University of California Press, 2008), 113.

85. Epstein, *Minsk Ghetto*, 115.

86. Hersh Smolar, *The Minsk Ghetto: Soviet-Jewish Partisans against the Nazis* (New York: Holocaust Library, 1989).

87. Smolar, *Minsk Ghetto*, 71.

88. Epstein, *Minsk Ghetto*, 143.

89. Lester Eckman and Chaim Lazar, *The Jewish Resistance: The History of the Jewish Partisans in Lithuania and White Russia during the Nazi Occupation, 1940–1945* (New York: Shengold Publishers, 1977), 69.

90. Ainsztein, *Jewish Resistance*, 267.

91. Ainsztein, *Jewish Resistance,* ch. 19.

92. Alexander Werth, *Russia at War, 1941–1945* (New York: E. P. Dutton, 1964), 718.

93. Werth, *Russia at War*, 718.

94. Haestrup, *European Resistance Movements*, 430.

95. Alexander Brakel, "Partisans and the Belorussian Population, 1941–4," in *War in a Twilight World: Partisan and Anti-Partisan Warfare in Eastern Europe, 1939–45*, ed. Ben Shepherd and Juliette Pattinson (London: Palgrave Macmillan, 2010), 94.

96. Matthew Cooper, *The Nazi War against Soviet Partisans* (New York: Stein and Day, 1979), 143.

97. Werth, *Russia at War*, 724.

98. Van Creveld, *Supplying War,* ch. 5.

99. Van Creveld, *Supplying War*, 162.

100. Van Creveld, *Supplying War*, 174.

101. Overy, *Russia's War*, 150.

102. Cooper, *Nazi War*, ch. 8.

103. Dov Levin, *Fighting Back: Lithuanian Jewry's Armed Resistance to the Nazis, 1941-1945* (New York: Holmes and Meier, 1985), 197.

104. Paul Allen, *Katyn: Stalin's Massacre and the Triumph of Truth* (DeKalb: Northern Illinois University Press, 2010).

105. Stefan Korbonski, *The Polish Underground State* (New York: Columbia University Press, 1978).

106. Haestrup, *European Resistance Movements*, 423.

107. Michael Borwicz, "Factors Influencing the Relations between the General Polish Underground and the Jewish Underground," in *Jewish Resistance during the Holocaust*, ed. Meir Grubsztein, 347.

108. David Widowinski, *And We Are Not Saved* (New York: Philosophical Library, 1985).

109. Borwicz, "Factors Influencing," 348.

110. Yehuda Bauer, *They Chose Life: Jewish Resistance in the Holocaust* (New York: American Jewish Committee, 1973).

111. Israel Gutman, *Resistance: The Warsaw Ghetto Uprising* (New York: Mariner Books, 1998).

112. Jewish Virtual Library, "The Stroop Report: The Warsaw Ghetto Is No More," April 1943, http://www.jewishvirtuallibrary.org/jsource/Holocaust/nowarsaw.html.

113. Marian Apfelbaum, *Two Flags: Return to the Warsaw Ghetto* (Jerusalem: Gefen, 2007).

114. Jewish Virtual Library, "Stroop Report."

115. Korbonski, *Polish Underground State*, 135-36.

116. Jozef Garlinski, *Poland in the Second World War* (New York: Macmillan, 1985), 172.

117. Eckman and Lazar, *Jewish Resistance*, 71-82.

118. Garlinski, *Poland*, 173.

119. Borwicz, "Factors Influencing," 350.

120. Shmuel Krakowski, *The War of the Doomed: Jewish Armed Resistance in Poland, 1942-1944* (New York: Holmes & Meier, 1984), ch. 1.

121. Krakowski, *War of the Doomed*, ch. 13.

122. Wladyslaw Anders, *An Army in Exile: The Story of the Second Polish Corps* (Nashville, TN: Battery Press Reprint, 2004).

123. Callum McDonald, *The Killing of Reinhard Heydrich* (New York: Da Capo, 1998).

124. Yeshayahu Jelinek, "The Role of the Jews in Slovakian Resistance," in *Jewish Resistance to the Holocaust*, ed. Michael R. Marrus (Westport, CT: Meckler, 1989), 356.

125. Jelinek, "Role of the Jews," 358.

126. Jelinek, "Role of the Jews," 359.

127. Sorge, *Other Price*, 55.

128. Liberman, *Does Conquest Pay?*, 49.

6: AFTERMATH AND AFTERWARD: FROM TRAGEDY TO FARCE

1. Irving Abells and Harold Troper, *None Is Too Many: Canada and the Jews of Europe, 1933-1948*, 3rd. ed. (Winnipeg: Lester Pub. Ltd., 1997).

2. Howard M. Sachar, *A History of the Jews in America* (New York: Knopf, 1992), 582.

3. Alan L. Berger, "Harry S. Truman and Jewish Refugees," in *Israel and the Legacy of Harry S. Truman*, ed. Michael Devine, Robert Watson, and Robert Wolz (Kirksville, MO: Truman State University Press, 2008), 3-10.

4. Donald Bloxham, *Genocide on Trial: War Crimes Trials and the Formation of Holocaust History and Memory* (New York: Oxford University Press, 2001).

5. John Loftus, *America's Nazi Secret* (Waterville, OR: TrineDay, 2010).

6. Richard Breitman et al., *U.S. Intelligence and the Nazis* (New York: Cambridge University Press, 2005). Also Alain Finkielkraut, *Remembering in Vain: The Klaus Barbie Trial and Crimes against Humanity* (New York: Columbia University Press, 1992).

7. Tom Bower, *The Paperclip Conspiracy: The Hunt for the Nazi Scientists* (Boston: Little, Brown, 1987).

8. Gerald Steinacher, *Nazis on the Run: How Hitler's Henchmen Fled Justice* (Oxford: Oxford University Press, 2011).

9. Harold Troper, *Old Wounds: Jews, Ukrainians and the Hunt for Nazi War Criminals in Canada* (Chapel Hill: University of North Carolina Press, 1989).

10. Benjamin Pinkus, *The Soviet Government and the Jews, 1948–67* (Cambridge: Cambridge University Press, 1984), 140–42.

11. Yakov Rapoport, *The Doctors' Plot of 1953* (Cambridge, MA: Harvard University Press, 1991).

12. Neil Gabler, *An Empire of Their Own: How the Jews Invented Hollywood* (New York: Crown, 1988), chs. 9 and 10.

13. Samuel Walker, *In Defense of Civil Liberties: A History of the ACLU* (New York: Oxford University Press, 1990), 212.

14. Mitchell Cohen, "Anti-Semitism and the Left That Doesn't Learn," *Dissent*, September 10, 2007, http://www.dissentmagazine.org/article/?article=987.

15. NPR, "Cornel West Outlines 'Pull toward Princeton' and 'Push from Harvard' in Exclusive Interview with NPR's Tavis Smiley," January 7, 2002, http://www.npr .org/about/press/020415.cwest.html.

16. Bernard Harrison, *The Resurgence of Anti-Semitism: Jews, Israel and Liberal Opinion* (Lanham, MD: Rowman & Littlefield, 2006).

17. Gabriel Schoenfeld, *The Return of Anti-Semitism* (San Francisco: Encounter Books, 2004), 96.

18. Schoenfeld, *Return of Anti-Semitism*, 89.

19. See, for example, the 2009 Goldstone Report: United Nations Fact Finding Mission on the Gaza Conflict, "Human Rights in Palestine and Other Occupied Arab Territories: Report of the United Nations Fact-Finding Mission on the Gaza Conflict," Office of the High Commissioner for Human Rights, www2.ohchr.org/ english/bodies/hrcouncil/specialsession/9/FactFindingMission.htm. For a critique of the Goldstone Report, see Peter Berkowitz, "Blaming Israel First," *Weekly Standard*, January 18, 2010, 14–16.

20. David Shulman, *Dark Hope* (Chicago: University of Chicago Press, 2007).

21. Jacqueline Rose, *The Question of Zion* (Princeton, NJ: Princeton University Press, 2005).

22. Schoenfeld, *Return of Anti-Semitism*, ch. 3.

23. Alison Weir, "Israeli Organ Harvesting," *Counterpunch*, August 28–30, 2009, http://74.125.93.132/search?q=cache%3Awww.counterpunch.org%2Fweir08282009 .html.

24. Israel Shamir, "Bloodcurdling Libel (a Summer Story)," http://www .israelshamir.net/English/blood.htm.

25. Adam Holland, "Alison Weir Continues to Promote Blood Libel," *Your View*, October 12, 2009, http://www.hurryupharry.org/2009/10/12alison-weir-continues-to-promote-blood-libel.

26. Harold Evans, "The View from Ground Zero," in *Those Who Forget the Past*, ed. Ron Rosenbaum (New York: Random House, 2004), 36–56.

27. Hillel Fendel, "Survey: Jews Are Blamed for Economic Crisis," Arutz Sheva, May 7, 2009, http://www.israelnationalnews.com/News/News.aspx/131238# .UMeKwaXi7ww.

28. RT, "Study: Europe Blames Jews for Crisis," February 12, 2009, http://rt.com/ news/study-europe-blames-jews-for-crisis.

29. Benjamin Ginsberg, *The Fatal Embrace: Jews and the State* (Chicago: University of Chicago Press, 1993), 8.

30. Christopher Caldwell, *Reflections on the Revolution in Europe: Immigration, Islam and the West* (New York: Doubleday, 2009).

31. Dore Gold, "Why the UN Has Failed," *FrontPage Mag*, January 7, 2005, http:// hnn.us/roundup/entries/9530.html.

32. Malise Ruthven, "The Big Muslim Problem!" *New York Review*, December 17, 2009, 62.

33. Jonathan Freedland, "As British Jews Come under Attack, the Liberal Left Must Not Remain Silent," Guardian.co.uk, February 4, 2009, http://www.guardian.co.uk/ commentisfree/2009/feb/04/gaza-jewish-community.

34. Lorenzo Vidino and Erick Stakelbeck, "Along Came Sharia: Islam and European Secularism Clash," *National Review*, February 19, 2004, http://www.nationalreview .com/comment/vidino_stakelbeck200402190906.asp.

35. Alex Callinicos, "The European Radical Left Tested Electorally," *International Viewpoint*, 2004, http://www.internationalviewpoint.org/spip.php?article10.

36. Bret Stephens, "Islamosocialism: The European Left Makes Common Cause with the Muslim Right," WSJ.com, March 18, 2007, http://www.opinionjournal.com/wsj/?id=110009802.

37. Callinicos, "European Radical Left."

38. Robert S. Wistrich, *Muslim Anti-Semitism* (New York: American Jewish Committee, 2002), 11.

39. Matthias Kuntzel, *Jihad and Jew Hatred* (New York: Telos, 2007), 136.

40. Kuntzel, *Jihad and Jew Hatred*, 151.

41. Wistrich, *Muslim Anti-Semitism*, 12.

42. Wistrich, *Muslim Anti-Semitism*, 14.

43. Wistrich, *Muslim Anti-Semitism*, 19.

44. Kuntzel, *Jihad and Jew Hatred*, 151.

45. Fox News, "How Central Is Muslim Anti-Semitism?" *On the Record with Greta Van Susteren*, January 24, 2002, http:www.danielpipes.org/426/how-central-is-muslim-anti-semitism.

46. Daniel Schwammenthal, "Europe Reimports Jew Hatred," WSJ.com, January 13, 2009, http://online.wsj.com/article/SB123180033807075069.html.

47. Schoenfeld, *Return of Anti-Semitism*, ch. 3.

48. Schoenfeld, *Return of Anti-Semitism*, 69–71.

49. Andrew Bostom, "The Islamization of European Anti-Semitism," *American Thinker*, September 7, 2006, http://www.americanthinker.com/2006/0.

50. Anti-Defamation League, "ADL Survey in Seven European Countries Finds Anti-Semitic Attitudes Steady," February 2009, http://www.adl.org/PresRele/ASInt_13/5465_13.htm.

51. Gabriel Schoenfeld, "Israel and the Anti-Semites," in Rosenbaum, *Those Who Forget the Past*, 104.

52. Schoenfeld, *Return of Anti-Semitism*, 34.

53. Harrison, *Resurgence of Anti-Semitism*, 106.

54. Schoenfeld, *Return of Anti-Semitism*, 98.

55. Robert Jan Van Pelt, "The Case for Auschwitz," in Rosenbaum, *Those Who Forget the Past*, 396.

56. Mark Strauss, "Antiglobalism's Jewish Problem," in Rosenbaum, *Those Who Forget the Past*, 276.

57. Strauss, "Antiglobalism's Jewish Problem," 281.

58. Schoenfeld, *Return of Anti-Semitism*, 74.

59. Anti-Defamation League, "Blaming the Jews: The Financial Crisis and Anti-Semitism," November 18, 2008, http://www.adl.org/main_Anti_Semitism_International/Blaming_Jews_Financial.htm.

60. Max Fisher, "Why Home-Grown Islamic Terrorism Isn't a Threat," *The Atlantic*, November 11, 2009, http://politics.theatlantic.com/2009/11/why_home-grown_islamic_terro.

61. Ben Harris, "Israel Apartheid Week Kicks Off," *Canadian National Post*, March 2, 2009, http://blogs.jta.org/telegraph/article/2009/03/02/1003389/israel-apartheid-week-kicks-off.

62. Joe Kaufman, "On Campus Anti-Semitism, Pro-Terrorism," *FrontPage Mag*, April 10, 2009, http://archive.frontpagemag.com/readArticle.aspx?ARTID=35204.

63. Kaufman, "On Campus Anti-Semitism."

64. Edward Alexander, "Ward Churchill and the Politics of Campus Extremism," *FrontPage Mag*, February 7, 2005, http://archive.frontpagemag.com/readArticle.aspx?ARTID=9663.

65. Alain Goldschlager, "The Canadian Campus Scene," in *Academics against Israel and the Jews*, ed. Manfred Gerstenfeld (Jerusalem: Jerusalem Center for Public Affairs, 2007), 157–58.

66. AboutJudaism.com. http://judaism.about.com/library/2_americanjewry/bl_campus_palconf.htm.

67. Lawrence Summers, "Address at Morning Prayers, Memorial Church, Harvard University, Sept. 17, 2002," in Rosenbaum, *Those Who Forget the Past*, 59.

68. See, for example, Rebecca Leibowitz, "Defeating Anti-Israel and Anti-Semitic Activity on Campus: A Case Study: Rutgers University," in Gerstenfeld, *Academics against Israel and the Jews*, 83–94.

69. John J. Mearsheimer and Stephen M. Walt, *The Israel Lobby and U.S. Foreign Policy* (New York: Farrar, Straus and Giroux, 2007).

70. Schoenfeld, *Return of Anti-Semitism*, 90.

71. Steven Erlanger, "French Protest of Israeli Raid Reaches Wide Audience," *New York Times*, June 13, 2010, 6.

72. Mearsheimer and Walt, *Israel Lobby*, vii.

73. Mearsheimer and Walt, *Israel Lobby*, 6.

74. James Petras, *Rulers and Ruled in the U.S. Empire: Bankers, Zionists, Militants* (Atlanta, GA: Clarity Press, 2007), 103.

75. See Bob Woodward, *Bush at War* (New York: Simon and Schuster, 2003).

76. Gary Felton, *The Host and the Parasite* (Mesa, AZ: Dandelion Enterprises, 2007).

77. Rasmussen Poll, "Americans Clearly Divided over Gaza," December 31, 2008, http://ibloga.blogspot.com/2008/12/rasmussen-americans-closely-divided.html.

78. WorldPublicOpinion.org, May 23, 2009, http://btvshalom.org/resources/poll_20090523.shtml.

79. Vocal Minority, "End the Occupation! Cynthia McKinney Preaches Hate and Silences Opposition at Binghamton," November 20, 2009, http://vocalminority .typepad.com/blog/2009/11/end-the-occupation-cynthia-mckinney-preaches-hate-and-silences-opposition-at-binghamton.html.

80. Ginsberg, *Fatal Embrace*, 146.

81. Dan Gilgoff, "Rev. Jeremiah Wright Says Jews Are Preventing Obama from Talking to Him," *U.S. News & World Report*, June 11, 2009, http://www.usnews .com/blogs/god-and-country/2009/06/11/rev-jeremiah-wright-says-jews.

82. Seth Lipsky, "Zero-Sum Politics," WSJ.com, August 23, 2000, http://www .opinionjournal.com/columnists/slipsky/?id=65000141.

83. Lipsky, "Zero-Sum Politics."

84. Ginsberg, *Fatal Embrace*, 167.

85. Jinjirrie, "End Apartheid, Slavery, Caste & Racism—Support WCAR 2009," Kadaitcha, March 3, 2009, http://www.kadaitcha.com/2009/03/03/end-apartheid-slavery-caste-racism-support-wcar-2009-2.

86. Harold Cruse, *The Crisis of the Negro Intellectual* (New York: Quill, 1984), 147–70.

87. Alvin H. Rosenfeld, *Progressive Jewish Thought and the New Anti-Semitism* (New York: American Jewish Committee, 2006).

88. Otto Weininger, *Sex and Character* (New York: Putnam's, 1908) (translation of *Geschlecht und Charakter*, 1903).

89. David Aaronovitch, "The Ironies of Hating Oneself," *Jewish Chronicle*, August 6, 2009, http://www.thejc.com/comment/columnists/the-ironies-hating-oneself.

90. Southern Poverty Law Center, "Neo-Nazis: Fugitive 'Aryan' Making Life Miserable for His Parents—Again," fall 2006, http://www.splcenter.org/intel/intelreport/article.jsp?aid=662.

91. Ruth Wisse, *If I Am Not for Myself: The Liberal Betrayal of the Jews* (New York: Free Press, 1992).

92. Norman Podhoretz, *Why Are Jews Liberals?* (New York: Doubleday, 2009).

93. Edward Alexander, "Introduction," in *The Jewish Divide over Israel*, ed. Edward Alexander and Paul Bogdanor (New Brunswick, NJ: Transaction, 2006), xiv–xvi.

94. Alexander, "Introduction," xv.

95. Tony Judt, "Israel: The Alternative," *New York Review of Books*, October 23, 2003, http://www.nybooks.com/articles/archives/2003/oct/23/israel-the-alternative.

96. Ilan Pappe, *The Ethnic Cleansing of Palestine* (Oxford, UK: Oneworld Publications, 2006).

97. Noam Chomsky, *Fateful Triangle: United States, Israel and the Palestinians* (London: Pluto Press, 1999).

98. Michael Neumann, "What Is Anti-Semitism?," in *The Politics of Anti-Semitism*, ed. Alexander Cockburn and Jeffrey St. Clair (Oakland, CA: AK Press, 2003), 2–10.

99. Norman Finkelstein, *The Holocaust Industry*, 2nd ed. (London: Verso, 2003).

100. Judith Butler, "No, Its Not Anti-Semitic," *London Review of Books*, August 21, 2003, http://www.lrb.co.uk/v25/n16/but102_.html.

101. Alexander, "Introduction," xxi.

Selected Bibliography

Abells, Irving, and Harold Troper. *None Is Too Many: Canada and the Jews of Europe, 1933–1948*. 3rd ed. Winnipeg: Lester Pub. Ltd., 1997.

Ainsztein, Reuben. *Jewish Resistance in Nazi-Occupied Eastern Europe*. London: Elek Books, 1974.

Arad, Yitzhak. *In the Shadow of the Red Banner: Soviet Jews in the War against Nazi Germany*. Jerusalem: Gefen Publishing, 2010.

Arendt, Hannah. *Eichmann in Jerusalem: A Report on the Banality of Evil*. Rev. ed. New York: Penguin, 1963.

Berger, Alan L. "Harry S. Truman and Jewish Refugees," in *Israel and the Legacy of Harry S. Truman*, ed. Michael Devine, Robert Watson, and Robert Wolz, 3–10. Kirksville, MO: Truman State University Press, 2008.

Bowman, Steven. *Jewish Resistance in Wartime Greece*. Edgware, Middlesex, UK: Vallentine Mitchell, 2006.

Brownlee, W. Elliot. *Federal Taxation in America: A Short History*. 2nd ed. New York: Cambridge University Press, 2004.

Budiansky, Stephen. *Battle of Wits: The Complete Story of Codebreaking in World War II*. New York: Touchstone, 2002.

Chadwin, Mark Lincoln. *The Warhawks: American Interventionists before Pearl Harbor*. Chapel Hill: University of North Carolina Press, 1968.

Cohen, Naomi W. *Not Free to Desist: The American Jewish Committee, 1906–1966.* Philadelphia: Jewish Publication Society of America, 1972.

Cole, Wayne S. *America First: The Battle against Intervention, 1940–1941.* Madison: University of Wisconsin Press, 1953.

Dawidowicz, Lucy S. *The War against the Jews, 1933–1945.* New York: Holt, Rinehart & Winston, 1975.

Dunn, Walter S., Jr. *Hitler's Nemesis: The Red Army, 1930–1945.* Westport, CT: Praeger, 1994.

Epstein, Barbara. *The Minsk Ghetto, 1941–1943: Jewish Resistance and Soviet Internationalism.* Berkeley: University of California Press, 2008.

Foster, Arnold. *Square One: A Memoir.* New York: Donald Fine, 1988.

Gabler, Neal. *An Empire of Their Own: How the Jews Invented Hollywood.* New York: Crown, 1988.

Glantz, David M. *Stumbling Colossus: The Red Army on the Eve of World War.* Lawrence: University Press of Kansas, 1998.

Glantz, David M., and Jonathan House. *When Titans Clashed.* Lawrence: University Press of Kansas, 1995.

Habeck, Mary R. *Storm of Steel: The Development of Armor Doctrine in Germany and the Soviet Union, 1919–1939.* Ithaca, NY: Cornell University Press, 2003.

Haestrup, Jorgen. *European Resistance Movements, 1939–1945: A Complete History.* Westport, CT: Meckler Pub. Co., 1981.

Harrison, Bernard. *The Resurgence of Anti-Semitism: Jews, Israel and Liberal Opinion.* Lanham, MD: Rowman & Littlefield, 2006.

Haufler, Hervie. *Codebreakers' Victory: How the Allied Cryptographers Won World War II.* New York: New American Library, 2003.

Hilberg, Raul. *The Destruction of the European Jews.* New York: Holmes and Meier, 1985.

Hondros, John L. *Occupation and Resistance: The Greek Agony, 1941–44.* New York: Pella, 1983.

Hughes, Matthew, and Chris Mann. *Inside Hitler's Germany: Life under the Third Reich.* Dulles, VA: Brassey's, 2000.

Jones, John B. *The Songs That Fought the War: Popular Music and the Home Front, 1939–1945*. Waltham, MA: Brandeis University Press, 2006.

Kaufman, I. *American Jews in World War II*. Vol. 1. New York: Dial Press, 1947.

Koppes, Clayton R., and Gregory D. Black. *Hollywood Goes to War: How Politics, Profits and Propaganda Shaped World War II Movies*. Berkeley: University of California Press, 1990.

Lash, Joseph. *Dealers and Dreamers*. New York: Doubleday, 1988.

Leyda, Jay. *Kino: A History of the Russian and Soviet Film*. 3rd ed. Princeton, NJ: Princeton University Press, 1983.

Liberman, Peter. *Does Conquest Pay? The Exploitation of Occupied Industrial Societies*. Princeton, NJ: Princeton University Press, 1996.

Marrus, Michael, and Robert O. Paxton. *Vichy France and the Jews*. New York: Basic Books, 1981.

Merridale, Catherine. *Ivan's War: Life and Death in the Red Army, 1939–1945*. New York: Metropolitan Books, 2006.

Milward, Alan S. "The Economic and Strategic Effectiveness of Resistance," in *Resistance in Europe, 1939–1945*, ed. Stephen Hawes and Ralph White. London: Allen Lane, 1975.

Ossad, Steven L., and Don Marsh. *Major General Maurice Rose: World War II's Greatest Forgotten Commander*. New York: Taylor, 2006.

Overy, Richard. *Russia's War: A History of the Soviet Effort, 1941–1945*. New York: Penguin, 1998.

Parrish, Michael. *Felix Frankfurter and His Times*. New York: Free Press, 1982.

Paxton, Robert. *Vichy France: Old Guard and New Order, 1940–1944*. New York: Knopf, 1972.

Pinkus, Benjamin. *The Jews of the Soviet Union*. Cambridge: Cambridge University Press, 1988.

Poznanski, Renée. *Jews in France during World War II*. Boston: Brandeis University Press, 2001.

Rapoport, Louis. *Stalin's War against the Jews*. New York: Free Press, 1990.

Reese, Roger R. *Why Stalin's Soldiers Fought: The Red Army's Military Effectiveness in World War II*. Lawrence: University Press of Kansas, 2011.

Rhodes, Richard. *The Making of the Atomic Bomb*. New York: Simon & Schuster, 1986.

Samuel, Lawrence R. *Pledging Allegiance: American Identity and the Bond Drive of World War II*. Washington, DC: Smithsonian Institution Press, 1997.

Samuelson, Lennart. *Tankograd: The Formation of a Soviet Company Town: Cheliabinsk, 1900s–1950s*. New York: Palgrave Macmillan, 2011.

Schapiro, Leonard. "The Birth of the Red Army," in *The Red Army*, ed. B. H. Liddell Hart, 24–32. New York: Harcourt, Brace and Company, 1956.

Schoenfeld, Gabriel. *The Return of Anti-Semitism*. San Francisco: Encounter Books, 2004.

Shogan, Robert. *Prelude to Catastrophe: FDR's Jews and the Menace of Naziism*. Chicago: Ivan Dee, 2010.

Slepyan, Kenneth. *Stalin's Guerillas: Soviet Partisans in World War II*. Lawrence: University Press of Kansas, 2006.

Slezkine, Yuri. *The Jewish Century*. Princeton, NJ: Princeton University Press, 2004.

Sorge, Martin K. *The Other Price of Hitler's War: German Military and Civilian Losses Resulting from World War II*. New York: Greenwood Press, 1986.

Sugarman, Martin. *Fighting Back: British Jewry's Military Contribution in the Second World War*. London: Valentine Mitchell, 2010.

Synott, Marcia Graham. *The Half-Opened Door: Discrimination and Admissions at Harvard, Yale and Princeton, 1900–1970*. Westport, CT: Greenwood, 1979.

Tarrant, V. E. *The Red Orchestra: The Soviet Spy Network inside Nazi Europe*. London: Cassell, 1995.

Van Creveld, Martin. *Supplying War: Logistics from Wallenstein to Patton*. 2nd ed. New York: Cambridge University Press, 2004.

Webster, Paul. *Petain's Crime: The Full Story of French Collaboration in the Holocaust*. Chicago: Ivan Dee, 1991.

Werth, Alexander. *Russia at War*. New York: Discus Books, 1970.

Wistrich, Robert S. *Muslim Anti-Semitism*. New York: American Jewish Committee, 2002.

Zuccotti, Susan. *The Holocaust, the French and the Jews*. New York: Basic Books, 1993.

Index

Abbott and Costello, 49
Abel, Rudolph, 87
abortion rights, 145
Abrams, Elliott, 159
Abwehr (German military intelligence),
  71
Acheson, Dean, 41, 136
Adelman, Kenneth, 159
Afghanistan, 146, 156, 159
Africa, 165. *See also* North Africa; South
  Africa
African American anti-Semitism,
  161–66
Afrika Korps, 51, 93
agricultural collectivization, 14, 32
Ahmadinejad, Mahmoud, 151, 165
Aktion, 3, 122
Alexander, Edward, 168
Alexander, Hugh, 75
Alexander II of Russia, 8
Alexander Nevsky (film), 34
Ali, Abdul Malik, 153

Allies, Allied powers, 6, 70, 74–75, 81,
  92–97, 131–33; and partisan warfare,
  102–10, 116, 130
Alsop, Joseph, 41
America First Committee, 40, 45–46
American Civil Liberties Union
  (ACLU), 135, 137
American Jewish Committee (AJC),
  46–47, 50, 135, 161
American Office of Strategic Services
  (OSS), 94–97, 110
Amsterdam, 3
Amsterdam News, 163
Anders, Wladyslaw; "Anders's Army,"
  128
Anglo-Saxons, 37; "WASPS," 4, 40
Anielewicz, Mordechaj, 126
animal rights, 145
antiaircraft fire, 21, 29
Anti-Defamation League (ADL), 46, 50,
  161, 165
antiglobalism, 150–51

About the Author

Benjamin Ginsberg is the David Bernstein Professor of Political Science and chair of the Center for Advanced Governmental Studies at the Johns Hopkins University. He is author or coauthor of a number of books, including *The Fall of the Faculty: The Rise of the All-Administrative University and Why It Matters*; *Moses of South Carolina: A Jewish Scalawag during Radical Reconstruction*; *The American Lie: Government by the People and Other Political Fables*; *Presidential Power: Unchecked and Unbalanced*; *Downsizing Democracy: How America Sidelined Its Citizens and Privatized Its Public*; *Politics by Other Means*; *The Fatal Embrace: Jews and the State*; *The Consequences of Consent*; *American Government: Freedom and Power*; *We the People*; and *The Captive Public*. Ginsberg received his PhD from the University of Chicago in 1973. Before joining the Hopkins faculty in 1992, Ginsberg was professor of government at Cornell.